Rousseau and the Republic of Virtue

LA FRANCE RÉPUBLICAINE.

Ouvrant son Sein à tous les Français.

Republican France bares her breast to all Frenchmen.
(Courtesy of the Bibliothèque nationale, Paris)

ROUSSEAU AND THE REPUBLIC OF VIRTUE

The Language of Politics in the French Revolution

CAROL BLUM

Cornell University Press

ITHACA AND LONDON

Copyright © 1986 by Cornell University Press

First published 1986 by Cornell University Press.
First published, Cornell Paperbacks, 1989.
Second printing 1990.

International Standard Book Number 0-8014-1857-7 (cloth)
International Standard Book Number 0-8014-9557-1 (paper)
Library of Congress Catalog Card Number 86-6396
Printed in the United States of America
*Librarians: Library of Congress cataloging information
appears on the last page of the book.*

∞ *The paper used in this publication meets the minimum requirements of the
American National Standard for Permanence of Paper for Printed Library
Materials Z39.48–1984.*

To my family this book is lovingly dedicated.

Contents

Plates

Frequently Cited Sources
and Abbreviations

All references to the works of Rousseau, except as otherwise indicated, will be to the *Oeuvres complètes,* published under the direction of Bernard Gagnebin and Marcel Raymond.

Volume 1: *Les Confessions. Autres textes autobiographiques.* Ed. Bernard Gagnebin, Marcel Raymond, Robert Osmont. Paris: Pléiade, 1959, rep. 1969.
Volume 2: *La Nouvelle Héloïse. Théâtre. Poésie. Essais littéraires.* Ed. Henri Coulet, Bernard Guyon, Jacques Scherer, Charly Guyot. Paris: Pléiade, 1961, rep. 1969.
Volume 3: *Du Contrat social. Ecrits politiques.* Ed. François Bouchardy, Jean Starobinski, Robert Derathé, Sven Stelling-Michaud, Jean-Daniel Candaux, Jean Fabre. Paris: Pléiade, 1964, rep. 1970.
Volume 4: *Emile. Education. Morale. Botanique.* Ed. J. S. Spink, Charles Wirz, Pierre Burgelin, Henri Gouhier, Roger de Vilmorin. Paris: Pléiade, 1969.

I also cite:
Lettre à d'Alembert: Du contrat social...Lettre à M. D'Alembert. Paris: Garnier, 1954.
PW: The Political Writings of Jean-Jacques Rousseau. Ed. Charles Vaughan. 2 vols. New York: J. Wiley, 1962.

Rousseau's letters are cited in two editions:
C.g.: Correspondance générale. Ed. Théophile Dufour and Pierre-Paul Plan. 20 vols. Paris: Colin, 1924–34.

C.c.: Correspondance complète. Ed. R. A. Leigh. Vols. 1–14, Geneva: Institut et Musée Voltaire, 1965–71. Vols. 15–46, Oxford: Taylor Institution, 1967.

References to the speeches and writings of Robespierre that appear in the text are to the *Oeuvres complètes.*

Volume 1: *Robespierre à Arras. Les Oeuvres littéraires en prose et en vers.* Ed. E. Déprez and E. Lesueur. Paris: Leroux, 1910–12.

Volume 2: *Oeuvres judiciaires.* Ed. E. Lesueur. Paris: Leroux, 1913.

Volume 3: *Correspondance.* Ed. G. Michon. Tome 1, Paris: Alcan, 1926; Tome 2, Paris: Nizet, 1941.

Volume 4: *Le Défenseur de la Constitution.* Ed. G. Laurent. Paris: Alcan, 1939.

Volume 5: *Lettres à ses commettans.* Ed. G. Laurent. Gap: Louis Jean, 1961.

Volume 6: *Discours* (1789–90). Ed. M. Bouloiseau, G. Lefebvre, and A. Soboul. Paris: Presses Universitaires de France, 1950.

Volume 7: *Discours* (Jan.–Sept. 1791). Ed. M. Bouloiseau and A. Soboul. Paris: Presses Universitaires de France, 1954.

Volume 8: *Discours* (Oct., 3, 1791–Sept. 18, 1792). Ed. M. Bouloiseau, G. Lefebvre, and A. Soboul. Paris: Presses Universitaires de France, 1953.

Volume 9: *Discours* (Sept. 1792–July 1793). Ed. M. Bouloiseau, J. Dautry, and A. Soboul. Presses Universitaires de France, 1958.

Volume 10: *Discours* (July 27, 1793–July 27, 1794). Ed. M. Bouloiseau and A. Soboul. Presses Universitaires de France, 1967.

References to the speeches and writings of Saint-Just are to the *Oeuvres complètes.* Ed. Charles Vellay. 2 vols. Paris: Charpentier and Fasquelle, 1908.

Abbreviations used in citing secondary sources:

ACR: Actes du Colloque Robespierre. Vienne, Sept. 3, 1965. Paris: Sociétés Etudes Robespierristes, 1967.

ACSJ: Actes du Colloque Saint-Just. Paris: Société des Etudes Robespierristes, 1968.

AHRF: Annales Historiques de la Révolution Française.

AJJR: Annales de la Société Jean-Jacques Rousseau. Vols. 1–39. Geneva: Julien, 1905–77.

Barny: *Jean-Jacques Rousseau dans la Révolution française.* Ed. Roger Barny. 19 documents. Paris: EDHIS, 1977.

BN: Bibliothèque nationale.

BR: P.-J.-B. Buchez & P. C. Roux, *Histoire parlementaire de la Révolution française.* 40 vols. Paris: Paulin, 1834–38.

Sources and Abbreviations

DHS: Dix-huitième Siècle.

DS: Diderot Studies.

ECS: Eighteenth-Century Studies.

Jaurès: Jean Jaurès. *Histoire socialiste de la Révolution française.* Edited and revised by Albert Mathiez. 8 vols. Paris: Editions de la Librairie de l'Humanité. 1922–27 (orig. 1900–1903).

JECS: Journées d'Etudes sur le "Contrat social" de Jean-Jacques Rousseau [actes des journées d'études organisées à Dijon pour la commémoration du *200ᵉ anniversaire du Contrat social*] Paris: Société les Belles Lettres, 1964.

Moniteur: Moniteur universel. 9 vols. (1789–11 nivôse, an III).

OM: Oeuvres de Jean-Paul Marat. Ed. Vermorel. Paris: Décembre-Alonnier, 1869.

SECC: Studies in Eighteenth-Century Culture.

SVEC: Studies on Voltaire and the Eighteenth Century.

Preface

The drive to display a self radiant with "virtue" provided the generative thrust of Jean-Jacques Rousseau's works. His two great discourses indict the loss of virtue in the modern world; his political writings trace the contours of the virtuous state; his tract on education instructs how one individual might be raised to virtue; his novel describes virtue as "sweetest sensuality"; and his autobiographical writings focus around the critical moment when he became "drunk with virtue."

The fictional construction labeled "Jean-Jacques Rousseau," a hero molded on virtue, is a cultural artifact knowable through the works in which it is depicted, through texts of contemporaries reacting to this personage, and, to a lesser degree, through its copious iconography. The mind of the author, the individual behind the persona, can be the subject only of speculation, however, and ultimately resists adequate explanation.

The arresting *figure* of "Jean-Jacques Rousseau" and the virtue associated with his name inform both the private writings and the public discourse of some revolutionary leaders: Robespierre, Saint-Just, and many of their lesser colleagues and rivals repeatedly produced texts in which the self-referential "I" claimed identification with the virtuous Jean-Jacques Rousseau and legitimacy because of this connection. They attributed galvanizing personal, moral, and political insights to the recognition of a powerful bonding with the persona of the virtuous Rousseau.

[13]

How is the function of Rousseau's concept of virtue to be under-stood? In what way can we form an adequate representation of a word that has ceased to function in our own ideational and affective language?

For the word "virtue" no longer sits well in the academy. Despite the immoderate amount of ink which has been spent on Rousseau's thought, what Raymond Trousson refers to as the "tidal wave" of recent scholarship, little serious effort has been applied to defining this indisputably central term. As Paul Valéry noted, "this word *virtue* is dead, or, at least, it is dying. Virtue is hardly even mentioned any more. It is no longer one of those immediate elements of the vocabulary living in us, the ease and frequency of which manifest the true demands of our temperaments and our intellects."[1] To the extent it has been dealt with at all, it has been declared a redundant sign. "Renunciation,"[2] "chastity,"[3] "devotion and sacrifice to the public goods"[4]—these have been suggested as appropriate modern equivalents of the referent in question.

If the significance of virtue in Rousseau's writings has eluded definition, its meaning in the utterances of his self-proclaimed revolutionary disciples is a subject that has been, by and large, broached only to be dismissed. Albert Soboul's comment typifies an

---

[1]*Oeuvres complètes* (Paris: Pléiade, 1942), 1: 940.

[2]Albert Schinz, *La Pensée de Jean-Jacques Rousseau* (Paris: Alcan, 1929), p. 144. Schinz further drew attention to the wealth of referents implicit in Rousseau's use of the word "virtue" in the *Premier Discours* alone. "But what is there to be understood by *virtue?* No one of the passages cited permits us to guess definitively, and Rousseau, guided no doubt by the idea that 'the principles of virtue are engraved in all hearts,' believes he can abstain from all explanations." Therefore, according to Schinz, either the concept is rational or it is not. He goes on to define "virtue" in three different ways: as "moral wisdom," in the Socratic sense, as Christian renunciation of this world, and as innocence. He concludes that "it would seem that Rousseau means to defend virtue most frequently as the means to happiness, be it virtue-wisdom or virtue-innocence" (pp. 144–147) Schinz's argument is to some extend valid (even though he ignores the patriarchal, aggressive virtue that permeates the discourse), as long as the phenomenon is regarded from *outside* Rousseau's fusion with his own goodness; illuminated from within, however, "virtue" assumes a different set of shapes. Lester Crocker defines one aspect of the term very succinctly as "a word that does not refer to moral standards, as such, but to devotion and sacrifice to the public good. Morals having been absorbed into politics, the one virtue that matters is thinking of oneself only as a part of the whole." *Rousseau's Social Contract* (Cleveland: Case Western Reserve University Press, 1968), p. 28.

[3]E. M. Zimmermann, "Vertu' dans *La Nouvelle Héloïse*," *MLN,* 76 (March 1961), 251.

[4]Crocker, *Rousseau's Social Contract*, p. 28.

attitude prevalent until very recently: "Incapable of analyzing the economic and social conditions of his time, Robespierre, like Rousseau, like Saint-Just, believed in...appeals to virtue."[5]

As though semantic difficulties did not suffice to muddy the waters, partisan political interpretations of the Revolution have imposed further obfuscation in the form of a priori and a posteriori definitions placed upon men and events. These have imparted confusion to such an extent that comprehension of questions as problematic as what Rousseau's virtue signified and why the discourse of prominent revolutionaries cleaved to that meaning with such unflagging constancy is rendered difficult indeed. Moreover, because this subject is alien from a twentieth-century perspective, because virtue is dead or at least dying, there is a tendency to wish to assimilate it to the history of Catholicism and dechristianization, or to the emergence of middle-class values corresponding to bourgeois ascendancy, or to the class struggle latent in Montagnard constituencies, or to the problem of individualism; in short, to something more familiar, more rational, and more understandable in contemporary terms.

The aim of this book, then, is to analyze a powerful and complex representational structure that emerged from a literary canon, to demonstrate how it was radically simplified into a folk saga, making it accessible to segments of the population otherwise little influenced by the literature of the Enlightenment and, finally, to explore what expression "Rousseauvian virtue" found in revolutionary discourse. This story belongs in the realm of cultural investigation, a treacherous area, nonetheless richly rewarding for its dangers. Robert Darnton, in his introduction to *The Great Cat Massacre*, put forth a cogent rationale for attempting to understand the emotional significance and intellectual content of a strange cultural relic from an earlier time. He pointed out that it is precisely where past preoccupations seem the most obscure—and certainly the revolutionary obsession with "Rousseau's virtue" makes most modern commentators feel uncomfortable—that "we know we are on to something. By picking at the document where it is most opaque, we may be able to unravel an alien system of meaning."[6]

---

[5]"Jean-Jacques Rousseau et le jacobinisme," *JECS*, p. 417.
[6]*The Great Cat Massacre and Other Episodes in French Cultural History* (New York: Basic Books, 1984), p. 5.

For purposes of this book, the boundary between literature and politics has been ignored. That is to say, speeches, journalistic writings, and correspondence are all treated as segments of discourse, on the same level of explicability as any other prose. This subjection of political text to literary analysis is especially appropriate both in the case of Rousseau, who used nearly all the literary genres of his day as vehicles for extraliterary concerns, and, conversely, in that of his admirers, whose political writings also function as literature.

My "opaque" and esoteric subject—Rousseau's *virtuous self* as a model for political discourse during the Revolution—lies immediately adjacent to a much broader, more obvious, and more popular subject: the influence of Enlightenment thinkers in general and Rousseau in particular on the French Revolution. *This* subject has been treated most often from the political perspective of the historian, and the history of who said what about the Enlightenment's role in the Revolution would be, in effect, a recapitulation of political thought in Europe and America over the last two centuries. Great swings of the pendulum have marked attitudes toward this topic. Early critics of the Revolution, such as Burke and Carlyle, blamed the fermentation of ideas produced by the Enlightenment for inciting ignorant masses to dangerous excesses. Romantics such as Jules Michelet, on the other hand, credited Rousseau and the Encyclopedists with providing the ideas the people needed in order to move into the next phase of history, while Louis Blanc nuanced the attribution of responsibility by distinguishing between Voltaire as the patron of individualism and Rousseau as the proponent of fraternity. Hippolyte Taine's great flawed account, which, according to Alfred Cobban, "established for a time beyond challenge the belief that the propaganda of the *philosophes* was the cause of the Revolution,"[7] was superseded by the histories of Jean Jaurès and Henri Sée, in which emphasis shifted from seeking intellectual "causes" for the Revolution toward documentary research into economic, political, and social factors. Thus historians had, by the beginning of this century, slowly moved away from conceptualizing the Revolution as a theory-driven entity.

Albert Mathiez, Alphonse Aulard, and Georges Lefebvre still further reduced the role of the writer in laying the groundwork for

---

[7]*Aspects of the French Revolution* (New York: Braziller, 1968), p. 47.

the Revolution. The divorce of literary text from political act reached
its apogee in Daniel Mornet's admirable study *Les Origines intellectuelles
de la Révolution française* (1933). Mornet attempted to ascertain the
relative importance of philosophic ideas in stirring up revolutionary
sentiment, and he came to the conclusion that they played only a
minor role. In a similar vein, Frank Kafker investigated the careers
of former Encyclopedists during the Revolution and concluded that
they were remote from political power during the Terror.[8] Thus, the
philosophes were found to be without influence on revolutionary
events, in their writings and their persons alike. Peter Gay summa-
rized that attitude by asserting that "the ideas of Voltaire, of the
Encyclopedists, and of Rousseau played a relatively minor part in
revolutionary speeches and thought."[9]

From this denial of continuity between discourse and revolutionary postulate, the pendulum swung in the opposite direction in the
works of J. L. Talmon and Lester Crocker, both of whom found
blueprints for modern totalitarian societies in the writing of eighteenth-
century thinkers, especially Rousseau. *This* reading, in turn, produced reactions of dismay both from liberal admirers of Rousseau,
indignant that he was being blamed for events and patterns of
behavior which he had never imagined, and from Marxists, who
objected to the word and the concept "totalitarian."

Between the two poles, however, between the affirmation that
Rousseau and some other eighteenth-century thinkers had somehow
provided a model for the Revolution, the Terror, and subsequent
manifestations of totalitarianism, and the denial of any connection
between literature and events, the distance has begun to close.
Within the past ten years a number of works have appeared in which
the partisanship and moralism of earlier histories have begun to
subside, and in which the following question is being considered
more dispassionately: in what specific ways did the ideational material
of the Enlightenment contribute to structuring the texts of which the
Revolution was made? From the *cahiers* of 1789 to the Napoleonic
Code civil, the Revolution now is itself seen as an intellectual construction inseparable from its discursive representations. There is no
appeal from the texts to the Revolution for illumination; rather it is

[8]"Les Encyclopédistes et la Terreur," *Revue d'Histoire Moderne et Contemporaine*, 14
(July-Sept. 1967), 294.
[9]*The Party of Humanity* (New York: Knopf, 1964), p. 176.

the documents themselves that must serve to evaluate the subjective creation called "the French Revolution."

Jan Marejko approached the question from a new perspective in his study *Jean-Jacques Rousseau et la dérive totalitaire* (1984), in which he examines the paradigmatic Rousseauvian self as a model for the text as revolutionary act. This illumination of Rousseau's structures from inside the feeling-states rather than from outside the document-as-object opens the way to new findings and, inevitably, to new distortions as one subjectivity both reveals and obliterates another.

To explicate the structures of Rousseau's thought from the inside while respecting the integrity of his subject, however, has been the contribution of the most universally respected contemporary critic of Rousseau: Jean Starobinski. Moving cautiously forward from the careful foundations of current Rousseau scholarship which he established in *La Transparence et l'obstacle*, Starobinski draws attention to a continuum between the structures of the Rousseauvian self as displayed in the confessional writings and those of the state as enunciated during the period of Jacobin hegemony: "I am thinking here of the Terror. Certainly not in order to see Rousseau as its theoretician (although Robespierre drew his essential ideas from him), but because the Terror seems to me to be, on the political level, homologous with what occurs on the mental level in the autobiographical works of Rousseau."[10]

While all these related strands are woven together in such a way that it is often difficult to distinguish one from the other, I would ask the reader's patience in teasing out the specific thread of Rousseau's *virtue* to examine at leisure. It is a phenomenon worthy of our attention, no less intriguing for its strangeness.

It is not my intention to *recount* the Revolution nor to *account* for any leader's career or events; rather I am trying to illuminate an aspect of eighteenth-century thought and feeling which has been largely denied, disavowed, or denigrated since Thermidor. My hope is that this book will remove the word "virtue" from the category of embarrassing excesses to which people in the past were inexplicably prone and which require translation into a more acceptable termi-

---

[10]"La Mise en accusation de la société," *Jean-Jacques Rousseau* (Neuchâtel: Baconnière, 1978), p. 34.

nology, and permit the word to live again in its historical specificity, with all its foreign and luxuriant richness.

A number of colleagues and friends have contributed to the preparation of this book through their encouragement and suggestions. I especially thank Frederick Brown, Otis Fellows, and Frederick Keener for their unflagging interest through the many years this work has been in progress, as well as the members of the Columbia University Seminar on Eighteenth-Century European Culture, who have been both patiently and constructively critical of various portions of the book. Thanks are also due to Elizabeth Fox-Genovese and Aram Vartanian for their thoughtful readings, recommendations, and guidance and to Berenice Hoffman for her much-appreciated enthusiasm.

I am grateful to the Research Foundation of the State University of New York at Stony Brook, to the National Endowment for the Humanities, and to the John Simon Guggenheim Foundation for their generous support.

The chairpersons of the Department of French and Italian at Stony Brook during the years I worked on this book, Joseph Tursi, Mark Whitney, and Eléonore Zimmermann, were unfailingly helpful, as were our librarians, particularly Gerhardt Vasco and Hélène Volat-Shapiro.

I am grateful to my family for their affection and understanding during this decade-long enterprise, and most particularly to my husband, who kept a steady vision of my subject in his mind when I lost sight of it in my own, and was kind enough to remind me of it when I needed reminding.

Portions of this book were read at meetings of the Modern Language Association, the American Society for Eighteenth-Century Studies, a National Endowment for the Humanities Seminar at Columbia University, the Radcliffe Institute, and the Columbia Seminar on Eighteenth-Century European Culture.

In translating French quotations into English, I have been here and there obliged to sacrifice stylistic considerations to ensure the most accurate possible rendering of the original text.

CAROL BLUM

Great Neck, New York

Rousseau and the Republic of Virtue

Prologue

Louis XIV offered his vision of monarchical virtue when he congratulated himself on the fortunate conjunction of qualities which made him not only the highest ranking man in the world but also the most personally excellent.

> To be King is to be the summit of superiority and the elevation of rank is all the more assured when it is supported by unique merit. The great interval which virtue puts between [other men] and him [the king], exposes him in the most beautiful light and with utmost glitter in the eyes of the whole world. All eyes are attached to him alone...everything else crawls, everything else is impotent and sterile.[1]

Thus he asserted, in the most straightforward way, the equation of virtue and competitive display. Virtue was that quality which, when added to rank, reduced the observer to the status of an awestruck, crawling nonentity. Part of the Sun King's genius lay in his understanding of the possibilities for grandiosity and humiliation in the world he inherited. He heightened them, with the subtlest sensibility, into a political weapon of astonishing capabilities, turning nobility into self-esteem and commoners' status into shame. To be noble in the France he created was to shine: the sovereign radiated his glory toward those whose birth was honor, and they, because of their rank and virtue, reflected the glow on those beneath them in the social

---

[1] *Oeuvres de Louis XIV* (Paris: Treuttel & Wurtz, 1806), 2: 67–68.

pyramid. The highest reward to which the occasional worthy commoner could aspire was a ritual rebirth into the ranks of the nobility.

The aristocracy, with a few conservative or liberal exceptions,
proclaimed a value system that equated virtue with blood and
respected as truly virtuous only those activities specifically relegated
to their class, such as military leadership and personal service to the
king. As Louis-Sébastien Mercier expressed it during the Revolution,
"The nobles had really separated the nation into two castes; those to
whom were owed the incense, the homage, the opulence, and the
authority; . . . The common people could have the work, the disdain,
the contempt."[2]

The self-infatuation of the aristocracy and the terrible resentment
it engendered fueled the writers of the period, from Molière to
Beaumarchais. Envy inevitably coupled with resentment, and those
who had the resources pressed forward into the channels leading to
the circle of light. The most effective assets of the ambitious commoner were money, sex, and talent. The rich bourgeois, snubbed for
lacking ancestors and tone, attempted to compensate for social
inferiority by an increasingly exhibitionistic use of money. As the
eighteenth century progressed, financiers, bankers, and wealthy mer-
chants became ever more ostentatious in the display of the luxuries
they purchased with their fortunes, often buying the properties and
titles of nobles in order to add the pleasures of commanding feudal
servility to those of conspicuous consumption. Seductive women
were also able to achieve both social standing and wealth even if they
began with neither. Mme Du Barry was only one in a long line of
courtesans who used personal magnetism to enter upon a way of life
and a position of social eminence largely indistinguishable from
those of the noble lovers they enthralled. In addition, a few exceptional individuals, writers, composers, artists, and actors such as
Voltaire, Rameau, and Mlle Clairon, had achieved celebrity through
the creativity which lifted them out of the masses, made them the
center of admiring attention, and endowed them with at least some
of the existential status of the nobility.

Apart from these radiant beings were the ordinary people who
made way for their carriages or else risked being crushed, who stood

---

[2]*De J.-J. Rousseau, considéré comme l'un des premiers auteurs de la Révolution* (Paris: Buisson, 1791), 1: 39. Barny, 6034–35.

open-mouthed at the splendor of their costumes, their houses, their array of lackeys and footmen. The very ostentation of the privileged demanded an audience of the undistinguished, a mass lacking the power and charisma before which everything else crawled. Would the noble pursuit of the boar have been as self-aggrandizing had the trail not led across the fields of amazed peasants, forced to witness, cap in hand, the destruction of their crops by the elegantly arrayed hunting party? In Tocqueville's words, "the noble loved to console himself for the loss of his real power by the immoderate use of his apparent rights."[3] The aristocracy had largely rejected the responsibilities that had once justified it and now insisted imperiously that its crushing superiority, aped in megalomania by the monied class, constituted noble virtue.

As well as being trained by his betters to have contempt for his own social inferiority, the commoner was instructed in metaphysical self-loathing by his religion. "The true and unique virtue," said Pascal, "is to hate oneself, for one deserves to be hated for one's lust." Between ignoble blood on the one hand and an irrevocably tainted soul on the other, the run of humanity was left with meager comfort for its self-esteem.

The charge of moral corruption, however, broadly desseminated by the church, remained a standard by which the monarchy and the aristocracy were judged long after they had ceased to employ it in judging themselves. The moral superiority to which the ascendant classes laid claim was undermined during the Regency and the reign of Louis XV by the behavior of the sovereign himself. Indulging his sensual temperament in public, the patron of the Deer Park so diminished the respect adhering to his role that recognition of his virtue became a sham indulged in only because of private interest or ac-quiescence to force. Even the defenders of the monarchy were reduced to pleading for a separation between the reverence due the throne and the contempt owed the man, as if they were combating a secular version of Donatism. They were echoed by the Abbé Proyart, writing after the Revolution about what he saw as the decay of the regime:

> Scandal is at its peak when it is a king who occasions it; when he provides an entire people with the spectacle of his incontinence. Do not

[3]*L'Ancien Régime*, trans. M. W. Patterson (Oxford: Oxford University Press, 1947), p. 96.

even attempt to enumerate the results of such disorder: they are incalculable. Let a prince cease to flatter himself that he still enjoys the same place in the hearts of his subjects: the ignorant are unable to distinguish, in their esteem, the dignity of the ministry from the weakness of the minister; and by the will of Providence, the moral conduct the great display before the eyes of the people becomes the measure of the consideration which supports their grandeur."[4]

The lofty public tone which Louis XIV had always maintained, even during his love affairs, that carefully contrived majesty which made him, in Bolingbroke's words: "if not the greatest King, the greatest impersonator of royalty who ever lived,"[5] was debased in the reign of his grandson. Imitating the new king, the nobility and many of the princes of the church jettisoned the exemplary, publicly displaying their lust, venality, and frivolity, at the same time insisting on the moral prerogatives of their stations. For the rest of society, any contact with them was, barring an unusually stolid self-sufficiency, a source of humiliation and impotent rage.

The avenues to social self-esteem were so narrow and so tightly controlled by the aristocracy that the system was strained to the breaking point. The question of virtue was a sore festering under the skin of the Bourbon monarchy, and as much as any issue of taxes, hereditary privileges, or budgetary imbalances it was the source of a despair and resentment which would eventually undermine the whole social order. Before that could happen, however, the resentment had to be legitimized by a new morality in the name of which the aristocratic claims to moral authority could be negated. Such an ethic would inevitably also set itself against aristocracy's companions: wealth, sexual appeal, and wit. The man who forged the vocabulary of this new virtue was Jean-Jacques Rousseau.

---

[4]*Louis XVI détrôné avant d'être roi* (Paris: published by the author, 1803), p. 31.

[5]"Considérations sur Louis XIV," *Oeuvres de Louis XIV,* 1: 31. Nannerl O. Keohane refers to the Marquis d'Argenson's description of the Sun King as a *beau comédien* "attracting applause for the splendor of his court while presiding over the ruin of his country." *Philosophy and the State in France: The Renaissance to the Enlightenment* (Princeton: Princeton University Press, 1980), p. 377.

CHAPTER ONE

Rousseau's Virtue and the Revolution: A Statement of the Problem

A profound shift of focus occurred during the creation of the scholarly representation of the French Revolution. The secondary literature largely concerns itself with political, economic, and social analysis. In contrast, the original texts, and in particular those of the Jacobins, were apt to invoke virtue and Jean-Jacques Rousseau.

Robespierre, the leader of the Jacobins, declared that "the soul of the republic is virtue,"[1] and he used this essentially mystical principle to separate himself from those of his compatriots he denigrated as merely political and hence immoral and counterrevolutionary. He announced that all of history illustrated the great struggle: "Vice and virtue control the destiny of the earth: they are the two opposing spirits warring for it."[2] The role of the revolutionary state was to legislate virtue. On the 18th of floréal, year II (May 7, 1794), he had virtue made the "order of the day." He reflected proudly upon that act: "Of all the decrees which saved the Republic," he said, "the most sublime, the only one...which freed people from tyranny, is the one which made probity and virtue the order of the day" (10: 519).

As scholars of the French Revolution have progressively moved from moral to more modern political, social, and economic models, the discursive insistence on virtue has more and more tended to be

[1]*Oeuvres de M. Robespierre,* ed. G. Laurent (Gap: Louis-Jean, 1961), 5: 17.
[2]*Oeuvres de M. Robespierre,* ed. M. Bouloiseau and A. Soboul (Paris: PUF, 1967), 10. 446.

treated as a screen rather than as sign. That is, virtue has been redefined within a materialist problematic or largely ignored. Scholars have resisted accepting that Robespierre believed that the foundation of freedom was an official commitment to virtue. In consequence, what the revolutionaries meant by the virtue they invoked has not been systematically investigated, although the topic has been touched upon frequently, with especial acuity in Crane Brinton's works on the period,[3] in studies of the influence of the Enlightenment in general and Jean-Jacques Rousseau in particular upon the Revolution,[4] in biographies of such figures as Robespierre and Saint-Just, and in specific studies such as J. L. Talmon's and George Armstrong Kelly's.[5]

---

[3]*A Decade of Revolution, 1789–1799* (New York: Harper, 1934), ch. 4, "The Republic of Virtue," and ch. 7, "Reigns of Terror and Virtue."

[4]In addition to Daniel Mornet's fundamental study *Les Origines intellectuelles de la Révolution française: 1715–1787* (Paris: Colin, 1933), Joan McDonald provides a bibliography of works dealing with Rousseau's influence on the Revolution in *Rousseau and the French Revolution: 1762–1791* (London: Athlone, 1965), pp. 175–83, of which the most indispensable are the following: three studies appearing around the time of the bicentenary, Edme Champion's *J.-J. Rousseau et la Révolution française* (Paris: Armand Colin, 1909), Albert Meynier's *Jean-Jacques Rousseau, révolutionnaire* (Paris: Schleicher, 1912), and L. Cahen, "Rousseau et la Révolution française," *Revue de Paris* (June 1912); plus Alfred Cobban's *Rousseau and the Modern State* (Hamden, Conn.: Archon, 1964 [1934]); and André de Maday's "Rousseau et la Révolution," *AJJR*, 31 (1946–49). To these should be added the following studies: Gordon H. McNeil, "Robespierre, Rousseau, and Representation," *Ideas in History* (Durham: University of North Carolina Press, 1965); Henri Peyre, "The Influence of Eighteenth-Century Ideas on the French Revolution," *Journal of the History of Ideas*, 6 (1949); L. Sozzi, "Interprétations de Rousseau pendant la Révolution," *SVEC*, 64 (1968), 187–223; and Sozzi, "*LeContrat social* et la pensée européenne de 1762 à nos jours," from *JECS* (which contains a group of relevant articles, including those of Albert Soboul and Louis Trénard). Roger Barny's unpublished major thesis, the 5-volume "Jean-Jacques Rousseau dans la Révolution française, 1787–1791: Contribution à l'analyse de l'idéologie révolutionnaire bourgeoise" (University of Paris X, 1977) contains a wealth of documentation concerning the influence of Rousseau in the period preceding the Terror. Barny published several articles drawing on the materials of his thesis which I have cited in this book. In addition, he edited a volume of nineteen rare texts from the period in *Jean-Jacques Rousseau dans la Révolution française (1789–1801)* (Paris: EDHIS, 1977), and also put together a collection of thirty-five documents available on microfiche: *Rousseauisme: 1788–1797* (Paris: Microéditions Hachette, 1977). These documentary collections have been of great help in assessing the significance of Rousseau in the Revolution, and their publication attests to the growing interest in variations of "influence."

[5]Talmon, *The Origins of Totalitarian Democracy* (New York: Praeger, 1960); Kelly, "Conceptual Sources of the Terror," *ECS*, 14, no. 1 (1980), 13–36.

All these works acknowledge that the topic had authentic meaning to the Jacobins without attempting to examine that significance in detail. More frequently, however, commentators have dismissed virtue as a valid category of intellectual inquiry. A reluctance to deal with revolutionary virtue as a legitimate object of modern scholarship has led many scholars to pour their discussions of it into molds provided by their own political orientations. Post-Marxists, for example, find the preoccupation with virtue to be a mark of historical limitations, an inadequate conceptual framework arising from the inability to make a materialist analysis. Galvano della Volpe, writing after World War II on Marxism-Leninism's debt to Rousseau, comments that "Rousseauan, contractual, natural law, an ultimately *moralistic* outline of the problems of democracy, has been shown insufficient . . . and replaced by a radically different treatment and method, like the materialist ones of class struggle."[6] Nevertheless, for della Volpe, besides Rousseau's "inter-class" and hence outmoded moralism, the outlines of universal *equality* are to be found beneath his insistence on virtue, and this is socialism's true debt to Rosseau, one that Marx, according to della Volpe, failed to acknowledge sufficiently.

Albert Soboul regarded the virtue invoked by both Rousseau and Robespierre as an indication of their pre-Marxian intellectual limitations: "Incapable of analyzing the economic and social conditions of his time, Robespierre, like Rousseau, like Saint-Just, believed in . . . appeals to virtue."[7] Despite paying greater attention to the importance of virtue than most other commentators, Talmon still claimed that moral concerns merely camouflaged economic failures. "The Jacobins lacked the courage to make a frontal attack on the property system. This is why the 'reign of virtue' postulated by them appears so unsatisfactory and so elusive an ideal as almost to be meaningless" (p. 62).

Others have seen the appeal to virtue as an inappropriate political solution to a social and economic problem. For Lester Crocker, "the Jacobin rule was in many ways an attempt to realize the total collectivist State of the Social Contract in which 'virtue-patriotism' would rule. Reasoning juridically, both [Rousseau and Robespierre]

[6]*Rousseau and Marx* (London: Lawrence & Wishart, 1978; 1st pub. 1964), p. 49.
[7]"Jean-Jacques Rousseau et la jacobinisme," *JECS*, p. 417.

were guided by purely political concepts when an economic analysis was needed."[8]

Thus the word "virtue" itself has functioned opaquely for modern scholars within the texts of Rousseau and his revolutionary followers. It has been treated as a white space into which other, more meaningful, signs were to be inserted. This rejection of the word has hindered the assimilation of denotations and connotations into adequate conceptual frameworks as well. The term as cipher inevitably befogs ancillary propositions.

The most striking of these clouded substantives is "terror." In a much-quoted phrase from his discourse of 17 pluviose, year II, Robespierre announced that the Republic was founded on two principles, "virtue and its emanation, terror." According to the architect of the Committee of Public Safety, the existence of the one necessitated the other. "Virtue without terror is impotent," he declared, "terror without virtue is malignant" (10: 357). This careful theorem of the nature of virtue and terror has not been dealt with successfully in modern scholarship.

To the conservative historian Hippolyte Taine the welding of virtue and terror was moral hypocrisy, the abuse of an ethical term to polarize political life and justify repression. "Since he is virtue," Taine fulminated, "one cannot resist him without crime . . . the Jacobin canonized his murders and now he kills through philanthropy."[9] What Taine decried was the transmutation, and thereby the loss, of what had been one of the great rallying cries of eighteenth-century liberal thought in its battles with the inequities and corruption of the *ancien régime*. The philosophes had countered the aristocratic definition of virtue with one of their own, still recognizable today as alternately a compromised bourgeois ideology or a viable liberal morality. How, in any case, could this same idealistic concept, now invoked with a repetitiousness bordering on obsession by Robespierre, Saint-Just, and some of their Jacobin colleagues, be turned into an explicit rationale for "terror"?

[8]*Rousseau's Social Contract*, p. 120. In a review in *AJJR*, Jean Starobinski, while respecting Crocker's analysis of Rousseau's political ideas, characterized it as "maximalist," that is, pushing the manipulative aspects of his thought farther than a more balanced reading might warrant (37 [1966–68], 262–65).

[9]*Les Origines de la France contemporaine: La Révolution, la conquête jacobine* (Paris: Hachette, 1911), p. 36.

Taine denounced what he saw as hypocrisy; this explanation reduces a powerful and forceful idealism to the level of an opportunistic tyranny. Taine's diatribes did not suffice to clarify the phenomenon they described. Other scholars have tried to evade the difficulty by denying that terror was an essential component of virtue to the Jacobin leadership. It has been proposed that virtue *mitigated* terror and was not an integral part of it. According to Roger Barny, "virtue given as a corrective of terror is obviously the sign of the difficulty rather than the solution."[10] Another form of the same argument asserts that not only could Robespierre's virtue not have had terror as an emanation, neither could Rousseau's: As Soboul stated it, Robespierre "gave the terror virtue as a corrective, virtue in the Rousseauistic sense, civic virtue, 'that virtue which is nothing more than love of the fatherland and its laws.'"[11]

Although this interpretation distorts the clear import of Robespierre's words, it does connect the concept of virtue with the name of Rousseau, reflecting the unusual devotion to that author which marked the decade before 1789 and which the Revolution only intensified. He was the idol of a generation at once sentimental and violent. Plays, poems, and essays were written about him, pilgrimages were made to his tomb at Ermenonville, there was a fervid fascination with every aspect of the Sage's life. According to Raymond Trousson: "The revolutionary period is the era of solemn apotheoses, of mass ceremonies orchestrated by the high priest of the new cult [of the Supreme Bring]. Rousseau will have a large part in these grandiose manifestations of gratitude and civism: he has become a god."[12]

Despite the constant invocation of his name, however, the nature and the extent of Rousseau's influence on the French Revolution have been the subject of controversy since the convocation of the Estates General. Disputes over whether the Gironde or the Mountain was Rousseau's true spiritual heir, whether Rousseau's teachings were basically aristocratic, monarchial, liberal, or proto-Marxist, whether he was an authentic source of political inspiration or merely a shibboleth have reflected the political and social convictions of nearly two centuries of partisans in France and abroad.

[10]"Rousseau dans la Révolution," *DHS*, 6 (1974), 73.
[11]"Jean-Jacques Rousseau et la jacobinisme," p. 410.
[12]*Rousseau et sa fortune littéraire* (St. Médard en Jalles; Ducros, 1971), p. 66.

Bernard Groethuysen described the Revolution as torn between two conflicting impulses, one toward collectivism and the other toward individual rights, the one seeking to guarantee the integrity of the individual according to the Declaration of the Rights of Man and the other to establish a supraindividual state which would become the paramount entity in the lives of its citizens. The latter impulse he saw stemming from the writings of Rousseau.[13]

Two political critics writing around the same time as Groethuysen labeled those two conflicting impulses liberalism and democracy. According to della Volpe's traditional division, "liberalism derived from Locke, Kant, Humboldt, Constant, etc., and democracy from Rousseau, Marx, and Engels" (p. 48). Writing after World War II, Talmon found a rationale for what della Volpe called "democracy" in the thought of Morelly, Mably, and especially Rousseau. He traced the development of these ideas in the period of Jacobin hegemony, culminating in the theories of Babeuf and the Conspiracy of Equals. For Talmon, ideas move through history under the impetus of their own vital force: "dictatorship...is the outcome of the synthesis between the eighteenth-century idea of the natural order and the Rousseauist idea of popular fulfillment and self-expression. Rousseau's 'general will' becomes the the driving force of totalitarian democracy..." (p. 6).

The introduction of the word "totalitarian" and Talmon's pejorative use of "dictatorship" cast his analysis into an indictment both of Rousseau's thought and of Eastern block socialism. This accusatory reading aroused antagonism from more than one quarter. At present Jean-Louis Lecercle's comment suffices to express the low exteem in which Talmon's thesis is held: "I reject with dispatch the 'totalitarian' image of Rousseau. To my knowledge not one Rousseauist, at least in Europe, accepts it any longer. It is the preoccupation with safeguarding liberty that is the first thought of Rousseau."[14]

Further, such syntheses have been forcefully challenged because of the vagueness of the connecting link between Rousseau's thought and revolutionary events. Peter Gay criticized Talmon's thesis because it "plays games with the subtlest of problems to which the intellectual historian must devote his best efforts: the problem of

[13]*Philosophie de la Révolution française* (Paris: NRF, 1956), p. 253.

[14]"Rousseau et Marx," *Rousseau after Two Hundred Years* (Cambridge: Cambridge University Press, 1982), p. 76.

influence. Rousseau influenced the widest variety of political thinkers, and by no means all of them were extremists, virulent terrorists."[15]

The correction that the Jacobins were not the only revolutionaries
influenced by Rousseau did not challenge Talmon's thesis as decisively
as the complaint that he had slid past the conceptual issues underlying his argument: Joan McDonald says: "To select ideas from the
Social Contract or from other works of Rousseau and then compare
these ideas with those expressed during the Revolution, as a means
of establishing the influence of Rousseau's theories, is to take for
granted precisely what the argument is purported to prove. How the
revolutionaries thought about Rousseau can only be discovered by
studying what they themselves said and thought about him" (p. 20).
In line with her own demands, McDonald analyzed the content of a
group of revolutionary publications and speeches and showed that
revolutionaries on all points of the political spectrum referred to
Rousseau with enthusiasm and even veneration but that the *Social
Contract* was little read and its tenets frequently contradicted even by
those invoking its prestige. Not one of the central political concepts
discussed in the *Social Contract* was understood by the revolutionaries
in the terms that Rousseau had formulated. She concluded that the
"cult of Rousseau" was independent of the contents of the *Social
Contract,* which had, after all, been read only after the fact by
revolutionaries who had already proclaimed themselves his spiritual
heirs.

This contention, however, has been subsequently challenged by
Roger Barny, who asserted that "on the eve of Revolution, Mme
Roland, Brissot, and Mirabeau knew the political works of Rousseau
perfectly well," but who agreed that "the image of the personage of
Rousseau himself was as important, practically, as the major themes
of the *Contract.*"[16]

McDonald asked why, in the face of their refusal to follow Rousseau's
advice, the revolutionaries persisted in dedicating themselves to him,
quoting him in speeches and articles, erecting statues of him and
renaming places after him, his works, and the characters he created.
She concluded, surprisingly enough, that it was *not* his political
thought at all which so impressed the revolutionaries, but his person-

[15]*The Party of Humanity,* p. 281.
[16]"Rousseau dans la Révolution," pp. 60–63.

al "myth," centering on his martyrdom: "the actual contents of the *Social Contract* were for a very large number of people immaterial; the *Social Contract* itself was part of the myth, and it was the myth of Rousseau rather than his political theory which was important in the mind of the Revolutionary generation" (pp. 172–73).

Similarly, Raymond Trousson also concluded that Rousseau's prestige had little to do with his political writings, which on the contrary owed their influence to the adoration of Jean-Jacques's personality. He showed the difference between the homage rendered to Rousseau and the respect paid to other eighteenth-century thinkers: "Rousseau's personage struck the imagination in a different way from those of Raynal, Mably, or Montesquieu and it benefited from the preexisting moral, literary, and personal cult consecrated to the author of *Emile* and *La Nouvelle Héloïse*. Jean-Jacques became the symbol of the just man persecuted by tyranny and privilege,... without there being ... a necessary or profound connection with his political writings" (p. 68).

Daniel Mornet added that "in order to convert to the new morality, Rousseau had exalted forces which better than any others can transform the moral world, that is to say, mystical forces" (p. 95). Groethuysen indicated that these forces corresponded to "an immediate emotional content. It is not enough to say: 'man has rights, the people have rights.' The words 'man' and 'people' must... awaken a warm feeling in the one who pronounces them ... [Rousseau] described the people with love and that is where the exceptional significance of the influence exercised by Rousseau on the French Revolution resides" (pp. 296–97).

Thus Groethuysen, like McDonald, Trousson, and Mornet, saw Rousseau's influence as crucial but primarily nonintellectual. Whether in the form of a "personal myth of martyrdom," a "mystical vision," or the emotional meanings with which such words as "man" and "people" were invested, these interpretations tend to reinforce one another. Yet they remain incomplete when compared to the firsthand testimony.

Robespierre, shortly after being elected deputy from Arras to the Estates General in April 1789, wrote what he called a "Dedication to the Shades of Jean-Jacques Rousseau." This unfinished text, published posthumously, reveals the high-minded gravity with which he be-

gan his career as a representative of the nation.[17] He invoked
Rousseau as his spiritual mentor. "Divine man! You taught me to
know myself; while I was still a young man you made me appreciate
the dignity of my nature and reflect on the great principles of social
order." Robespierre called Rousseau "divine," thus underlining
Trousson's comment "[Rousseau] has become a god." The first debt
of gratitude which Robespierre wished to discharge, however, concerned his belief that Rousseau had taught him to know himself.
The meaning of this noetic apprenticeship was made explicit in the
second part of the sentence: "You made me appreciate the dignity of
my nature." Robespierre felt indebted to Rousseau therefore because
his readings of the master had shown him the worth of his own
being, and he equated this state of heightened self-esteem with
"knowledge." It was only after this internal transformation that he
was moved to "reflect upon the great principles of the social order."
Thus it was not a body of information or the tenets of a political
system which Robespierre absorbed from Rousseau, but a compelling vision of himself. "Your example is there," he continued, "there
before my eyes. Your admirable *Confessions,* that honest and courageous exhalation of the purest soul, will go to posterity less as a
model of art than as a model of virtue. . . . I want to follow your
venerated steps . . . happy if I can remain faithful to the inspirations I
imbibed from your texts." Robespierre did not claim to find political
inspiration in the *Social Contract* or the discourses. What was significant to him was Rousseau's "virtue" as displayed in the *Confessions.*
For the next five years, until he went to the guillotine in July 1794,
he was to remain faithful to that vision. In the words of his English
biographer J. L. Carr, Robespierre's "identification [with Rousseau]
was in fact almost total."[18] As Jean Starobinski has noted, however,
there were several Rousseaus with whom it was possible to identify:
"Rousseau as natural man, as musician-poet of the Golden Age, as
Republican orator of the virtuous society."[19] Among these figures

[17]*Oeuvres de M. Robespierre,* ed. Laponneraye (Paris: published by the editor, fau-
bourg St. Denis, 1840), 2: 473–74. Bernard Gagnebin discusses the allegation that this
dedication may be apocryphal and concludes that it is probably, although not unquestionably, authentic in "L'Etrange Accueil fait aux 'Confessions,'" *AJJR,* 38 (1969–71).
[18]*Robespierre* (London: Constable, 1972), p. 119.
[19]*Jean-Jacques Rousseau: La Transparence et l'obstacle* (Paris: Gallimard, 1957), p. 379.

embodied in the works, Robespierre's identification was centered around the last, the republican orator of the virtuous society.

In this way one of the Revolution's greatest leaders, who as a scholarship student at Louis-le-Grand had suffered humiliating contact with the aristocracy, emerged from a state of self-contempt through contact with the virtue that "exhaled" from Rousseau and thereafter found himself able to appreciate his own dignity. As it will become apparent in chapter 8, his experience was far from unique in his generation. No wonder that the man who made it possible was venerated.

CHAPTER TWO

The Magnetism of Virtue

That Rousseau was the source of the cult of Rousseau and only secondarily an intellectual leader to his followers was no accident. His admirers were replicating, in their relation to his myth, the very relationship that Rousseau had established with his own self-representation. If one is to understand both Rousseau and the generation following him, it is that relationship which must be comprehended, for it constitutes virtue in and of itself. Not an ethical system in any usual sense, Rousseau's virtue was rather a state of being that could be entered by the willing disciple. The noncognitive qualities of this state are those which have given rise to difficulties for many commentators. Before there could be a public cult of Rousseau, there had to be Rousseau's own myth of himself. The enthralling image, the beginning of the Rousseau who mattered to those who invoked his virtue, was established with the publication of the *Premier Discours*, when the author was thirty-seven years old.

Before that, he displays himself in the autobiographical writings as a child thrice abandoned, first when his mother died, then when his father deserted him, and finally when he was ejected from his uncle's home.[1] His early self-esteem he depicted as rooted in largely

---

[1] Pierre-Paul Clément has reconstructed the family constellation of Rousseau's early years, laying special emphasis upon Suzanne Bernard, his father's sister, who served him as a substitute mother. When the family abruptly collapsed in 1722, Clément points out, Jean-Jacques lost this maternal figure as well as his father. *J.-J. Rousseau, de l'Eros coupable à l'Eros glorieux* (Neuchâtel: Baconnière, 1976), chs 1–6.

imaginary pictures of himself as a Plutarchian hero. "I became the person whose life I was reading: the account of courageous and intrepid acts which struck me made my eyes shine and my voice strong," he wrote in the *Confessions* (1: 9). As he was progressively demoted from his position as his father's favorite son to that of a pensioner at his uncle's house and finally to the level of an apprentice to an engraver, his situation became incompatible with his need for affirmation of his own merit. His quest for admiration and the anguish he experienced at denigration led him to quit his apprenticeship. "The contempt of the engraver humiliated me extremely," he remembered. M. Ducommun succeeded in "reducing me in my mind as well as in my fortunes to the status of an apprentice." Debased by the engraver's lack of regard for him, Rousseau found that his father too looked down on him: "My father, when I went to see him, did not find me his idol anymore." Describing himself as crushed at being viewed as a lowly apprentice by his master and his father, he abandoned Geneva and set out to travel, filled with the certainty that his inner worth would be recognized by those he met: "I was entering the wide world confidently, my value was going to fill it. By showing myself I was going to be the center of attention of the entire universe" (1: 44).

The day he left Geneva, he began a life of wandering, intent on dazzling the world by showing himself to it. At one point he and a friend he had picked up dreamed of exhibiting a toy fountain. He imagined the reaction the toy would elicit in the villages where they would stop: "In every village we would gather the peasants around our fountain and meals and delicious dishes would rain down upon us."

A few years later, the fountain long broken and discarded, Rousseau essayed a different gambit in his quest for instant admiration. He had become so fascinated by a musician friend, Venture de Villeneuve, that his head was "venturized": "I made an anagram of the name of Rousseau in the name Vaussore, and I called myself 'Vaussore de Villeneuve.'" After seizing upon his hero's name, he went on to expropriate his profession as well: "Venture knew composition, although he didn't talk about it; I, without knowing it, told everybody about it and although incapable of annotating the least ditty, I presented myself as a composer" (1: 148). He actually mounted a "concert," where, in his role as composer, he passed to the musicians sheets of paper-sprinkled with notes in no particular order. It was only after the uproar of the astonished musicians and spectators struck his ears that he realized what he had done. The next day the city was laughing at him; his reaction was shame.

His wish to become fascinating in a magical way conflicted with his ambitions to achieve celebrity by more conventional means. The impulse to captivate the world by showing himself, to rivet attention by exhibitionism, lay dormant for periods, only to emerge in manifestations as diverse as his exposure of his buttocks in the courtyards of Turin and his public readings of his *Confessions*. The pressure toward these eruptions of display was the greater because he cut a shy and inarticulate figure when he was not carried away: "the desperate need I had to be the object of other people's thoughts was precisely what robbed me of my courage to show myself" (1: 287).

His wanderings, which took him through the Savoy, in and out of the home of his mistress-protectress, Madame de Warens, and through Turin as a convert to Catholicism, eventually led him to Paris. There the question of how to become the center of attention again occupied his mind. He frequented the coffee houses where the great chess-masters played, surrounded by admirers. "I did not doubt that in the end I would become better than all of them and that was enough, in my opinion, to support me. I used to say to myself: whoever is best at something is always sure of being sought after. Let's be best then, at no matter what; I shall be sought after, opportunities will present themselves, and my worth will do the rest" (1: 288).

He drifted away from chess and back to music, hoping to create a new system of notation: "I persisted in wanting to make a revolution in music with it and achieve in that way a fame which in Paris is always linked to fortune" (1: 286). He wrote an opera. Much of what Rousseau did and attempted during his period inverted the values of his early environment. He discredited the Calvinist morality according to whose tenets he was a failure and worse. According to Walter Rex: "The one rule governing virtually all of Rousseau's conduct was a determination not only to reject his Genevan training but to embody himself the exact *opposite* of Genevan values."[2]

It was not, eventually, either chess or music that plucked him from

---

[2]"On the Background of Rousseau's *First Discourse*," SECC, 9 (1980), 138–39.

his obscure, Bohemian, anti-Calvinist existence to hurtle him into the quintessentially Parisian limelight of which he had so long dreamed, but letters, his prize-winning response to the question set by the Academy of Dijon as to "whether the reestablishment of the sciences and the arts has contributed to purifying morals." This savagely brilliant piece made him what he had always wished to be, the object of rapt attention, the magnetic center drawing all gazes, in short, someone as fascinating as the nobleman was because of his birth, the rich man because of his money, or the courtesan because of her charms.

The original core of the *Premier Discours* was the passage entitled the "Prosopopée de Fabricius." It was this speech which he had received as a revelation while walking to Vincennes to visit his friend Diderot (at that time imprisoned for publishing the *Lettre sur les aveugles*) and had later dictated, while lying in bed, to his mistress's mother. In this harangue, a resurrected Plutarchian republican lectures the degenerate inhabitants of Imperial Rome:

"Gods!" You would have said, "what has become of those thatched roofs and those rustic homes where moderation and virtue used to dwell? What baleful splendor has replaced Roman simplicity? What is this alien language? What are these effeminate ways? What is the meaning of these statues, these paintings, these buildings? Fools, what have you done?...Romans, make haste to overthrow these amphitheaters, smash these marbles, burn these paintings, drive away these slaves who are subjugating you and whose ominous arts corrupt you. Let other hands win fame with their vain talents; the only talent worthy of Rome is that of conquering the world and making virtue reign." [3: 14–15]

The speech of Fabricius is founded on a nostalgic vision of a time gone by when men were better and happier. It presents a guilt-provoking tableau. The founding father returns to view the works of his children and is appalled by their sophistication, which he condemns as reflecting the degeneration of their morals. Intrinsic to this contempt for the civilized is the glorification of virile militarism: "Is it to enrich architects, painters, sculptors, and actors that you have steeped Greece and Asia in your blood? Are the spoils of Carthage the prey of a flute-player?" There was only one proper response to the hegemony of intellect and art in Rome. The Romans must overthrow, break, and burn in order to cleanse themselves for their proper role, that of world conquest and domination in the name of virtue. The exhortation ended with an evocation of what was meant by "making virtue reign": Cyneas, the Thessalian of whom Plutarch had written, mistook the Roman senate for an assembly of kings. "Oh citizens," said Fabricius, "he saw a spectacle that your riches and all your arts will never provide; the most beautiful spectacle ever to appear beneath the sun, the assembly of two hundred virtuous men, worthy of commanding Rome and governing the earth."

This prosopopeia contains within it all of the elements of the *Premier Discours* and beyond that, the essence of much of his future writing. François Boucharrdy commented: "The *Premier Discours* did not exhaust the intuition, Rousseau declared it inseparable from the *Second* and from *Emile*. Why not add also: inseparable from the *Lettre à d'Alembert,* from *La Nouvelle Héloïse,* and from the *Contrat social,* all works which we can understand better today by relating them to this programmatic discourse?"[3] In subsequent texts Rousseau often substituted Sparta for Rome as the locus of "patriarchal virtue," Sparta being even more stark, warlike, and anti-intellectual. But all the elements of the new myth were already in place. Virtue had been awarded ultimate prestige and, detached from both theology and ethics, was now equated with military masculinity, dominance, simplicity, frugality, ignorance, and a preference for the archaic; in short, the antithesis of every value prevailing among the influential classes of French society in the eighteenth century. The whole essay provided a language in which imperial France could be condemned as Fabricius had condemned Imperial Rome. As Jean Starobinski put it, "Modern *accusatory thought* found its language . . . in the illumination of Vincennes."[4] A vast array of objects and beings now awaited Rousseau's accusations.

For he had become a man doubly transformed, both inwardly and outwardly. He returned repeatedly to the emotional meaning of that vision for the rest of his life. One of his own selves, one of the Plutarchian identifications which had been his source of strength in childhood, had broken through to him and provided him with an ecstatic experience of internal unification. In receiving the speech of Fabricius (who was a childhood self) he became a prophet and, like

---

[3]Introduction to Pléiade edition (3: xxxiii).
[4]"La Prosopopée de Fabricius," *Revue des Sciences Humaines,* 161 (1976), 96.

all prophets, consecrated. He, usually so anxious to make a good impression that he could not put himself forward at all, had now become a charismatic being, one through whom an apparently external gift manifests itself. He felt energized and organized, powerful, superior, and marked by supernatural favor. Pierre-Paul Clément called him "moved by poetic inspiration, as if the sacred mission of regenerating humanity by a new baptism had been imposed on him" (p. 245). Rousseau described his transformation using the third person:

> From the lively effervescence which then took place in his soul came those sparks of genius which have dazzled in his writings during ten years of delirium and fever, a genius no trace of which had appeared until that time, and which in all likelihood would not have shone again if he had continued to write once this paroxysm had passed.... For a time he astonished Europe by the works in which ordinary souls saw only eloquence and intellect, but where the souls who inhabit the ethereal regions recognize with joy one of their own. [1: 829]

Simultaneously, he underwent a second transformation. The same aspect of his personality which had permitted him to "become" the Plutarchian figure he read about or to "become" Vaussore de Villeneuve now allowed his amorphous personality to coalesce as the austerely virtuous man he had projected in his discourse: "The news [of winning the prize] reawakened in me all the ideas which had dictated [the discourse] to me, animated them with a new strength and started fermenting in my heart that first yeast of heroism and virtue which my father and my fatherland and Plutarch had put there in my childhood. I no longer saw anything great and beautiful except to be free and virtuous, above contingency and public opinion, and to suffice unto myself" (1: 356).

The unprecedented success of the work created in its readers the image of a superhumanly virtuous author, Rousseau-Fabricius, adored by the *beau monde*, whom Rousseau could now call himself. His wish to fascinate the world was abruptly realized by his transfiguration into a man of virtue. "It would," he noted, "be a question of exciting desire and facilitating the means of attracting the same admiration to oneself with virtue that nowadays one can only attract with money" (3: 502; "De l'honneur et de la vertu"). The *Premier Discours* performed precisely that function; it endowed him with a prestige which hitherto had been the prerogative of the rich and powerful. "I would rather be forgotten by the human race than regarded as an ordinary man," he remarked in an autobiographical fragment (1: 1123), and he was now transformed into Europe's most extraordinary individual, the living wellspring of goodness in a wicked world. Enthralled with the picture of himself he had created, he resolved to become consubstantial with the arresting figure of moral superiority his discourse had projected: "Determined to spend the few years remaining to me in independence and poverty, I applied all the strength of my soul to breaking the chains of opinion and courageously doing everything which seemed good to me" (1: 362).

His "personal reform" included freeing himself from his rich protectors and earning his living copying music, giving up the fashionable costume, complete with sword, which aped aristocratic garb, in favor of simple attire, and selling his watch. These changes in his personal life did not take place overnight, but were the result of a long struggle to bring his being into accord with his writings. According to Michel Launay: "It was no less than five years before Rousseau could consider himself faithful, deep in his heart, to 'that first germ of heroism and virtue that his father, his fatherland, and Plutarch had put there in his childhood.'"[5] He was now not merely interesting but sensational. The nobles, the rich, the elegant women of Paris were at his feet, and he made the astonishing discovery that the more contempt he showed for them, the more devoted they were. "The success of my first writings had made me fashionable. The state I had adopted excited curiosity: people wanted to know this bizarre man who avoided everyone and cared about nothing except living free and happy in his way: that was enough to make it impossible. My room was never empty of people who, under various pretexts, came to take up my time. Women used a thousand ruses to have me to dinner. The more rude I was to people, the more stubborn they became" (1: 36).

To be admired, even adored, for his austere virtue was only half the triumph of this stage in Rousseau's life, however, for looking down on his adulators left him feeling lonely. He needed other

---

[5] *Jean-Jacques Rousseau, écrivain politique (1712–1762)* (Grenoble: ACER, 1971), pp. 178–79. Also see M. Raymond, "Rousseau et Genève," *Jean-Jacques Rousseau* (Paris; Corti, 1962), pp. 225–37.

experiences in addition to those of moral superiority. It was the success of his opera, *Le Devin du village*, which provided him with the warm sense of fusion in goodness he desired.

If the author of the *Premier Discours* exerted an austere patriarchal magnetism upon fashionable Paris, the composer of the *Devin du village* seduced his audience through feelings that Rousseau identified as feminine. In the autobiographical writings, Rousseau describes its composition as an act of innocent revenge. Reducing the audience to a state of passive enthrallment, the opera served to render Rousseau master where previously he spoke of being enslaved. He characterized himself as having long been subject to states of helpless bondage that certain women easily induced in him. He described the sensation as one of losing his will to the spell cast by an overwhelmingly attractive woman, as if she exerted a power he was unable to resist. His depiction of Madame Dupin at her toilette was typical: "Her arms were bare, her hair was loose, her dressing gown was carelessly arranged. This type of reception was new to me; my poor head could not cope with it, I became confused, bewildered, in short, there I was, smitten with Madame Dupin" (1: 291).

This loss of will in the presence of an alluring woman was an essential attribute of the mythic Rousseau, and, in his self-representations, he both resented the enticement of women and coveted it. Bernardin de Saint-Pierre, in his memoirs of his friend, recounts an anecdote that Rousseau told him during a walk they took together. Rousseau related the story as a joke: "Once a young country boy came to Paris and was invited to a party given by the duchesse de Berry. He had never before glimpsed such opulence. The music, the glittering lights and the brilliant jewels, Madame de Berry's perfume and above all her magnificent *décolletage* took such a hold upon the simple fellow that, shedding decorum, he fell upon his glamorous hostess, hands and mouth glued to her breast."[6]

If Rousseau found this story amusing, as Bernardin reports, it was because the magnificent, affluent duchess was punished rather than rewarded for her charms. She was made the focus of an embarrassing episode by an innocent who had reacted directly to the provocation she offered. Rousseau verbalized male anger at the social convention that permitted women to expose their bosoms invitingly while men

[6]*La Vie et les ouvrages de Jean-Jacques Rousseau* (Paris: Cornély, 1907), p. 58.

were supposed to look but maintain strict control of their public behavior and, inhibiting arousal, never respond directly to the stimulation.

When Voltaire and Diderot made use of similar episodes, they did so in quite different contexts. In Voltaire's *L'Ingénu*, a young Indian, inflamed at the sight of the lovely Breton Mlle de St. Yves, prepared to consummate their union on the spot, much to the scandal of the young woman's relations. In Diderot's *Supplément au voyage de Bougainville*, a girl who had successfully passed herself off as a sailor during Bougainville's whole voyage, was instantly assaulted by native men when she stepped off the boat in Tahiti. Unlike the Europeans, the Tahitians immediately recognized and responded to a woman. For both Diderot and Voltaire the point was that sexuality had, in civilized countries, become overlaid by other concerns, so that the European man acted artificially in such matters, unlike the primitive, who was capable of a direct, "natural" response. For Rousseau, very differently, it was the socially corrupt misuse of organs of nutritive function as objects of sexual display that was repudiated when it evoked the gesture of an imperious infant.

Rousseau began *Emile*, his treatise on education, with a denunciation of childrearing practices among the upper classes in France as being both physically dangerous and morally degrading. By giving newborn infants to nurses to be cared for, women sacrificed their children's wellbeing, failed to develop the bond breastfeeding provided, and discouraged their husbands from assuming the proper paternal role.[7] Women neglected their duties, according to Rousseau, in their pursuit of pleasure. Wishing to escape the tedium of the taboo which prohibited them from engaging in sexual relations while nursing, they contrived to have their doctors and husbands excuse them from their natural function. "I have sometimes witnessed the little strategy of young women who pretend to want to nurse their infants. They know how to make people coax them into renouncing this whim: adroitly they make the husbands, the doctors, above all their mothers intervene. A husband who would dare to consent to his wife nursing her child would be ruined. You are

---

[7] See Nancy Senior, "Aspects of Infant Feeding in Eighteenth-Century France," for an evaluation of Rousseau's contribution to the breastfeeding movement in Europe. *ECS*, 16 (1983), 367–88.

Revolutionary pictorial homage to Rousseau.
(Courtesy of the Bibliothèque nationale, Paris)

fortunate if you find women in the country more chaste than yours!" (4: 256).

In their unbridled lubricity, women went beyond rejecting their infants and practiced birth control. "Not satisfied with having ceased to nurse their infants, women stop wanting to have them.... They want to perform a fruitless act in order to repeat it, and they channel the appeal [nature] gave them to multiply the species to the prejudice of the species" (4: 256).

Wetnurses further endangered the health of their charges by swaddling them and "hanging them on a hook" so as not to be bothered with them. "Civil man is born, lives, and dies in slavery: at birth they sew him into swaddling, when he dies they nail him into a coffin; as long as he retains a human face he is enchained by our institutions" (4: 253).

This grim picture, however, could be completely reversed if only women would breastfeed their infants. "Let mothers deign to nurse their babies, morals will reform themselves, feelings of nature will reawaken in all hearts, the State will be repopulated" (4: 258).

With moving immediacy, Rousseau evoked the sensations of the nursing infant, giving each reader empathic access to a long hidden part of himself, a buried self in whom innocence still existed, unsullied by the incursions of time and men. As he had spoken of primitive man in the *Second Discours,* now he spoke of the child, a lost, fundamental referent, who antedated social relations.[8] Raising a male child to virtue meant preserving his self-absorption intact into adult life. The reabsorption of the sexually active woman into the lactating mother, the substitution of a nutritive for a genital function, was a bold and daring provocation in the eighteenth century, where an egalitarian attitude toward women had become fashionable in enlightened and aristocratic circles.[9]

---

[8]Francesco Orlando, in *Infanzia, memoria e storia da Rousseau ai romantici* (Padua: Liviana, 1966), and "La Découverte du souvenir d'enfance," *AJJR,* 37 (1966–68), 149–73, described how original and in a sense courageous Rousseau was to treat material from his own childhood, for its intrinsic value, with seriousness and respect.

[9]In her introduction to *French Women and the Age of Enlightenment,* ed. S. I. Spencer, Elizabeth Fox-Genovese discusses the complex shifts in attitude of nineteenth- and twentieth-century historians toward the aristocratic as opposed to the bourgeois woman in the eighteenth century, and the recent attention of social historians and feminist scholars to the vast majority of French women belonging to the lower echelons of society, whose existence had little in common with "the galaxy of notable

When the *Devin du village* was presented at Versailles, Rousseau was carried away, he writes, by the sensation of moving the elegant woman in the audience as they had so often moved him: "All around me, I heard whispering women who seemed to me beautiful as angels and who said to one another, this is charming, this is ravishing. The pleasure of causing emotion in so many enticing women made me shed tears myself, and at the first duet, I could no longer control them, when I observed that I was not the only one to weep." He was moved at the sight of the fashionable women in tears: "Sexual sensuality entered into it much more than an author's vanity, for had there only been men present, I would not have been devoured, as I was, with the desire to gather with my lips the delicious tears which I was causing to flow" (1: 379).

Sentiment was the means by which a beautiful woman could be converted into one who oozed a "delicious" secretion. The wish to lick tears from an emotionally aroused woman's face was the reverse side of the preference for the "sweet happiness" of weeping which was such an essential element of the mythical Jean-Jacques. Pleasurable weeping in a state of heightened self-esteem was the sensual outlet given highest prestige in his works, a desired accompaniment and at times a preferred substitute for sexual relations with a woman. In *La Nouvelle Héloïse* Rousseau described how his two self-projections, Julie and Saint-Preux, enjoyed moments of "virtuous love" when, tearfully struggling with prolonged ungratified sexual temptation, they were overwhelmed with ambiguously pleasurable sensation. Emile and his fiancée, Sophie, found greater sensuality in libidinized crying than in intercourse. "Sometimes in raptures which must be held in check they shed tears which are purer than the dew, and these sweet tears are the enchantment of their lives; they are in the most spell-binding, charming delirium ever experienced by human souls. You, sensual people, you bodies without souls, they will know your pleasures some day, and they will long the rest of their lives for the happy times when they refused those pleasures themselves" (4: 792).

The very first description of pleasure in the *Confessions* occurred when Rousseau recounted how his father used to take his son in his

---

eighteenth-century women who have mesmerized historians and critics since their own day" (Bloomington: Indiana University Press, 1984), p. 5.

arms and tell him that he resembled his dead mother. "He believed he saw her again in me, without being able to forget that I had taken her from him, never did he hug me that I did not sense in his sighs, his convulsive embrace, that bitter regret colored his caresses, which were all the more tender for it. When he said 'Jean-Jacques, let us speak of your mother,' I used to say to him: 'Very well, father, now we are going to weep'; and this word alone reduced him immediately to tears" (1: 7).

In the fourth *Promenade* Rousseau recounted an accident of his childhood to demonstrate that, in the *Confessions*, he had inexplicably omitted certain stories, such as the following, which showed "the happy qualities with which my heart was endowed." His playmate had accidentally hit him on the head. "He thought he had killed me. He threw himself upon me, embraced me, held me tightly while dissolving into tears and uttering piercing screams. I was hugging him too, with all my might, weeping like him in an emotional bewilderment not without a certain sweetness" (1: 1037). "Jean-Jacques" experiencing simultaneously sensual arousal and wronged innocence forms the core of his literary persona. He gave the world erotized tears as a prelude to, and even a substitute for, more usual avenues of discharge for libidinal impulses.

Rousseau had thus melded the figure of the sternly virtuous author of the *Premier Discours* with that of the melting creator of the *Devin du village*. What is most extraordinary, however, is that he then presented a figure of himself, enchanted by the success of his two self-projections: "Until then I had been good; from that time on I became virtuous, or at least drunk with virtue. This intoxication had begun in my mind but it had passed into my heart. I was not playing at it in the least; I became in effect what I appeared and during the four years this effervescence lasted in all its force nothing great or beautiful can enter a man's heart of which I was not capable, between heaven and me" (1: 416).

To be "drunk with virtue" was to be in a magical state, suffused with passive pleasure. Jean Starobinski describes how Rousseau "found himself swept away by a dizzying wave. . . . He gave himself up to the paradox of a virtuous intoxication; . . . [his] soul's energy was entirely absorbed by the giddiness of the fascination."[10] This fascination with

[10]*La Transparence et l'obstacle*, p. 80.

himself as virtuous man, which entirely engrossed him, caused each of his works, no matter what its ostensible topic, to have his own personage as its actual core: "Aristotle's system or that of Spinoza detaches itself from the author," noted J. L. Lecercle. "Nothing of the kind with Rousseau: his ideas adhere to his person."[11] As a result, G.-A. Goldschmidt observed, "In Rousseau everything proceeds from a center to which everything returns: a center from which the diversity of the world can only be excluded."[12] The fully achieved exclusion of the diversity of the world would be the topic of his next major work.

He had up to this point achieved a presentation of himself that combined claims of moral superiority with a covert erotic (if infantile) invitation, a "seductive magic which did not jeopardize itself in the act of love," as Starobinski puts it, and the seduction was "inseparable from virtuous exaltation; the two reinforce each other and create an ambiguity which understandably can appear to be impure."[13]

At this point the virtue of the Father and the virtue of the Mother had been described; two of the three legs of his tripod were in place. There remained only the discovery and celebration of the natural self: the goodness of the baby.

A second essay competition proposed by the Academy of Dijon presented him with the opportunity he needed. He retired to the forest of St. Germain with his mistress, Thérèse Levasseur, for a week's stay during which he roamed the woods, contemplating his response to the question: "What is the source of inequality among men?"

> Deep in the forest I sought and I found the image of earliest times whose history I proudly presented; I destroyed the petty lies of mankind, I dared to strip their nature bare. My soul, exalted by these sublime contemplations, raised itself to the divinity, and from that point, seeing my fellow beings following the blind route of their errors, of their misfortunes, of their crimes, I called to them: "Madmen, who complain about nature endlessly, learn that all your woes come from yourselves." [1: 389]

[11]"Réflexions sur l'art de Rousseau," *Europe*, no. 391–92 (1961), 91–92.
[12]*Jean-Jacques Rousseau ou l'esprit de solitude* (Paris: Phoebus, 1978), p. 23.
[13]*La Transparence et l'obstacle*, p. 212.

One of the "souls who inhabit the ethereal regions," he could "raise [himself] to the Divinity" and destroy "the petty lies of mankind." His claim echoed and rivaled the pretensions of the king to rise above mankind and understand its morally defective nature. Louis XIV had said: "As he [the king], is above other men like God, he seems to share in His omniscience as well as His authority."[14] Louis's claim to superiority was founded on blood; Rousseau's rested on virtue.

As befits an author whose soul had raised itself above mankind, in the *Second Discours* Rousseau placed his authorial voice at a point removed in time and detached in attitude from the society around him. He spoke, with magisterial assurance, to the entire human race, dismissing the conclusions of other thinkers contemptuously, since the source of his teaching was none other than nature itself: "Oh man, from whatever country you may be, whatever your opinions are, listen: here is your story as I believed I read it, not in the books of your fellow men, who are liars, but in Nature, who never lies" (3: 133). From this lofty vantage, Rousseau depicted a time before time, when men had not yet formed societies. He described an infancy of the race which in fact recapitulated the infancy of the individual, a period of total self-absorption which present society had forgotten.

Rousseau's unusual psychic development had kept him in touch with a stratum of human experience that the rest of humanity had forgotten or refused to acknowledge: the mentality of the child before its introduction into the world of social relations. When he described the presocietal, preverbal innocence of the species, his audience responded with an inchoate sense of recognition, which generated an utter conviction all the more compelling for not being objectively verifiable. The presentation of the past of every man as the situation of primitive man invested Rousseau's writings with a stamp of indubitable and mysterious authenticity.

Scattered thinly among the great forests covering the world, men, Rousseau maintained, were totally good because they were not in conflict with one another or with themseles. Nature, like a kindly mother, saw to each man's needs and left him free to experience himself alone. "His soul, which nothing agitates, gives itself to the

[14]*Oeuvres de Louis XIV,* 1: 8.

feeling of its momentary existence alone." This was a state of primal innocence in which men were not, as Hobbes had claimed, "naturally wicked," but "having no sort of moral relationship among themselves, could be neither good nor wicked,... unless one were to call vices in the individual those attributes which can harm him, and virtues those attributes that can protect him, in which case one would have to call the man virtuous who least resisted the simple impulses of Nature" (3: 152). In this premoral condition man already had "the only Natural virtue, which even the most fervid Detractor of human virtues must recognize. I speak of Pity" (3: 154). Pity was defined as that involuntary movement which causes all animals to suffer the pains which they witness, and from this principle as we shall see, Rousseau drew far-reaching conclusions. The central insight into the human condition, however, was the inherent conjunction of primitive goodness with utter solitude, and it was here that Rousseau departed most radically from the usual eighteenth-century picture of primitive existence. Whereas Buffon, for example, had seen sexual relations as leading to a natural partnership between men and women and hence to the first social organization, the family, Rousseau remained faithful to his intuition of the underlying infantile organization of the human mind, and insisted that sexuality was a purely physical impulse, which, in a state of nature, forged no link between partners:

> Let us begin by distinguishing between the moral and the physical in the feeling of love. The physical is that general desire which leads one sex to unite with the other; the moral is what determines that desire and fixes it upon a single object exclusively. It is easy to see that the moral in love is an artificial feeling, born of society's usages, and celebrated by women with a great deal of cunning and skill to establish their sway and to render dominant the sex which should obey. [3: 158]

Rousseau denied the "naturalness" of love, seeing it as an arbitrary social convention, a perverse creation of women designed only to usurp the dominance of the male sex. Joel Schwartz points out how Rousseau's pseudoscientific depiction of primitive undifferentiated sexuality yielding to exclusive erotic attachments forged basic political structures: "Because it alters the status quo, romantic love is of political importance. It impels men and women to transcend the original family unit, thereby bringing about the total socialization of the human species."[15]

In a natural state, however, far from mating for life, men and women coupled by chance and then parted; women carried their babies about with them as undifferentiated appendages only until they were able to walk, when they wandered off to assume their own solitary existences. Sexuality, "that blind need, deprived of all feeling of the heart, produced only an animal act. The need satisfied, the two sexes no longer recognized each other, and even the child was nothing to the mother once he could get along without her" (3: 164).

This state of self-contained happiness came to an end ultimately owing to population growth. When the powers of reproduction outstripped the bounty of nature, the originally scattered individuals were pressed in on each other: "As the human race grew, troubles multiplied with men" (3: 165). The greater masses of humanity imposed the necessity for cultivating the soil, engaging in an energetic search for sustenance, and eventually forming cooperative enterprises.

With this picture of origins as background, he could then in the second part of the discourse, depict the inevitable parallelism between technological and intellectual progress and moral decay. The need for increased efficiency in providing for life's necessities brought men together and produced the family; a sort of silver age resulted, when people knew the pleasures of "conjugal and paternal love," but their simple inventions for rendering existence less onerous became "the first yoke that they imposed upon themselves without knowing it, and the first source of the woes that they prepared for their descendants" (3: 168).

In this part of the discourse, Rousseau presented a whole brilliantly original theory of how what was to be called the means of production shaped the economic structure of human life, and how the resultant economic organization controlled and degraded man's political and private existence. In those few pages Rousseau traced every aspect of man's relation with himself, with nature, and with his fellow men as he emerged from the natural state of total independent goodness to his modern artificial condition of dependency,

[15]*The Sexual Politics of Jean-Jacques Rousseau* (Chicago: University of Chicago Press, 1984), p. 27.

unhappiness, and vice. He demonstrated that inequality, the subject proposed by the Academy of Dijon, had come about through a tragic fall into social relations, and that what was vaunted as the achievement of civilized man was a world of unrelieved physical and moral bleakness. Where men were forced to obey the will of others, as in modern political states, a kind of horrible new equality was established: that of slavery. "This is the last term of inequality, and the extreme point which closes the circle and touches the point where we began. It is here that all private individuals become equal again because they are nothing. It is here that everything returns to the one law of the strongest, and therefore to a new law of nature, different from the one with which we began because one was a law of nature in its purity and the latter is the fruit of an excess of corruption" (3: 191).

It was a savage indictment of every existing society, of every real government, of every living being except the fictional primitive. From the utter isolation which this argument urged, the authorial personage of the discourse turned abruptly back to Rousseau's native city and to his father. Geneva, which he had described as so humiliating when he was an apprentice to M. Ducommun, was now illuminated with a retrospective glow of the virtue he found in himself, and his father, who had exiled himself and abandoned his son rather than stand before the city's tribunal, now reappeared as the exemplification of his city's virtue.

He composed a "Dedication to the Republic of Geneva," addressed to the "MAGNIFIQUES, TRES HONORÉS, ET SOUVERAINS SEIGNEURS." He declared a new self-definition: "Convinced that only the virtuous Citizen is entitled to render unto the Fatherland honors which it can accept, I have been working for thirty years in order to be worthy of offering you public homage" (3: 111). Following the publication of the *Premier Discours*, Rousseau had begun signing the title "Citizen of Geneva" after his name, although he was not entitled to use it since he had abjured his religion and with it his rights to citizenship. The logic of his "moral and intellectual reform," however, demanded that the public realities of his life be reconciled with his claims. In this first sentence of his Dedication, he attempted to state by fiat the situation he wished to see come into being: that Geneva should once more accept him as a citizen, and that it should regard him as "virtuous." In the rest of the Dedication, a small essay of its own, he painted a portrait of Geneva which was the positive reverse image of the bitter picture he had drawn of the rest of Europe.

Geneva and Geneva alone was exempt from the corrupting inequality that corroded life in other nations. In reality, Geneva was a rigidly stratified society, possessing five different categories of persons—subjects, inhabitants, natives, bourgeois, and citizens—and was governed by three legislative bodies, composed exclusively of the citizen class and locked in constant struggles for authority so devastating that it had to rely on foreign powers to guarantee its constitution. Rousseau nonetheless addressed himself to its republic as if it were a united entity, which had resolved all problems of polity. He spoke of the rights of "citizens" in such a way that the term appeared to signify all members of the state, and not merely a privileged minority. Thus Geneva was a "state where all the individuals know one another, so that the obscure maneuvers of vice and modesty could not hide from public view and public judgment; a state where this endearing habit of seeing and knowing one another made the citizens' love that of fatherland rather than that of territory" (3: 112).

He exhorted the Genevans, always under the equivocal title of "citizens," to make their happiness "durable by the wisdom of employing it well." He warned them against the least sign of divisiveness: "If there remains among you the faintest hint of bitterness or suspicion, hasten to destroy it as a sinister seed from which, sooner or later, will result your misfortunes and the ruin of your state" (3: 116). Geneva was an example and a source of humiliation to other governments, it showed "the whole universe the example of a proud and modest people, as jealous of their glory as of their liberty" (3: 117).

He invoked the memory of his father, "the virtuous citizen who gave me life," and he upheld his father's right to respect, because, although Isaac Rousseau belonged to the lower echelon of the citizen class, the Genevans were obliged to hold him in esteem since he was "your equal in education, as well as by right of nature and birth; your inferior by will and by the preference accorded your merit...for which you in turn owe a sort of gratitude" (3: 118).

It was an extraordinary document, a triumph of will over fact. Ostensibly designed to flatter Geneva, it was a covert indictment of the existing city as compared with Rousseau's vision of its ideal form. As if excited by his own dream of it, he returned to his native city and, rejecting Catholicism, arranged to be reinstated in his citizenship. He decided against remaining there, however, perhaps because Voltaire had taken up residence in the city, and perhaps also, as Jean Guéhenno suggests, because in that small republic where no dubious personal ties could "hide from public view and public judgment" he found his relationship with Thérèse a source of anxiety.[16] Instead of settling down in Geneva, he accepted the hospitality of Mme d'Epinay, who had remodeled a little house called the Hermitage, in the forest of her chateau at Montmorency.

[16]Guéhenno recounts how difficult it was for Rousseau to reintegrate himself into the religious community of Geneva, to explain "the presence of this woman who was living at his side and, what's more, sleeping in his room." *Jean-Jacques*, vol. 1, *En Marges des "Confessions"* (Paris: Grasset, 1948), p. 296.

CHAPTER THREE

A Society of Perfect Beings

In the *Confessions,* Rousseau depicted himself as a man somehow passively trapped in a persona he had himself created. Having equated the virtuous, the natural, and the asocial, yet, according to his self-referential texts, needing to dazzle and to fascinate, he was in a dilemma of his own making. His retreat to the Hermitage, in April 1756, would have been a suitable act for the author of the *Second Discours,* but it precipitated the exhibitionary Rousseau into a depression. In three senses, he described an unbearable isolation.

Surrounded by forest, immured in nature, he could no longer view the Parisian turpitude he spoke of needing to sustain his posture of accusatory virtue. Settled into Mme d'Epinay's country retreat, he sank into a somber lethargy: "This change began as soon as I left Paris and the spectacle of the vices of that great city ceased to nourish the indignation which it had inspired in me" (1: 417).

At the same time he had lost the friendship of the philosophes, who had been his sustaining social matrix for many years. Diderot, d'Alembert, and Grimm accepted neither the premises of the discourses nor the persona Rousseau was enacting. His increasing distance from the philosophes included estrangement from his hostess, Mme d'Epinay, whose lover was Grimm. Diderot, who had been closest to him, was as obsessed with the subject of virtue as Rousseau, but denied a claim to virtue based only on inner sensations of goodness.[1] During his arduous, largely practical, work with the *Encyclopédie*, he had replaced a morality of intention and sensibility with one based solely on socially useful action: "It is not the thoughts, it is the acts which distinguish the good man from the wicked one. The secret story of all souls is about the same."[2] Voltaire had never departed from the attitude he defined in his *Dictionnaire philosophique:* "What is virtue, my friend? It is to do good: let us do it, and that's enough. But we won't look into your motives."

Rousseau's claims to exceptional moral purity made his friends uncomfortable. Diderot could condone striking a moral posture for rhetorical purposes in a literary work but he found Rousseau presumptuous in taking the posture for reality: "Let us not think either too well of ourselves or too ill without being authorized in our judgments by repeated trials. Let us await the last moment before pronouncing upon our fate and our virtue."[3]

In addition, Rousseau's attacks upon civilization, science, literature, and the arts as the enemies of virtue had been a terrible blow to the Encyclopedists. The accusation that they and their works were immoral, coming not from Catholic orthodoxy but from a former comrade in arms, aroused a bitterness that Rousseau, committed to his axiomatic goodness, labeled incomprehensible.

As Rousseau withdrew progressively into the role of self-sufficing Sage, Diderot, who craved frequent affectionate contact with his friends, expressed anger at being wanted and needed less. The tension between them erupted publicly when Rousseau decided that a statement in Diderot's play, *Le Fils naturel*, "only the wicked man is alone," referred to him. The remark occurred in a discussion of the importance of fulfilling social responsibilities, particularly toward one's children. Rousseau said that Diderot, always the more active party in the friendship, was attacking him: "In our altercations you have always been the aggressor," he told him in a letter. "I am sure I

---

[1]In *Diderot: The Virtue of a Philosopher* (New York: Viking, 1974), I discussed the conflict between Rousseau and Diderot over the significance of the word "virtue." Diderot gradually substituted a morality of socially useful action for one based on subjective sensations of goodness; a system of value which both men had shared in their youth and to which Rousseau remained faithful.

[2]Diderot, *Correspondance*, ed. G. Roth and Jean Varloot (Paris: Minuit, 1955–70), 11: 149.

[3]Diderot, "Réfutation suivie de l'ouvrage d'Helvétius intitulé *L'Homme*," *Oeuvres philosophiques* (Paris: Garnier, 1956), p. 611.

never did you any harm other than not enduring patiently enough the harm you liked to do me, and there I admit I was wrong. I was happy in my solitude; you took it upon yourself to trouble my happiness and you did a good job of it. Besides, you said that only the wicked man is alone, and to justify your sentence you must, at any price, see to it that I become wicked" (C.g., 1: 237).

The third factor that increased Rousseau's sense of isolation at this time, according to the *Confessions*, was his renunciation of sexual relations with Thérèse. He wrote of feeling uneasy, both about having placed his five children in the foundling hospital and about becoming sexually exhausted: "Fearing still another incident and not wishing to run the risk, I preferred to condemn myself to abstinence rather than expose Thérèse to finding herself in the same situation again. Moreover I had noticed that relations with women made my health perceptibly worse" (1: 595). He did not, however, mean abstinence in its fullest sense. In the Paris manuscript he added: "The equivalent vice of which I was never able to cure myself seemed to affect my health less" (1: 495).[4]

With himself as sexual partner, Rousseau wrote of turning to his own fantasies for sensual pleasure, withdrawing from the real world and plunging into his own mind to maintain the feelings of virtue which he called necessary to his well-being. In his youth, some twenty-five years before, when he was living as the protege of Mme de Warens, his masturbation had been so obvious that she, alarmed at his habits, took him to her bed. He reacted to this change in their relationship "with an invincible sadness which poisoned the charm" (1: 197). His autobiographical writings place the origins of the problem of whether it was better to masturbate or to enter into a real affair with a woman during those years. It was at this time, probably around 1729, while he was living at the home of Mme de Warens, that Rousseau wrote his first play, *Narcisse*.

The plot centers on the instantaneous state of enthrallment the self-absorbed hero experiences when he sees his own portrait over which has been drawn a feminine headdress. "Here is the prettiest face I have ever seen in my life," he exclaims, and within minutes he

---

[4]Georges Dupeyron commented that Rousseau's onanism "emerges by means of a momentarily "perverse' progress into that ideal of 'virtuous sublimation' which Jean-Jacques dreamed of attaining as the goal of his amorous enterprises." "Jean-Jacques et la sexualité," *Europe*, nos. 391–92 (1961), 33–42.

is ready to break off his engagement to pursue the lovely "stranger."
A friend says of the portrait: "Although he is the prettiest man in the
world, here he shines as a woman with new charms," but his sister
insists he has always been "a kind of woman hidden under a man's
clothes, because of his delicacy and the affectation of his dress. This
portrait...seems less to disguise him than to bring him back to his
natural state" (2: 978). Valère is both a beautiful man *and* a beautiful
woman, a self-contained sexual partnership.[5] Although his fiancée
loves him and wishes to disentangle him from his self-embrace, her
attitude is more maternal than amorous. "What can one reproach
him with, except the universal vice of his age?" she asks, using a
phrase which, in Rousseau's autobiographical writings, refers to
autoerotism. The play goes on to a conventional ending. The hero
allows himself to be persuaded to choose his real fiancée over
himself as a girl and thanks her for having cured him "of a
ridiculous habit which was the shame of my youth" (2: 1018).

Now in his mid-forties, Rousseau was again faced with the conflicts
that had given rise to *Narcisse,* but this time he chose his own
self-representations, not the outer world. Turning inward for pleasure, he was inundated with erotic memories. Images of women
from all periods of his life came to people his imaginary world. He
was surrounded by a "seraglio of Houris" (1: 427). This portion of
Rousseau's autobiography echoes the tale of his father's separation
from his wife and his years in Constantinople as watchmaker in a
harem. Surrendering to life in a seraglio, however, even an imaginary one, was incompatible with Rousseau's self-created myth of the
exemplary virtuous man. To elicit the pleasure without sacrificing
the self-esteem, he developed a fantasy that mediated the two
demands, a situation that was permanently to alter the eighteenth
century's concept of both erotism and virtue.

He invented a situation that brought together a group of desirable
and desiring young people, attracted to one another but restrained
by their virtue. He described himself entering into the world of this

---

[5]Jacques Scherer pointed out that the character must have been connected "in
reality to homosexual tastes to which the proprieties of the theater forbade allusion"
(2: 1861). It would seem, however, that the inclination Rousseau was depicting was not
so much homosexuality but, as the title suggested, narcissism. P.-P. Clément (p. 143)
comes to the same conclusion regarding Rousseau's self-portrait in the *Confessions*:
"We are given to understand less the presence of latent homosexuality than a
narcissistic fixation."

plot and being seized by a new elation: "Forgetting the human race altogether, I made myself societies of perfect beings as celestial by their virtue as by their beauty, sure, tender, faithful friends such as I never found here below" (1: 427). Little by little the "society of perfect beings" became two lovely young cousins, Julie and Claire, and their amorous tutor, Saint-Preux. The central daydream of *La Nouvelle Héloïse*, of the virtuous lovers who live together but may neither yield to their passion nor overcome it, took shape in Rousseau's mind as a private fantasy, for he had not yet thought of utilizing it to write a novel.

Just as, in the past, he had become a figure from Plutarch, or Vaussore de Villeneuve, or Rousseau-Fabricius, so now the boundaries between his real being and what he fantasized dissolved under the impact of his longing. He began imagining himself to *be* alternately Julie, Claire, and Saint-Preux. He wrote letters expressing their emotions and then copied the letters onto beautiful gilt-edged paper, so that he might take them to the woods and open and read them, his heart beating "with as much pleasure as if he had received them from an adored mistress."[6] He himself was that society of perfect beings which he had imagined. He could feel, as Julie, passionate love for himself as Saint-Preux; as Saint-Preux he was overwhelmed with desire for himself as Julie. He alternately externalized his characters and fused himself again with them so successfully that he was intoxicated by "torrents of the most delicious feelings which have ever entered the human heart" (1: 427).

In a final triumphant negation of all separation between creator and created, he encountered Mme d'Epinay's sister-in-law, Sophie d'Houdetot, and cast her to play out in actuality the role he had delineated for Julie in fantasy. He read her Saint-Preux's letters during their long walks in the woods; they achieved a throbbing intimacy that never reached consummation despite burning kisses and a night spent together in a thicket. Now Rousseau was able to drink deeply of the cup of sentiment, for he had established a universe in which all the elements were designed for his delectation. So protean was his personality at this point, according to his account, that he became inflamed by Sophie's avowals of her passion for Saint Lambert and: "without my noticing it and without her noticing it she

---

[6]Cited by René Pomeau, introd. to *La Nouvelle Héloïse* (Paris: Garnier, 1960), p. viii.

inspired me with the same feelings for her which she expressed for her lover" (1: 440). In thus loving a woman with a woman's love for a man, he completed the synthesis begun by animating memories of his former mistresses with his own distaff identity. He had illuminated Mme d'Houdetot with this phantom radiance and finally appropriated her passion for her lover as a source of emotional vitality. All boundaries had become blurred. In his ecstasy Rousseau could move easily back and forth between subject and object, male and female, lover and beloved. He had triumphed over the challenges of the Hermitage and recaptured the state of being "drunk with virtue" when he was "capable of every great and beautiful thing that can enter a man's heart."

Just as Rousseau had insisted, in the *Premier Discours,* that the truth he was seeking was to be found not "in the facts" but in his "own heart," now he found the superior universe of *La Nouvelle Héloïse* not in the world but in himself. The novel depicted no one but Rousseau in a variety of guises, enticing himself. The slender givens of *Narcisse* were fleshed out to encompass a complex world. And all the while, his identification with Julie, Claire, Saint-Preux, and Wolmar denied the conflicts of his own life as depicted in the autobiographical works: his abandoned children, the derisive attitude of his friends, and the chains of dependency binding him at once to Thérèse and to heterosexual abstinence. He had created a paradise where, as each character in turn, he was not only free from remorse, but so innocent that his innermost thoughts and feelings were open to the scrutiny of others. When he assembled the letters he had written to himself, the collection constituted a "book without wickedness of any kind, neither in the characters nor in the actions" (1: 54). He considered that he had gone so far in that direction that the novel would be rejected by the worldly reader: "All the sentiments will be considered unnatural by those who don't believe in virtue" (2: 6).

The genius of his achievement may be indicated by looking at the difficulties involved. The underlying fantasy rested on the maintenance of an adulterous passion between Julie and Saint-Preux and the vaguely bisexual voyeurism of Claire and Julie's husband, Wolmar. Straightforward or direct expression of these themes would have rendered the characters vicious. On the other hand, concealing them would have made the characters opaque and deceptive. It would have destroyed that utter transparency which was the prerequisite of the total communion with them for which Rousseau yearned.[7]

His efforts to reconcile these opposed requirements resulted in the creation of a distinctive style of thought, feeling, and expression, marked by the characters' pervasive drive toward fusion with one another. His need, alternately, to eject his self-projections so as to watch them enact his daydreams, and then to redissolve them into himself in a mystical, ecstatic union, produced the sensation of a powerful undercurrent, constantly threatening to suck the characters back into their primal matter. "The closest union of bodies was never enough for me," he wrote in the *Confessions*, "it would have taken two souls in the same body; without that I always felt empty" (1: 416). Just as Rousseau's autobiographical persona was of a man whose real sexual object was himself, his fictional characters were obsessed with the same wish to melt and flow into one another. "Give me your heart, my Julie," said Saint-Preux, "to love you as you deserve!" (2: 150). Julie dreamed of marrying her lover to her friend and confessed that their hearts were already merged within her own: "let them fuse still more," she told Claire, "be but one person for you and for me" (2: 634). Claire replied that she was too absorbed in Julie, "from our earliest years . . . all my feelings have come from you, you alone take the place of everything for me" (2: 640). Saint-Preux spoke frequently of an amorphous sentiment enveloping both girls: "you are both more dear to me than ever; but my heart no longer can tell one from the other, and does not separate the inseparables" (2: 619).

At the same time, the emphasis on fusion was used for a second, protective purpose. The context of sentimental virtue served to ward off the image of the seductive and therefore controlling woman. As much as it was emphasized that Saint-Preux, Claire, and Julie were emanations of one flux, still it was Julie who threatened to tilt the balance and become dominant. In a second preface to the novel Rousseau remarked: "This Julie, such as she is, must be an enchant-

---

[7]Choderlos de Laclos, in *Les Liaisons dangereuses*, rendered the latent perversity of Rousseau's novel specific and explicit, deliberately ripping the "veil of delicious sentiment" with which Rousseau disguised the outlines of the core fantasy. See C. Blum, "Styles of Cognition as Moral Options in *La Nouvelle Héloïse* and *Les Liaisons dangereuses*," *PMLA*, 88 (1973), 289–98.

ing creature; everything approaching her must resemble her, everything around Julie must become her" (2: 28). Despite the multivalence of the characters, it was Julie who emerged as the center of a potent magnetism which held them all. She dominated her lover: "My Julie," he told her, "you were made to rule. Your empire is the most absolute I know. It extends to the very will; . . . you impose your will on me, you subjugate me, you overwhelm me, your spirit crushes mine, I am nothing in your presence" (2: 409). Everybody in Julie's entourage was similarly hypnotized by her, even her servants "drop everything at the least sign from her, they run when she speaks; her glance alone animates their zeal, in her presence they are happy; they talk about her among themselves and urge one another on to serve her." She exercises an "adorable and powerful sway" (2: 444).[8]

But despite these aspects of her character, she inspired not fear but tears. The novel extended and amplified the effects of the *Devin du village*. The social integration and surrender of the solipsistic impulse which had resolved the intrigue of *Narcisse* were now jettisoned in favor of a new solution, a veritable manual of the cognitive style necessary to reconcile pretensions of moral superiority with a high level of erotic stimulation. "Sentimental virtue" comprised a vocabulary of transparency, of prolonged, painfully pleasurable tension, of a ceaseless pull toward dissolution into another who was an idealized representation of the self, a compromise between struggling against and submitting to hypnotic female domination. It was a synthesis of sensuality and moral superiority in which the self longed for an erotized fusion that made genitality almost irrelevant. This hovering on the edge of dissolution was itself the state of virtue and, at the same time, the keenest source of libidinal sensations: "For a long time Julie loved virtue itself so dearly only as the sweetest of voluptuous pleasures" (2: 541).

This latest stage in the development of Rousseau's morality was savaged by a now thoroughly hostile Voltaire, who cruelly satirized the tone and the author in three "Lettres sur *La Nouvelle Héloïse*." He pointed out that Rousseau said "the Paris theater corrupted morals, and he just gave the public a novel about Heloise or Aloise of which

---

[8]As Jean Rousset pointed out, while Julie writes less and less frequently her presence looms ever larger in the novel: "She practically stops writing and yet the only question is Julie; she is the center and the others are the mirrors which reflect her." *Forme et signification* (Paris: J. Corti, 1962), p. 91.

several parts would make this young lady [a prostitute] blush, if she knew how to read."[9] Diderot sniffed that, "in preaching against license in morals, Rousseau wrote a licentious novel."[10] But the acerbic philosophes were in a distinct minority. The vast mass of the novel's readers found it a revelation, indifferently, of new standards of sexual morality or of a new intensity in sensuality. Rousseau received numerous letters thanking him for having saved the writer from moral degradation, such as that of Charles Panckouke, who wrote: "it took a god and a powerful god to pull me from the precipice and you are, sir, the god who just performed this miracle."[11] Simultaneously, he was deluged with erotic responses to the book's steamy atmosphere: "The women especially were intoxicated both with the book and its author to the point that there were few even in the highest ranks whose conquest I could not have made had I attempted it" (1: 545). Rousseau had emerged from the lonely forests of Montmorency a more arresting figure than ever.

The conceptual advances that had made it possible to write the *Nouvelle Héloïse* had implications extending far beyond the challenge of creating a novel at once erotic, sentimental, and virtuous. The glorious sensations which Rousseau depicted when in perfect fusion with emanations of his own multiplied self were potentially available to the rest of humanity as well. The secret of expelling evil from within oneself and thereby freeing oneself from the taint of guilt could be revealed to mankind at large, and his fictional representations showed others how to do it, thereby creating more beings like himself. Then, rather than placing their happiness in specious premises and shifting relations with others, they would embrace the true joy of blameless self-absorption. And, having tasted the joys of virtue, they would both admire Rousseau as a mentor and, knowing their own goodness, simultaneously acknowledge his.

In absorbing the atmosphere of the book, every reader was, at the same time, being instructed in the social organization of an ideal world: Clarens, Julie's domain. There a society of well-nigh perfect beings, each of whom, the *Confessions* related, was actually an emana-

---

[9]Voltaire, "Lettres sur *La Nouvelle Héloïse*," *Oeuvres*, ed. Beuchot (Paris: Lefèvre, 1830), 40: 228.

[10]Diderot, "Essai sur les règnes de Claude et de Néron," *Oeuvres complètes* (Paris: Garnier, 1875), 3: 98.

[11]Quoted by Trousson, p. 31.

tion of Rousseau himself, interacted in a way that could easily be expanded to form the paradigm of an ideal state. But the didactic import of the novel was hidden within the text itself. The book thereby exemplified what was to become one of Rousseau's most characteristic imperatives: leading someone to virtue in a covert way. What the fictional persona "Rousseau" was to his readers Julie was to the other characters of the novel.

His relations with Mme d'Houdetot having precipitated a rupture with Mme d'Epinay, Rousseau moved from the Hermitage to a residence in Montmorency belonging to the maréchal de Luxembourg. The maréchal and his wife for some time played the role of benevolent protectors in his life. Rousseau had planned to write a treatise, "Sensate Morality, or, the Materialism of the Sage," which would prescribe "an exterior regimen which according to circumstances could put the soul or keep the soul in the state which is the most favorable to virtue" (1: 409). Although it was never written, its central idea found expression repetitively; all his works expressed, as he told Christophe de Beaumont, "the same principles; always the same moral, the same belief, the same maxims, and, if you will, the same opinions" (4: 928). During the next years he produced the *Contrat social, Emile, Considérations sur le gouvernement de Pologne, Constitution Corse*, and the *Lettre à d'Alembert sur les spectacles*, which, while structurally dissimilar, all offered strategies by which men might be led to virtue, the operational substrate of the central problem of how to make virtue reign. In these works the mythic Sage Rousseau extended to all men the goodness he found within himself, while relieving them of the struggle with culpability that he described as so onerous. From all these works emerges a single paradigm by which either a whole state or a single individual could be trained to virtue without any struggle for domination. As Lester Crocker described this pattern: "The prime function of the state and of its 'guide,' 'leader,' or 'Legislator' [is] the control of the will, the acts, thoughts, and passions of the citizens, and . . . the means of controlling all these are essentially the same."[12]

Rousseau now formulated the conviction that man was incapable of becoming virtuous by his own efforts and must, instead, be molded. This training would be effective, however, only if the

---

[12]*Rousseau's Social Contract*, p. 26.

subject, or "patient" in the sense of the one being acted upon, had no awareness of obeying an alien will. The optimal situation would be one in which a benevolent agent arranged life so that the individual or group becomes virtuous without knowing about the training and without engaging in any struggle in order to achieve moral rectitude. P.-P. Clément connects this dominant theme in Rousseau's writings to a push toward an "a-conflictual" relationship with others, usually with an older, powerful man toward whom no opposition was to be expressed or even experienced (pp. 140–46).

This train of thought was already articulated in *La Nouvelle Héloïse*, where the domestics were made to behave virtuously and yet were totally ignorant of the pressure being placed upon them. "The whole art of the master," Rousseau explained, "is hiding this constraint under the veil of pleasure or of diversion in such a way that they think they want everything that one obliges them to do" (2: 453). From this beginning, the model continued to develop. Emile would be controlled so as to behave as his preceptor wished, but without his knowledge. "At ten he is led with sweets. . . . When will he pursue only good behavior? Fortunate is the one who is led to it in spite of himself!" (4: 799). Emile had the good fortune to be conditioned to virtue; he was not forced to submit to a dominating will as ordinary children were, his preceptor shaped his will to the good without Emile's even noticing. "Let him always believe he is the master but let it always really be you. There is no subjection so perfect as the one which retains the appearance of liberty, thus one captivates the very will itself. . . . He must want to do only what you want him to do, he must not take a step which you have not predicted" (4: 363). Emile, in turn, would exercise an unwitting control over his little friends: "Without wishing to command he will be the master, without believing they obey, they will obey" (4: 423).

Involuntary obedience was not only to be prized in the home and in private relationships; it was also the goal in theoretical politics: "If it is good to know how to use men as they are, it is much better yet to make them such as you need them to be; the most absolute authority is the one which penetrates to the interior of man" (3, 251; "Sur l'Economie politique"). When in 1764, Rousseau was asked to provide suggestions for the government of Corsica, he responded: "I will not preach morals at them, I will not order them to have virtues, but I will put them in such a position that they will have virtues without knowing the word for them" (3: 948). He who had written about the wish for self-display was now presenting himself in the role of a "stage director." Denise Leduc-Fayette described the character of Rousseau as a superhuman guide to virtue: "Like all great artists, he disappears behind the setting once it is in place, and leaves the child as he leaves the people the illusion of freedom of choice. The preceptor, pedagogue, or legislator, who has the task of forming the individuals entrusted to him, uses feelings as instruments, and plays on private sensibilities as well as public ones."[13]

Rousseau explained that man, just like his image of himself, was naturally good and could, as he himself had, learn, if properly trained, to experience virtue without recourse to deceitful books by mandacious or misled philosophers. The Sage Jean-Jacques's conviction that he was innately good, that his heart was always the seat of moral truth, that humanity was himself writ large and hence equally good—and could, if led to a "natural" unification with the self, enjoy equal access to moral truth—forms the basis of his theory of the state and the individual.

The mechanism for leading men to virtue covertly, for arranging situations in which their innate goodness could manifest itself, responded to the problem raised by the failure of exhibitionism described in the autobiographical works. That his display of himself as a virtuous man had not produced universal admiration, that there were still people in the world who criticized Jean-Jacques, after he had shown himself to be good in his writings consecrated to the truth, demonstrated the limits of virtuous exhibition:

> I knew that living alone among men, and men all more powerful than I, I could never, no matter how I went about it, protect myself against the evil they would wish to do me. There was only one thing I could do; it was to behave in such a way that when they wished to do me harm, they could only do so unjustly. Those people always so prompt to call adversity a crime would be surprised if they knew all the precautions I've taken in my life so that no one could say to me truthfully in my misfortunes: *"You brought them upon yourself."* [1: 424]

Voltaire had criticized *La Nouvelle Héloïse* on the grounds that Julie "cannot arouse sympathy because in her most painful struggles one

---

[13]"Le Matérialisme du Sage et l'art de jouir," *Revue Philosophique*, 3 (1978), 338.

can always say to her: if you are unhappy, it is you who brought it upon yourself."[14] If her pathetic situation was not the result of innocent circumstance but the product of culpable will, then the same indictment extended to Rousseau as author who put her in the situation and invited the reader to weep for her. Under these circumstances, Rousseau refused to accept the dictum he described as inspiring the *Second Discours:* "Learn that all your woes come from yourselves" (1: 389; *Confessions*). He had repudiated all wickedness at the time of his "reform" and was now free from evil. His virtuous image did not, however, transport everyone as it did him. There were those, and especially his former friends among the philosophes who mocked the virtuous persona he was presenting to the world. He began to express the sensation of being surrounded by wicked men. They were powerful and numerous, he was helpless and alone. His writings became concerned with deflecting guilt from himself onto them, and this concern become a preoccupation and eventually his central obsession. If only "they" had responded to his display of goodness by feeling at one with his literary self-presentation, rather than remaining neutral or ironical observers, then they would have formed a delightful society of perfect beings.

In his *Lettre à d'Alembert sur les spectacles,*[15] Rousseau explained how the theater, and by extension all art, ought to serve the cause of virtue. Incensed over d'Alembert's article "Genève" in the *Encyclopédie*, in which his former friend recommended the establishment of a theater in Geneva, Rousseau asked whether such an enterprise could possibly contribute to the virtue of the citizenry. He answered his own question with a resounding no: "As for me, even if I must once again be treated as wicked because I dared maintain that man is born good, I think so and I believe I have proven him to be so: the source of the interest which attaches us to what is honest and inspires us with an aversion to evil is in us and not in plays" (p. 139). He criticized Molière because "without ever getting us to love virtue...he troubles the order of society; with what scandal he reverses all the most sacred relations upon which it is based, how he derides the respectable rights of fathers over their children, of husbands over their wives, of masters over their servants!" (p. 149). He reserved his most severe criticism, understandably, for *Le Misan-*

---

[14]*Lettre de M. L. sur "La Nouvelle Héloïse"* (Geneva: N.p., 1762), p. 52.
[15]*Du Contrat social...Lettre à M. D'Alembert* (Paris: Garnier, 1954).

thrope. In that play virtue had been held up to mockery: "Molière after dramatizing so many other ridiculous traits, was left to dramatize the one the world pardons least of all, the ridiculousness of virtue: that is what he did in the *Misanthrope*." Alceste, the protagonist of Molière's play, hates the human race only because he finds it full of wickedness. "This character, virtuous as he is, is presented as ridiculous" (p. 152). Rousseau compares him to Philinte, Molière's foil in the play, who stands for the middle-of-the-road morality Rousseau found so galling among the philosophes.

> This Philinte is the sage of the play; one of these "decent men" of society whose maxims are so like those of scoundrels, one of those men who are so benign, so moderate, who always find that things are all right because they have an interest in seeing that things do not get better, who are always pleased with everyone because they do not care about anybody, who, sitting around a well-laid table, maintain that it is untrue that the people are hungry; those whose pockets being well lined are offended when someone speaks out in favor of the poor; those who, when their own houses are firmly protected, would see the whole human race robbed, pillaged, throttled and massacred without complaining, since God has endowed them with the most worthy patience in enduring the misfortunes of others. [Pp. 152–53]

In this unexpected, violent, and beautifully constructed antithesis Rousseau refused moderation or tolerance any part in his concept of virtue. In *Emile* he would defend the violence of the religious fanatic as being, ultimately, less harmful to virtue than the skeptic's lack of principles:

> Without faith, no true virtue exists. If atheism does not shed any human blood it is less through love of peace than through indifference toward the good: as long as everything goes along, what does the so-called sage care, provided he remains undisturbed in his study. His principles do not kill men but they keep them from being born by destroying the morals that multiply them... in reducing all affections to a secret egotism as harmful to population [growth] as to virtue. Thus fanaticism, although more painful in its immediate effects than what they call these days the philosophical spirit, is much less harmful in its consequences. [4: 633]

Geneva had no need of such lessons, nor would the eternal importance given to women and romantic love on the stage improve morality. "Do you think," Rousseau asked d'Alembert, "that in augmenting the ascendancy of women, men will be better governed?" (p. 159).

What Geneva needed was not a French theater, as d'Alembert had the impertinence to suggest, but a truly Republican form of spectacle. Not "exclusive performances which confine a small number of people in caverns of darkness," but instead "it is in the open air, under heaven that you must gather and give yourselves over to the blissful feelings of your happiness. Let your pleasures be neither effeminate nor mercenary.... Let the sun shine upon your innocent spectacles, you yourselves will form a spectacle, the most worthy it can illuminate" (pp. 224–25). Thus the primordial separation between actor and observer would be obliterated; Geneva would be both subject and object of its own celebration; like Narcissus it would find happiness in the contemplation of itself and that happiness would be virtue.

The good state was composed not of discrete individual persons, in whom Rousseau recognized evil, but of a single being, himself, inflated to the boundaries of a nation. As he described himself: "From his youth he had often wondered why he didn't find all men good, wise, and happy as they seemed to him made to be; he looked into his own heart for the obstacle which kept them from it and did not find it. If all men, he said to himself, were like me, they would live amongst themselves in a very pleasant society" (1: 828).

The organization of such a state was further examined in the *Contrat social.* Like the society at Clarens, or like the union of actor and observer at the true spectacle, Rousseau's self-state constituted one being, a true body politic: "The body politic, taken individually, may be considered as an organized body, alive and similar to that of man. The sovereign power represents the head; ... the citizens are the body and the members which make the machine move, live, and work" (3: 244). The life of the great body and its constituent members "is the ego common to all" (3: 245).

The citizens of the good self-state, far from being competitive individuals, would be utterly subsumed by the body politic, like cells in the human body.[16] His ideal "state" (*état* in French carrying the

---

[16]Many critics have been at pains to deny any particular signficance to what has been referred to as the "métaphore organiciste," perhaps because in the motion of the state as one great living creature, the primitive power of Rousseau's thought rises

double meaning of political organization and emotional condition) was now removed from the contingencies of historical development: "The state of happiness must be permanent."

Just as Rousseau knew that he, as virtuous individual, could find truth in his own heart, so could the good state, the virtuous body politic, find truth by looking at its own wishes, because "the General Will is always for the side which is most favorable to the public interest... so that it is necessary only to be just to be assured of following the General Will."

The "good" citizen was the one who fused most completely with the "good" state. "Each man is virtuous," said Rousseau, "when his private will conforms totally to the General Will" (3: 254). Since the state was an enlarged projection of Rousseau's own being, virtue was measured by the citizen's willingness to be subsumed by Rousseau.

In the *Premier Discours,* Fabricius had declared that the only talent worthy of Rome was that of conquest and "making virtue reign" (3: 15). Now, in Rousseau's theory of the legitimate state, the leaders had the same responsibility that he had attributed to Rome: they had to see to the citizens' "virtue." It was not the individual's conduct principally, but his *will* which had to be shaped. "Do you wish the General Will to be accomplished? Make all the private wills agree with it, and since virtue is only this conformity of the private will with the general, to say the same thing in other words, make virtue reign" (3: 252).

Where virtue reigned, for Rousseau, was where other men's wills were in preordained harmony with the mythic self he elaborated

---

uncomfortably close to conscious expression. The editors of the *Oeuvres complètes* ascribe to it only "the value of an image or a comparison, the inexactitude of which Rousseau carefully emphasizes" (3: 1393). However, as Charles Vaughan suggests (*PW,* Introduction, 1: 57–58), despite the disclaimer, the comparison between the human body and the body politic permeates the *Contrat social* and is elaborated at length in the *Economie politique*. Robert Derathé places the extended image in its historical context while dismissing its affective energies by remarking that "organicist images are never anything more than a last resort, a figurative language which one must not take at face value." *Jean-Jacques Rousseau et la science politique de son temps* (Paris: Vrin, 1970), p. 473. Raymond Polin also dismisses the importance of the metaphor, arguing that since Rousseau had found it in Hobbes, it meant little to him. What matters in the perspective of this study is not the comparison's provenance or its consistency but the specific meanings it carried in Rousseau's work, and as Polin pointed out: "What is decisive is that the body politic as such manifested itself as a moral being." *La Politique de la solitude* (Paris: Sirey, 1971), p. 143.

through his works. Since in his own heart he told of finding only goodness and truth, if others would unite with that same goodness and truth which was naturally present in their hearts, then his being would be generalized and virtue would be supreme at last.

In his ideal state, therefore, the bureaucratic rules and procedures that encumbered other governments would be unnecessary. Rather than relying upon complicated bookkeeping, for example, to check the venality of administrators, governments should recognize that "virtue is the only efficacious instrument. Therefore give up account books and papers, and put finances into faithful hands, that is the only way for them to be faithfully administered" (3: 265–66).

Although the *Contrat social* is a theoretical work on the principles of legitimate sovereignty, and *Emile*, written at nearly the same time, is a treatise on childrearing, it is generally recognized that the two are intimately related. In the political works the question was how to structure a "people" for virtue; in *Emile*, Rousseau showed how to raise one person to be virtuous.

CHAPTER FOUR

Virtue and Pity

Emile belongs to the great constructive phase in which Rousseau elaborated positive plans for a new integration of man into the political state. The child, Emile, was to be reared so as to be reconciled with himself, thus healing the moral split created by man's introduction into society. The author's concern for the conditions under which children were raised was also a defense against the accusation that he was an "unnatural father" because he had abandoned the five illegitimate children borne by his mistress.[1]

The specter of these children has hung over Rousseau's reputation during more than two hundred years of debate as to what meaning, if any, should be assigned to their fate. They have been used by some as pretexts to dismiss his thought, on the grounds that no man who fails in his duty to his children is entitled to present himself as a model of virtue. Dr. Théodore Tronchin, for example, wrote to the minister Paul-Claude Moultou expressing his revulsion at the juxtaposition of Rousseau's moral pretensions and the abandonment of his children:

---

[1]The connection between the documents in which Rousseau presented defensive arguments regarding the children's fate and the writing of *Emile* is not altogether clear. Pierre Burgelin comments (4: lxxvii): "There is no strictly contemporaneous allusion, that is, dating from 1759, which permits us to think that the fact of having placed his children in the asylum determined Rousseau to write a treatise on education. The declarations he made later are rather contradictory. He told Madame de Luxembourg in 1761 that the idea of his dereliction contributed to his meditations on his work." Cf. *C.c.*, 6: 146.

Every habitual act which shocks, which destroys at their foundations [those] principles of morality which are so important to me, is repellent to me, and I am all the more affected when the one who ought to reproach himself parades the most austere Virtue. I believe that chastity is essential to Virtue. Would that also be an error? But even if it were one, I respect paternity so much, the bond appears to me so sacred, that in my view he who breaks it injures the primary natural feeling, the one to which all the others are attached.[2]

On the other side, Mme de Staël absolved her "master," claiming the abandonment was for the sake of the children, blaming Thérèse, and citing Rousseau's own childlike nature:

The weightiest reproach which can be made against his memory, the one which will find no defender, is that of having abandoned his children; very well! This same man, however, would have been capable of furnishing the greatest examples of paternal love ... if he had not been convinced that he was sparing them the greatest of crimes by leaving them ignorant of their father's name ... The unworthy woman who spent her life with him ... the stories I have heard of the ruses she used to augment his fears ... these things are scarcely believable. It is undoubtedly a huge folly to listen to such a woman and to love her, but given that folly, all the others are understandable. ... It cannot be said that [he] was virtuous; but he was a man who should have been left to think, without asking anything more of him, who should have been led like a child and attended like a sage.[3]

Victor Hugo put forth a different apology in a statement made by Enjolras, a politically idealistic young student in *Les Misérables:* "Silence in the presence of Jean-Jacques! This man, I admire him, he denied his children; so be it, but he adopted the people."[4]

In the twentieth century, Albert Schinz viewed Rousseau's role as that of a passive victim of uncontrollable events: "We will not discuss this affair again. Let those who, placing themselves in the circumstances in which Rousseau found himself, would have done otherwise, cast the first stone."[5] Albert Meynier, writing in 1912, and attempting to establish Rousseau as the father of parliamentary

[2]June 17, 1762 (*C.c.*, 11: 106).
[3]*Lettres sur les écrits et le caractère de J.-J. Rousseau* (n.p., 1788), pp. 98–99.
[4]*Les Misérables*, 4 vols. (Paris: Nelson, 1937), 2: 378.
[5]*La Pensée de Jean-Jacques Rousseau*, p. 129.

L'ALAITEMENT MATERNEL ENCOURAGÉ.

Un Philosophe Sensible indique à la bienfaisance les objets sur les quels elle doit verser ses dons .
La Comédie, sous la figure de Figaro, tient des gros Sacs . Elle en répand un aux pieds de plusieurs mères qui donnent le se
à leurs enfans . Au dessus du Philosophe est la Statue de l'Humanité, portant ces mots . Secours pour les Mères nourri

A Paris, chez l'Auteur, rue de la Harpe, N.° 48 . vis-à-vis la rue Serpente

Engraving, 1784: "Maternal nursing encouraged. A sensitive philosopher shows Charity where she should bestow her bounty. Comedy, dressed as Figaro, spills a heavy sack at the feet of mothers breastfeeding their babies. Above the philosopher appears the statue of Humanity, bearing the words 'Aid for Nursing Mothers.'" (Courtesy of the Bibliothèque nationale, Paris) liberalism, took the position that Rousseau had made a sacrifice for the sake of his creativity: "He had to be himself or the father of Thérèse's children. He preferred to remain himself. The answer belongs to *Héloise*, to the *Social Contract*, to the *Emile*, for it is to these children of his mind that he sacrificed those of his flesh."[6] Jean Fabre went further yet. He regarded child-abandonment as an eighteenth-century norm (on the basis of a misreading of official encouragement to place those infants who *were* abandoned in asylums rather than leaving them on the street) but simultaneously claimed that Rousseau may not even have been aware that the woman he was living with was giving birth: "When *la mère* Levasseur took the four or five children born to Thérèse during the first years of her liaison with Rousseau to the *Enfants trouvés*, a customary step at the period, indeed, one recommended by the Church and the state, it is highly probable that the putative father felt hardly anything, even supposing he was told about it."[7] Fabre saw Rousseau's refusal to commit himself to his children as a mark of positive moral superiority over Diderot, who, as poverty-stricken as his erstwhile friend, was as earnest in embracing the paternal role as Rousseau in jettisoning it: "The curses [Diderot] heaps on the tasks and bores which prevent him, as well, from being himself, permit us to guess the obsessive but unavowed feeling aroused in him by his former friend, when the masterpieces which proved [Rousseau] right burst upon the scene: a feeling of envy. Never has one writer reminded another more expressively of the first duty of their vocation: don't commit yourself."[8]

Pierre Burgelin attempted to dismiss the whole problem: "Rousseau's life does not interest me in the least. What interests me is his work. Let's know nothing of his life as we know nothing of Homer's."[9] This posture of willful ignorance is difficult to maintain, however, because "Rousseau's life" is a *problem* almost exclusively because of its literary representation by Rousseau. The mythical reworkings of his own goodness are the core of his writings, and the question of responsibility for children permeates every work. What Walter Rex said of the *Premier Discours* applies to each of the works: the content "is not

---

[6] *Jean-Jacques Rousseau, révolutionnaire*, p. 30.
[7] "Le J.-J. Rousseau de Lester Crocker," *Revue d'Histoire Littéraire*, 75 (1975), 808.
[8] "Deux Frères ennemis, Diderot et Rousseau," *DS*, 3 (1961), 176.
[9] "L'Education de Sophie," *AJJR*, 35 (1962–63), 113.

philosophy but the most intimate sort of autobiography whose message is quite as personal as any to be found in the *Confessions*; in fact it is telling the same story."[10] Far from trying to separate himself as writer from his own personage, Rousseau placed the question of the children squarely in the middle of his work. It was crucial to him to demonstrate that Rousseau, the citizen, the Sage, the example of natural goodness, had not been *wicked* in consigning his children to an institution in which less than one baby in five survived for six months. He was answering charges, not only of child-abandonment, but also of infanticide, charges that mocked his persona of the virtuous man. He described himself having to cope with a paradoxical world in which other people could regard as immoral a series of acts which produced in him no inner sensation of wrongdoing. He wrote a string of defenses to demonstrate to these accusers that his actions in no way compromised his state of internal goodness.

His difficulties in justifying himself were compounded because he needed to defend not a single act, a moment of aberration, but rather, as Tronchin noted, a way of life that had been maintained for a period of ten years, from 1745 until 1755. During that time, he recounted how he had shared his life with Thérèse Levasseur (whom he called "my Aunt"), had sexual relations with her, and had placed their five children—or permitted them to be placed—in the Enfants trouvés, "despite her groans" (1: 345). Reviewing this pattern, he reported no sense of having done anything which was morally unacceptable:

> This arrangement seemed so good to me, so sensible and legitimate that the only reason I did not brag about it openly was respect for the mother, but I told it to everyone to whom I had confided our relations. I told it to Diderot, to Grimm, later I informed Mme d'Epinay and then Mme de Luxembourg of it, and I did so freely, willingly; I was under no pressure and I could have easily hidden it from everyone; for [Thérèse's midwife] was decent and very discreet, and I counted on her completely. I had reason to confide in only one of my friends, Dr. Thyerri [Thierry], who took care of my poor Aunt during a difficult delivery. In short, I made no mystery of my conduct, not only because I was never able to hide anything from my friends, but because I really saw no harm in it. All things considered, I made the best decision for my children, or

[10]"On the Background of Rousseau's First Discourse," p. 147.

I thought I had. I would have wanted, I still would like to have been raised and nurtured as they were. [1: 358]

Having examined himself and producing no evidence of an *inner feeling* of wishing to do harm, he moved inexorably to the conclusion that he was naturally good, prior to word or deed. The censure of actions for which he felt no guilt could only be an attempt to drive a wedge between him and his virtue. But he repeatedly explained that his happiness depended on his union with goodness and, therefore, that anything that made him unhappy must be evil and false. With this as a sure foundation, he could judge the truth-value of any assertion made about him or about his world by an immediate standard: it either harmonized with his feeling of goodness or it threatened it. His goodness was more an epistemology than an ethic. When Voltaire, in his poem on the Lisbon earthquake, argued that God must be either impotent or malevolent, Rousseau responded that he knew Voltaire to be wrong since, if he were right, that state of affairs would make Rousseau unhappy, and nothing that produced that effect could be true.

His own actions, since they were performed by him, were axiomatically good or, alternatively, lacked any moral significance. Thus, as he said, he saw nothing wrong with abandoning his children. This statement becomes a source of confusion if it is read to signify that he was convinced of the salubrity of the Enfants trouvés or the soundness of the education it provided. The literal meaning is that the literary representation he called himself experienced no guilt, that no feelings of self-reproach moved Jean-Jacques when the question of the children arose, and if he felt no remorse for his actions, it must have been because they were not morally wrong.

Nonetheless, the story of the children, though not the children themselves, challenged Rousseau's version of his own being; in an anonymous pamphlet circulated in 1764, Voltaire described Rousseau as a "pox-ridden clown," and revealed the story of the five abandoned children. The scandal caused people to refuse belief in Rousseau's goodness. His virtuous image was no longer reflected back at him. He could see contempt or irony replacing the admiration he had formerly elicited as "the Sage of Europe."

He attempted to explain the scandal away, to make it disappear so that he could once again gaze upon his good self mirrored in the regard of others. He offered many apologies for his behavior; they contradicted one another. Coherence, however, was not important since the function of his explanations was to redeem his image in the eyes of others. He could offer such divergent explanations of his acts because motives were improvised for the occasion, pressed to serve against some specific accusation and then tossed aside and forgotten. The matter of his inner goodness, however, his intrinsic worth as distinct from his actions, was of absolute and urgent importance. As Jean Starobinski pointed out, "going as far back as possible into his being, one finds him shameful and culpable, yet rejecting the guilt and the shame."[11] In order to change the ironic glances of his contemporaries back into stares of open admiration, he created texts that worked to undo the damage to his reputation which the story of his children had wrought. The "true" explanation of his actions was the one which, at a given moment, would staunch the flow of criticism, not one which corresponded to some externally perceived and hence irrelevant order of events.

In certain passages, Rousseau expressed contempt for the society that placed such burdens upon its members, claiming that part of his moral superiority lay in his refusal to permit himself to be constrained by the numerous obligations others sought to impose upon him. He spoke of his preference for the state of langorous passivity he cultivated: "Deliberately abandoning himself to his delicious idleness, he occupied his hours of leisure with his own kind of pleasures, neglecting the masses of so-called duties which human sagacity prescribes as indispensable" (1: 822).

In another text he referred to abandoning the children as a sort of painful affliction for which he should be pitied rather than blamed. "It is a misfortune which should make you feel sorry for me, not a crime with which to reproach me," he wrote to Mme de Francueil in 1751, explaining that if he had to support them "it would be necessary to have recourse to protectors, intrigue, to chase after some lowly job" (1: 1431).

Alternatively, he asserted that the abandonments were an example of philsophical civic spirit. It was not the good individual who looked after his own children, he argued, but the good society which

[11]"Jean-Jacques Rousseau et le péril de la réflexion," *AJJR*, 34 (1956–58), 140.

shouldered the burden. "Thus Plato wanted all children raised in the Republic; let each one remain unknown to his father and let all be children of the State" (1: 1431). His discourses had shown that the sexual impulse was not connected in any natural way with the financial, social, and legal responsibilities of paternity which were only more hateful links in the chain society placed around the neck of humanity. The good society would do for the citizen what nature had done for unfettered man: disassociate lust from responsibility.

His principal rebuttal was to demonstrate that, far from being cruel and insensitive, Rousseau's heart was filled with warmth, love, and paternal affection. He wanted to withdraw public attention from acts, for which he denied feeling responsible, and redirect it toward his emotions, where he was certain of his goodness: "Never for a single instant of his life, could Jean-Jacques have been a man without feelings, without heart, an unnatural father. I could have made a mistake but I could not have become callous" (1: 1430). It was merely a case of his tenderness not having had a chance to be aroused: "The wish to do harm did not enter my heart, and a father's love could not be very strong for children one has never seen" (1: 359).

He contrasted the beautiful feelings of goodness, generosity, and nobility which he found within himself with the contemptible acts of which he was accused, and denied absolutely that such a soul could wish to commit a crime: "This innate benevolence for my fellow man, this ardent love of the great, the beautiful, the just, this horror of evil in any form, this inability to hate, to harm, even to wish harm:... can all that ever be reconciled in the same soul with the depravity which allows the most precious of duties to be trampled underfoot without scruple?" (1: 357).

By the time his defense of himself had consolidated, it had become a paean to intention with a corollary devaluation of the significance of action. Intention alone was the appropriate measure of moral man, a just God would understand the essential quality of the soul, its purity or corruption, and would not be misled by irrelevant considerations of deeds: "I am weak, it is true, but what of it, if it is my intentions and not my actions that are counted. Only the wicked person wants evil and premeditates it, the wicked person alone will be punished" (*Emile*, 4: 227). Bad actions in the presence of a pure will were merely the evidence of frailty: "I blame my faults on my weakness and am consoled, for never has premeditated evil touched my heart" (1: 1075).

He marshaled corollary reasons to prove that action was an unreliable test of human worth. In some instances an individual might be so impassioned that his gestures would be disassociated from his character: "There are moments of a kind of delirium, when men must not be judged by their action" (1: 39). In his letter to Christopher de Beaumont, he adduced another mitigating circumstance: "Reason teaches us that a man is to be punished only for the faults of his will and that invincible ignorance could not be considered a crime" (4: 951). Weakness, overwhelming passion, or invincible ignorance could all produce the paradox of a wicked act performed by a good person, clouding the correspondence between the inner self and the outward manifestation. If "they" were to condemn such a discrepancy, "they" would be wrong: "the public is the judge of faults; its blame is the only punishment. Nobody can escape this Judge.... The public cannot punish the Author, for that would be punishing an offense which might be involuntary, and concerning evil one must punish only the will" (3: 692).

He promulgated this vital distinction through his literary characters. Julie forgives Saint-Preux his bout of debauchery on the grounds that "an involuntary error is easily forgiven and forgotten" (2: 305), and Emile "could do a great deal of harm without evil-doing, because the bad action depends on the intention to harm and he will never have that intention" (4: 322).

Coping with their criticism made Rousseau more aware of the moral flaws in other people. For them to cast blame on an innocent person, as he defined himself, seemed to him an incomprehensibly vicious act. He commented on Voltaire's libel; "I would prefer to have done what I am accused of in this passage to having written it" (*C.g.*, 12: 6).

It was Voltaire's piece, he claimed, which finally decided him to embark upon a project he had long entertained: that of writing his great and tragic *Confessions*. The work served two conflicting purposes and bears the mark of its duality; it would confront his lying critics by telling the true story of his unique life in all its details, sparing neither himself nor those he had known. This total unburdening would reveal Rousseau at last as a man without guile;

his utter frankness would compensate for any bad actions he had performed. At the same time, however, it would be an exemplary text which he could bring before God and upon which his moral value would be judged as the equal, if not the superior, of any man's.

> Let the trumpet of the last judgment sound when it will; I shall come, this book in my hand, to present myself before the sovereign judge. Eternal Being, gather round me the innumerable throng of my fellow beings: let them listen to my confessions, let them groan at my indignities, let them blush for my misfortunes. Let each of them in turn reveal his heart at the foot of your throne with the same sincerity and then let a single one tell you, if he dares: I was better than that man. [1: 5]

More than any other book, the *Confessions* brought to an end an era of rather brittle elegance and opened the gates through which all that was human, the noble and the sordid, the universal and the trivial, the tragic and the ridiculous, were to pass into literature with equal dignity. Rousseau produced the impression of holding back nothing of which he was conscious; and now, after nearly two hundred years of self-revealing literature, much of it infinitely more squalid than Rousseau's work, the reader who opens the *Confessions* for the first time still experiences shock. The incredible tour de force that Rousseau achieved in this work was to air the most unattractive aspects of his life before the public—his predilection for spankings, his constant wish to urinate, his preference for masturbation, his attempts to arouse his friend's mistress, his sordid relations with Thérèse and their pitiful consequences, his exhibitionism, his betrayals of confidence and his ingratitude toward his friends—and yet to present himself in such a seductive way that not only did he make all this acceptable to most of his readers, but the majority of them adored him for it. For what had he done? He had expressed all the queerness, the perversity, the psychosexual confusion which the prevailing culture disdained as unseemly and had given open voice to what thousands of Frenchmen and women had thought their unique and unspeakable shame. He ended the book as he had begun it, on a note of bravado: "Whosoever, even without having read my writings, will examine with his own eyes my nature, my character, my morals, my penchants, my pleasures, my habits, and can believe I am not a decent man, ought to be strangled" (1: 656).

[83]

He read the text before private groups at the homes of the Marquis de Pezay, the poet Dorat, and the Comtesse d'Egmont. News of the readings met with cold silence followed by fear and rage when his former friends whose foibles had been relentlessly revealed got wind of the work. In May 1771, Mme d'Epinay asked the lieutenant of police to forbid further readings of the *Confessions*. Rousseau's sense of persecution deepened and yet, once the book was published, the man who had revealed himself so openly before an astounded world was on his way to becoming the center of a cult bordering on adulation. Triumphant in his humiliation, he offered a whole generation a figure with whom an intoxicating identification in virtue was possible.

In the texts from the eight years remaining to him, he depicts himself as certain of his own goodness and increasingly aware of and uncomfortable with the difference between mankind, which he could love because it was intrinsically like himself, and other people, who inexplicably mocked him or made his acts turn out badly. "I think I know man," he remarked, "but as for men, I know them not" (1: 1232, note 3). "Men" were all those who were *not* the good Rousseau. To the extent that they differed, they were alien, opaque, and eventually threatening. As his persona became the object of raging controversy in France and in Geneva, he was forced to the conclusion that he was radically unlike other men and would be best able to experience his love for humanity far from the presence of real people: "I flee them because I love them, I suffer their misfortunes less when I do not see them. This affection for the species suffices to nourish my heart, I do not need particular friends" (1: 1144).

The insistence that goodness is equivalent to the absence of any inner wish to do harm and that actions are therefore irrelevant to morality caused a shift in Rousseau's vocabulary. In his later writings, in the last book of the *Confessions* and in the *Dialogues* the concept of "innocence" began to compete with "virtue" as the word for the warm feeling of inner goodness he depicted so movingly. Alone, retired from active struggle in the world of men, he stopped dressing as a Frenchman and started wearing Armenian dress. "It was not a new idea. It had come to me at various periods in my life, and returned often at Montmorency where, as the frequent use of [urethral] catheters condemned me to remain alone often in my bedroom, I preferred the advantages of the long robe." In point of fact, he found an increasing appeal in woman's mode of existence. "I learned to make lace . . . and, like the women, I went to work before my front door and chatted with the passers-by."

Although he described taking pleasure in this new mode of existence, especially in his relationship to Isabelle d'Ivernois, to whom he gave counsel and who "perhaps owes me her sanity, her husband, her life and her happiness" (1: 600–601), he enjoyed his own goodness best when he contrasted it with the wickedness of others. The very harshness and injustice of his enemies guaranteed his innocence: "I, who never offended anyone, what enemies can I have if not those who have offended me, but they are all the more implacable for being unjust" (4: 1027). Picturing his plight produced a bittersweet pleasure: "These reflections, sad but touching, caused me to fall back on myself with a regret not without sweetness. The feeling of my inner value made me feel this injustice, but it also comforted me for it in a way and made me shed tears which I loved to let flow" (1: 426).

Suffering paved the way for inner unity. The more outrage he elicited from the public, from government authorities, and from his former friends, the more isolated, condemned, and potentially ecstatic he felt. And, in a closed circle, his "invincible ignorance" paved the way for his suffering. The protagonist of the *Confessions* and the other autobiographical works is blind to his own provocativeness. In Jean Guéhenno's words: "Such was the violent candor of Jean-Jacques: he himself did not see the significance of his writings. The truth is that the *Emile*, the *Social Contract*, . . . were to unleash a sort of revolution."[12]

Besides, in relatively peaceful periods when he was not especially reviled or denigrated, he found it difficult to arouse himself. He had experienced staleness and boredom at the Hermitage when he had settled into that peaceful existence with Thérèse and her mother of

---

[12]*Jean-Jacques*, vol. 2., *Roman et vérité, 1750–1758* (Paris: Grasset, 1950), p. 48. In "La Condamnation de l'*Emile*," Marcel Françon, on the other hand, traced the reactions to Rousseau's most controversial writing and interpreted them as a systematic attempt on the part of the philosophes to denigrate their former collaborator: "The *Emile* affair is the beginning of the series of efforts which Voltaire and his clan made to destroy Rousseau." *AJJR*, 1 (1946–49), 245. Françon exemplifies Rousseau's ideal reader, who identifies with the conviction of interior goodness described by the author, rather than comparing his *text* with those of his adversaries to arrive at an independent evaluation.

which he had dreamed: "I no longer had any project for the future which could capture my imagination. It was not even possible for me to make any, since the situation I was in was precisely the one which united all my desires: I had nothing more to wish for and yet my heart was empty. This state was all the more cruel in that I couldn't imagine one which would be preferable to it" (1: 424). He described an anhedonia which could be overcome only in the excitement of states of fusion, either with someone he found thrilling or else with someone he pitied, a blameless person who was under attack. These moments of merging, however, did not intrude upon his solipsism, but rather sustained it; he did not recognize the other one, he expropriated him or her. Jan Marejko characterized this emotional state as an adhesion which "ends up in a fusion where he loses himself, not in an alliance where he would affirm the self by establishing the self's limits."[13] Seeing an innocent being hurt aroused in him an instantaneous identification with the victim. This was how his liaison with Thérèse had begun at the boarding house where he met her when he was thirty-three and she was ten years younger: "They teased the little one, I defended her. Even if I did not take to the poor girl naturally, I would have done so through compassion and contrariness. Having long been beaten by her brothers, by her sisters, even by her nieces, this unfortunate girl was now pillaged by them and could not defend herself any better against their thefts than against their blows" (1: 340). Rousseau was attracted to her less as another human being than as an emanation of himself: "I needed someone in whom I would find the simplicity, the docility which [Mme de Warens] had found in me" (1: 31).

Once Thérèse became his housekeeper-mistress, she lost much of her role as the scapegoat of her family and much of her interest for him. Unable to pity her, he increasingly pitied himself. Even when not feeling persecuted, he brooded over the emptiness of his life, feeling that he was growing old and would soon die "without having tasted this intoxicating sensual pleasure which I feel potentially in my soul. This sad but touching thought made me turn in on myself with a regret not without charm. It seemed to me that destiny owed me something it had not given me. The feeling of my inner worth, while it made me recognize the injustice, compensated for it in a way and made me weep tears which I loved to let flow" (1: 426).

[13]*La Dérive totalitaire* (Lausanne: L'Age d'Homme, 1984), p. 130.

As he described it, pity was for Rousseau a blending of sensual pleasure and enhanced self-esteem, a means of making himself weep as he had once delighted in making beautiful women weep. It was intrinsically related to identification, not to social interaction. If he did not identify with the "victim of injustice," suffering did not affect him, nor did he categorize the sufferer as a "victim." That was why he could observe his children being taken away from their mother "despite her groans" and remain unmoved.

On the basis of his self-observations, he constructed his theory of pity as a deflection of sexuality. It was only with the physical and emotional changes of puberty that boys became capable of experiencing pity. The beginnings of sexuality were equated with the capacity for perceiving pain: "The child, not imagining what others feel, knows no ills but his own, but when the first development of the senses lights the fire of imagination, he begins to *feel himself in others*, to be moved by their pleas, and to suffer their ills. It is then that the sad tableau of suffering humanity must bring to his heart the first compassion it has ever experienced" (4: 505).

Already, the preface to the *Second Discours* had laid the groundwork for this theory: "Meditating upon the first and simplest operations of the human soul, I believe I distinguish two principles which precede reason: one interests us urgently in our own well-being, and the other inspires a natural repugnance toward seeing any sentient creature suffer or die, and especially our fellow men" (3: 126).

Of all Rousseau's writings, this text is the most fundamental to understanding his vision of the nature of man and the corrupting influences of social relations. He is formulating a dual-instinct theory in this passage.[14] The first of the two principles, or instincts, is asocial self-love. On this point Rousseau was in harmony with virtually all eighteenth-century philosophers. Diderot, for example, in a

---

[14]For Victor Goldschmidt, the "two principles" represent a kind of dualism, "not metaphysical but methodological." He sees, however, that this duality is only apparent. "Rather than an antagonistic principle, pity, even in the state of nature, is the limit of self-love and forms an entity with it, as does the surface marking the boundary of a solid." *Anthropologie et politique: Les Principes du système de Rousseau* (Paris: Vrin, 1974), p. 354. As striking as Goldschmidt's metaphor is, it does not correspond to the explicit significance of pity for Rousseau. John Charvet defines the term more accurately in noting that it implies the *rejection* of the other and the appropriation of his suffering for the self. See *The Social Problem in the Philosophy of Rousseau* (Cambridge: Cambridge University Press, 1974), pp. 18–19.

letter to Sophie Volland, said: "I believe that nature is indifferent to good and evil. It acts toward two ends: the conservation of the individual and the propagation of the species" (*Corr.*, 4: 85). The difference with regard to the second principle is immediately apparent. For Rousseau, there was no inherent tendency toward propagating the species. Sexual desires were analogous to hunger or fear, simply factors that disturbed the well-being of the individual and could be dealt with by the self-love which seeks to avoid unpleasant feelings caused by the environment and to quiet uncomfortable sensations that arise within the self. What replaced the urge to have children, in Rousseau's theory, was the feeling of pity.[15]

Removed equally from interpersonal and generative implications, sexual desires were merely pressures which must be satisfied in order to maintain a state of contentment. The same pressures could be relieved by killing. Emile's preceptor would manipulate him into hunting: "Emile will develop a taste for [the hunt], he will enter into it with all the ardor of his age. [It] will harden his heart as well as his body; it will accustom him to blood and to cruelty. It will serve to suspend a more dangerous passion" (4: 644–45).

Rousseau had the courage to defy the prevailing cultural idealization of unflagging male sexuality. It was he who voiced, for the first time, the misgivings of the man unable or unwilling to follow in the wake of the century's Don Juans and Casanovas. Rousseau expressed the fears, the inhibitions, the anguish privately suffered by an era publicly devoted to gallantry. He revealed many men's secret when he depicted heterosexuality as dangerous. The preceptor was instructed to teach Emile the sufferings brought about by debauchery, and as an additional protection, should sleep "at least in the same room with him" (4: 663). "Thus through the clever use of examples, lessons, and images, you will blunt the spur of the senses and you will throw Nature off the scent, following Nature's own directions" (4: 518). Pubescent sexuality was a pack of hunting dogs to be deluded by a false scent; the adolescent was the quarry pursued by the hounds. Sexuality was not an integral part of the personality, it was

[15]Joel Schwartz discusses "sexuality in the state of nature," interpreting Rousseau's text as a statement of the natural feebleness of male libido. He says that for Rousseau "needs occasion reliance upon others." *The Sexual Politics of Jean-Jacques Rousseau*, p. 16. Rousseau's dual-instinct theory, however, is constructed precisely to eliminate natural "reliance upon others," and to restore masculine sex drive to the spontaneous level of an immediately gratifiable impulse.

an enemy, relentlessly seeking its prey. But it could be tricked into accepting a different victim and, instead of finding heterosexual expression, be induced to batten upon suffering.

When Rousseau spoke of an "age when the passions make themselves felt," he was using his terms concretely. If the passions could not really be held to arise *outside* the individual, nonetheless it was doubtful whether they would ever manifest themselves except in response to exterior provocation: "If no lascivious object had ever struck our eyes, if an indecent idea had never entered our minds, perhaps this so-called need would never have made itself felt to us, and we would have stayed chaste, without temptation, without effort, and without merit" (4: 662). Sexuality was like the other flaws that corrupted the purity of the child: "It is impossible that they would become disobedient, wicked, liars, greedy, unless somebody sowed in their hearts the vices that would render them so" (4: 341).

If sexuality was not innate, then it was an aggressive intruder "striking our eyes," "entering our brain," "making itself felt," unbidden. The good self was presexual, or at least had deflected its sexuality onto an expanded love of the self.

In any event, sexuality did not demand acknowledgement of the separate existence of another person. Thus it was that primitive people had "No kind of commerce among themselves" and the natural man having "no need of his fellow-beings . . . perhaps even without recognizing any of them individually . . . subject to few passions, [sufficed] unto himself." If he did have sexual relations, "for him, one woman is as good as another" (3: 157–58). In nature, men and women met fortuitously, coupled anonymously, and parted postcoitally, not even to recognize each other should they meet again.

The sensual and sentimental overtones that were thus stripped from genital sexuality were invested in the second instinct, pity. It made its appearance "when the first development of the senses lights the fire of imagination" and caused the shedding of tears which one loves to let flow. The intrinsic nature of pity would appear, at first glance to rescue the principle of sociability so dear to the Encyclopedists. In point of fact, Rousseau postulated the "natural repugnance toward seeing any sentient creature suffer," which he later called "pity," specifically in order to repudiate the idea that man is naturally sociable. The combination of the two instincts made it "unnecessary to introduce the [principle] of sociability" (3: 126).

[89]

Pity requires no awareness of other human beings because it is a feeling that causes the individual to experience the sufferings of others *as if they were his own.* It is merely an altered mode of experiencing the self by melting emotionally into the victim. Jan Marejko comments (p. 84) that for Rousseau: "Pity is really only an avatar of self-love, because it confirms the self in its autonomy by giving the illusion of movement toward others." Emile, the child raised to virtue, knew no one but himself: "He knows no attachment except those of habit; he loves his sister like his watch and his friend like his dog" (4: 500). When he became adolescent his love of himself could "be transmuted into pity. Let us extend self-love onto other beings, we will transform it into virtue" (4: 547). Self-love, then, was the natural source of virtue since it inspired benevolence (the Encyclopedic conception of virtue) in various forms: "What is generosity, clemency, humanity, if not pity applied to the weak, the culpable, the human race at large?" (*Premier Discours,* 3: 115). This automatic reaction of extending the self, "anterior to reason," was, for Rousseau, diminished and obscured by civilization. Thus, as Nannerl Keohane noted, "The savage deserves to be called a good man, not because he makes strenuous efforts to be virtuous, but because he is in the fortunate position of not having to deceive anyone to advance his goals."[16]

The more sophisticated and rational one becomes, the less one permits the natural impulses to dominate. Thus, according to Rousseau, it was the least cultivated, the least favored segment of society who experienced pity the most keenly. "During a riot, while street fights are going on, the prudent man walks away; it is the riffraff, the market women, who separate the brawlers and who keep the good fellows from throttling one another" (*Premier Discourse,* 3: 156).

Charles Bonnet, of Geneva, the celebrated naturalist, wrote an open letter expressing his disbelief and resentment of Rousseau's attribution of pity to the lower classes alone: "Why is it," he asked, "that the populace, to whom M. Rousseau accords such a great dose of pity, turns out so avidly for the spectacle of a poor fellow broken on the wheel?"[17] Rousseau's reply showed that what was a paradox to Bonnet was no paradox to him: "Pity is such a delicious feeling that

[16]*Philosophy and the State in France,* p. 432.
[17]"Lettre à M. Philopolis," *PW,* 1: 226. This is Rousseau's response, containing the quoted material, to Bonnet's letter in the *Mercure de France,* October 1755.

it is no wonder they are eager to experience it" (3: 236). It was not that he suggested the creation of such spectacles for the sake of the sensations they aroused, but there was nothing in his definition of pity to preclude their enjoyment. Pity was an internal sensation which could not be measured by external benevolence: "Even if it were true that commiseration is only a feeling that puts us in the place of the sufferer, an obscure vital feeling in the savage, developed but weakened in social man, what difference would that make to the truth of what I say, except to make my argument still stronger? In effect, the commiseration will be all the more intense as the Spectator animal identifies himself more deeply with the suffering animal" (3: 155).

Pity, however, could not be aroused simply by suffering, no matter how severe. Where the Spectator animal did *not* immediately identify with the suffering animal, little pity might be experienced. The prerequisite identification depended on whether the suffering animal was perceived as possessing the innate goodness the Spectator animal found within himself: "The soul has difficulty identifying with contemptible men one would be sorry to resemble and whatever ills they suffer, the pity they inspire is never very keen, but we like to put ourselves in the place of an unfortunate hero...who displays before us a virtue which we appropriate all the more willingly since we don't have to practice it" ("Fragments divers," 2: 1332).

If it is difficult to identify with the contemptible, it is not easy to place oneself in the position of the fortunate, either. "Imagination puts us in the place of the poor wretch rather than that of the happy man." The rich, too, are not to be pitied, for "the rich man's troubles do not come from his state, but from himself alone, who abuses his state. Even if he were more unhappy than the poor man, he is not to be pitied because his woes are all his own doing" (4: 509). All persons exerting power fell into the category of those who could suffer without arousing pity. Women, because of their magnetism had to be dealt with severely: "Girls must be thwarted early in life. This misfortune, if it is a misfortune for them, is inseparable from their sex...they must become accustomed to constraint so that it does not bother them. They must subdue all their own fantasies to submit them to the will of others...it is just that this sex share the difficulties it has caused in us. Do not permit them an instant of their lives free from bondage" (4: 709–10). Pity did not prevent prescribing enslavement for half the human race because, at the particular moment Rousseau was penning those lines, he was not experiencing the feeling which puts us in the place of the suffering animal.

Rousseau complained that unhappy people were forever bothering him, under the misapprehension that he was a well of sympathy. But where he did not identify, he felt nothing, had no interest, and refused the hypocritical posture of feigning one: "Once I became known through my writings, a terrible mistake no doubt, but more than expiated by my sufferings, from then on I became the general aid office for all the sufferers or so-called sufferers...who wanted to get hold of me one way or another" (1: 1052).

As more and more of the people he had known were added to the ranks of those with whom he could not identify, he was left with only two objects, ultimately identical, for whom he could feel pity: mankind at large and himself. Inevitably, the boundaries between the two began to erode, and he became convinced that he *was* mankind at large.

CHAPTER FIVE

Isolation and Fusion in Virtue

The great apologetic discourses of his later years show a Jean-Jacques convinced of the failure of his crucial enterprise. He had presented the world with images of his good self, which ought to have produced sustaining love and admiration. Surrounded by an audience that valued Jean-Jacques as he did, he would have been able to fuse with them into one infinitely valuable being.

In point of fact, as a reading of his correspondence demonstrates, he had succeeded to an astonishing decree in making himself an adored world figure, to whom thousands of readers poured out their gratitude, their feelings of oneness with him, and their love. Yet he wrote of finding it difficult to trust such homage to his genius, and instead, of brooding more and more upon himself as a figure of controversy, subject to ridicule and persecution. As his sense that he was surrounded by vicious adverseries deepened, he sought shelter within the contours of his own being, and simultaneously turned toward a world which was larger and more general than the world of real human beings, a biphasic mechanism of reduction and expansion in goodness. He described the phase of contraction in the *Emile:* "Let us begin by becoming ourselves once more, by concentrating ourselves in us, by circumscribing our soul within the same limits that nature has given to our being" (4: 1112). Once fully himself, freed of all dependency on the opinions of other people, once completely alone, he could then open himself to the forces of the universe and feel, in a delicious sweep of uplifting emotion, at one with all of creation:

> From the surface of the earth I would raise my ideas to all the beings in nature, to the universal system of things, to the incomprehensible being who embraces the whole. Then, my mind lost in this immensity, I was not thinking, I was not reasoning, I was not philosophizing, I experienced myself overwhelmed by the weight of this universe with a sort of voluptuous pleasure, I gave myself with rapture to the confusion of those grand ideas,...I was suffocating in the universe, I would have liked to hurtle myself into infinity. [1: 1141; *Lettres à Malesherbes*]

His expansion allowed him to meld into the world and once again experience the exaltation of that mystical union with the good which had always been his touchstone of virtue. As Jean Starobinski put it, "the ego abandoned itself to its ecstasies, it was equal to the imaginary totality of the world."[1] These privileged moments of exaltation were marked by sensations of reduction to the most elementary level of being and, at the same time, experienced as an immersion in the divine presence. As Georges Poulet has noted: "Ecstasy not only identifies actual men with the primitive being. It lifts him up toward God, up to a state similar to that enjoyed by the saints in the beatific vision."[2] Like many ecstatics, Rousseau identified his states of elation as direct contacts with God, contacts which could be achieved by other human beings if they freed themselves from the sterile contrivances of organized society, established religion, and intellectual pursuits.

The accusations of moral turpitude which he had heaped upon the monarchy, the affluent, and worst of all, his former friends, the philosophes, had earned him resentment where they had not elicited self-accusatory acquiescence. Rousseau reacted to the angry responses that he himself had provoked without seeming to understand their rationale. He saw himself as a blameless individual who was being inexplicably attacked by men more powerful than himself. Starobinski remarks on this inevitable underside of attributing total moral value to the self: "The certitude of personal innocence is inseparable from a no less unshakable faith in the guilt of others."[3]

[1]*La Transparence et l'obstacle*, p. 309.
[2]*Studies in Human Time* (New York: Harper, 1956), p. 171.
[3]"La Mise en accusation de la société," p. 35.

Rousseau's public readings of the *Confessions*, in 1770 and 1771, failed to produce the convincing affirmation of his goodness which he sought. They were, Bernard Gagnebin tells us, "badly received by the majority of French and English critics who were unable to discern the originality of this work."[4] This was his last major effort at forcing his contemporaries publicly to accept his value. The reception accorded the work caused him great anguish, and from then until his death in 1778 he was preoccupied largely with writings that defended the moral worth of Jean-Jacques.

In order to escape the unbearable isolation into which Jean-Jacques was thrust by his self-exculpating theodicy, Rousseau came to the notion of a *trial* as the only possible point of human contact between the accused and the accuser—"a trial," in Jan Marejko's words, "which would put an end to the malediction because whether reintegrating him into society or excluding him from it, the trial would finally show him that he had some connection to his fellow men" (p. 42).

The three lengthy dialogues entitled *Rousseau juge de Jean-Jacques* are trials of Jean-Jacques Rousseau's "guilt" or "innocence." They consist of a series of conversations between "Rousseau" and "a Frenchman" about "Jean-Jacques." Just as he had written letters to himself alternately as Julie and Saint-Preux in *La Nouvelle Héloïse*, he now projected himself into three separate personalities whose only preoccupation, in this instance, was Rousseau's moral value.[5] Thus

---

[4]"L'Etrange Accueil fait aux 'Confessions' de Rousseau au XVIIIe siècle," *AJJR*, 38 (1969–71), 126.

[5]This splitting of the self into various persona who play the roles of prosecution, defense, and accused, has aroused suspicions as to Rousseau's sanity. Dr. A. Hesnard labeled the tendency pathological in *L'Univers morbide de la faute* (Paris: Presses Universitaires de France, 1949). Robert Osmont, however, an editor of the Pléiade edition of these dialogues, denied the applicability of such a diagnosis: "As for the doublings which permit the fiction of the *Dialogues*, it seems exaggerated to attribute a morbid character to them." Further, Osmont suggests, "the doubling dissipates false appearances, it serves clarity" (1: lvi–ii). Hesnard is attempting to reconstruct a man and comprehend his mental status through his writings, as if they were the manifest content of a patient's dreams or utterances. Osmont, on the other hand, deals with the texts as opaque, self-referential objects, whose connection with any real person is ultimately unknowable. P.-P. Clément (p. 351) groups all three autobiographical works together, calling them efforts to "reestablish, each in its own way, a compromised unity; they show that the true Rousseau, despite his acknowledged errors, which were always attributable to society or to circumstances, has a pure and loving nature and could never recognize himself as that man 'plunged into the most sordid debauchery'

even the impulse to present his "self" to the impartiality of *others* was expressed by a form in which the others were emanations of his "self."

The character called "Rousseau" said "I have read the entire works claimed by Jean-Jacques several times, and the total effect on my soul was always to make me more human, most just, better than I was before. Never have I concerned myself with these works without profit for virtue. I am sure that the effect they produce on me would be the same on any decent man who would read them with the same impartiality" (1: 696). The "Frenchman," on the other hand, was convinced that "Jean-Jacques" was a "hateful rogue, the shame and opprobrium of the human race" (1: 692). "Rousseau" was devastated to learn that "Jean-Jacques" was wicked. He told the "Frenchman": "One man alone, thinking like me, nourished my confidence, one sole truly virtuous man made me believe in virtue, moved me to cherish it, to idolize it, to place all hope in it; and here it is that in depriving me of this support you leave me alone upon the earth" (1: 729).

It was a question of reconciling a tremendous disparity; how could the man not be consubstantial with the virtuous author of *La Nouvelle Héloïse*, the *Discours*, *Emile*, and the *Contrat social*? The two characters, equally motivated to arrive at the truth, struck a bargain. The "Frenchman" agreed to read all of "Jean-Jacques's" works, "despite his repugnance," and in exchange, "Rousseau" would pay a call upon "Jean-Jacques." He told the "Frenchman" "I want to find him innocent with all my heart" (1: 764). "Rousseau" immediately went to visit "Jean-Jacques," who was able to distinguish him from every other visitor by his sincerity. "He saw that all the others were searching only for evil, and that I was the only one who, looking for good, wished to see nothing but the truth" (1: 784). When "Rousseau" looked at "Jean-Jacques," he saw "the features of Emile's Mentor. Perhaps in his youth I would have found those of St. Preux" (1: 778). "Rousseau" and "Jean-Jacques" got on wonderfully well, as "Rousseau" told the "Frenchman." "Rousseau" decided "impartially"

---

his enemies depicted him as being." See also Jean-Marie Goulemot, "*Les Confessions: Une autobiographie d'écrivain*," *Littérature*, 33 (Feb. 1979), 58–74; J. F. McCannell, "The Post-Fictional Self: Authorial Consciousness in Three Texts by Rousseau," *MLN*, 89 (1974), 580–99; Robert Ellrich, *Rousseau and His Reader: The Rhetorical Situation of the Major Works* (Chapel Hill: University of North Carolina Press, 1969).

that "Jean-Jacques" was not really "virtuous, because he does not need to be, and for the same reason he will be neither vicious nor wicked" (1: 945). "Jean-Jacques" was morally neutral because he did not need anybody but himself, having "imaginary friends." His only vice, masturbation, "harms no one but himself": "Our man will not be virtuous because he will be weak and virtue belongs only to strong souls. But this virtue which he cannot attain, who admires it, cherishes it, adores it more than he?" (1: 824).

The "Frenchman," having fulfilled his end of the bargain, came to the conclusion that, all accusations to the contrary, "Jean-Jacques" was innocent. "I believe [him] innocent and virtuous, and this belief is so much at the bottom of my soul that it needs no other confirmation" (1: 945). As certain as he was, however, he would not defend Jean-Jacques in public for fear of arousing the wrath of his persecutors. He advised "Rousseau" to give "Jean-Jacques" some advice: "surrounded as he is by ambushes and traps awaiting his every step, the best thing is to stay immobile, if possible, not to act at all, . . . to resist even his own movements" (1: 962).

Convinced that "Jean-Jacques" was "innocent," "Rousseau" and the "Frenchman" expressed their hope that "his memory will be rehabilitated some day to the honor it deserves, and that his books will become useful through the esteem due their Author. Let us add to this hope the happiness of seeing two honest and true hearts opening to his. Thus let us temper the horror of that solitude where they force him to live amidst the human race" (1: 976).

When alone and troubled in the forests around the Hermitage, Jean-Jacques had made his society by decomposing into self-emanations who could then interact; now once again he had closed the psychic circle. Manifestations of himself had crystallized, this time to evaluate him, find him good, and then melt back into him.

He attempted to lay this manuscript upon the altar of Notre Dame Cathedral, with a note addressed to God: "My soul, exalted by the feeling of my innocence and by that of [men's] iniquities, elevated itself in a rush to the throne of all order and all truth, to seek the resources I no longer had here below" (1: 976). That enterprise having failed, Rousseau in despair took to the streets of Paris, distributing to sympathetic-looking passers-by a leaflet entitled "To all Frenchmen who still love justice and truth." In it he asked how the French could behave so cruelly toward him: "How you have changed

[97]

toward a poor foreigner, alone, at your mercy, with no support, no defender, toward a man without pretense, without bitterness, an enemy of injustice who endures injustice patiently, who has never done, or wished, or repaid harm to anybody, and who for fifteen years has felt himself weighed down with indignities unheard of until now in the human race, without ever being able to learn the cause!" (1: 990).

In these autobiographical works of the latter part of his life, the *Confessions*, the dialogues of *Rousseau juge de Jean-Jacques*, and finally the *Rêveries d'un promeneur solitaire*, the gap between the innocence of Jean-Jacques and the evil of the world gradually widened until it became unbridgeable.

Jean-Jacques had turned in upon himself, making himself small and still, in order to enjoy his sensations of goodness, but this pleasure exacted a price. The more intensely blameless Rousseau felt, the more culpable he experienced the rest of the world as being: he knew that he could not be guilty because his intentions had always been good, but this was not true of his enemies. They premeditated evil, even when they did not perform it. "They are not unjust and wicked toward me by mistake but rather willfully: they are wicked because they want to be" (1: 986). He could, says Starobinski, "will his innocence only by willing the cruelest persecution. For only the exterior burden of persecution relieves him of the interior weight of responsibility. Rousseau disculpates himself by accusing: all defect is outside."[6] As a result, he believed that he was alone because of the cruelty of the human race.

He could not make intellectual sense of his world, it was a terrible mystery, "an incomprehensible chaos" (1: 995). Why should an inoffensive being such as he inspire hatred? The moral anomaly troubled his mind. Referring to himself in the third person because "I wanted to know what I would look like if I were someone else," Rousseau described his anguish: "By a decree which it is not mine to fathom, he must spend the rest of his days in contempt and humiliation."

"He is absolutely alone and has only himself for help," and "such a singular position is unique in the existence of the human race" (1: 765). It seemed, logically, to go against all probability that the entire world would choose to persecute and revile one single innocent

[6]*La Transparence et l'obstacle,* p. 290.

person. Despite its inner emotional logic, his situation was impossible to comprehend rationally: "Who would believe that I would be considered without any doubt a monster, an assassin, that I would become the horror of the human race, the plaything of the rabble, that the only greeting passers-by in the street would offer would be to spit on me, that a whole generation would agree unanimously to bury me alive?" (1: 996). He seized on this last metaphor repetitively: "They enjoy themselves burying him alive," he said in the dialogues (1: 743), and "they have shut him up alive in a tomb" (1: 1055). He was surrounded by "black shadows" (1: 1009). His enemies were killing him slowly so that his sufferings would last longer: "they have erected around him walls of shadow, impenetrable to his eye; they have buried him alive amongst the living" (1: 706).

The situation left Rousseau with no choice but to withdraw further from people. No one could claim that he was obligated toward anyone, considering how he was being treated. Since the "plot" was "universal and without exception" Rousseau could find no one with whom to identify: "I would have loved men in spite of themselves. They could avoid my affection only by ceasing to be men. here they are then, alien, unknown, in a word nothing to me, since they wished it so" (1: 995).

The Spectator animal was denied pleasurable pity in regarding the suffering animal because the suffering animal was evil and hence unworthy of sympathy. Since Rousseau knew that mankind was, like him, good, he was forced to the awful but inevitable realization that the creatures who treated him so heartlessly were not *really people* at all, that the key to the mystery was that "my contemporaries were but mechanical beings in regard to me who acted only by impulsion and whose actions I could calculate only by the laws of movement" (1: 1078). He was now really alone, the only human being left amid a throng of automatons; the human race existed solely in him: "Alone, sick, abandoned in my bed, I can die there of poverty, cold, and hunger without anybody troubling himself about it" (1: 1080). Thérèse, it was true, was with him constantly, but he did not think of her as a separate person. Although, in his solitude, he could still be swept up in "ecstasies of indescribable deliciousness," he fell into despair when he recognized that his daydreams were not the same thing as reality. "I was made for living," he said in the second *Promenade,* "and I am dying without having lived." He cheered himself, however, by observing that "at least it is not my fault and I will bring before the Author of my being, if not the offering of good works which they would not let me perform, at least the tribute of good intentions" (1: 1004). Finally, convinced that even the little children in the streets were looking askance at him, he was reduced to searching "among the animals for the benevolent glance henceforth refused [him] among men" (1: 1089).

His quandary had become desperate. He envisaged a solution, one that would render him decisively "good" and yet shield him from attack. He began to long for the ultimate persecution. Only his immolation by the forces of evil would set the eternal seal upon his goodness. "I envy the glory of martyrs. If I have not altogether the same faith as they I have the same innocence and the same zeal, and my heart feels it is worthy of the same prize" (*C.c.*, 19: 261). That prize was the recognition, finally irrefutable and immutable, of his essential moral excellence. Martyrdom itself had become the ultimate goal, not martyrdom in the service of the divine Will or a sectarian dogma. To be killed by the wicked as punishment for goodness would resolve forever all questions about Rousseau's moral worth.

If Jean-Jacques were to die a martyr to goodness, however, surely such an event could not be without transcendental significance. He suspected that the enigma of his universal persecution would be revealed to him only after his death. The ubiquity of the animosity he experienced made him realize that it was part of God's design: "This universal agreement is too extraordinary to be completely fortuitous... all wills, all destinies, such a striking coincidence, like a prodigy, leaves me no doubt but that its outcome is written down in the eternal decrees. A large number of private observations...convinces me...to consider what I had up to now regarded as the fruit of man's wickedness henceforth as one of heaven's secrets, impenetrable to human reason. God is just. He wants me to suffer, he knows I am innocent, ...my turn will come sooner or later" (1: 1010). He had raised his lifelong certainty of inner worth to its ultimate conclusions. Jean-Jacques's pathos marked a divine mission.

Christianity, in the century preceding the Revolution, had inextricably allied its fortunes with those of the privileged ranks, whatever lip service was paid to the blessedness of the humble. The philosophes hacked away at this comfortable marriage with every literary weapon at their disposal, and in the last decades of the eighteenth century the grip of Christianity upon thought and feeling had been significantly loosened. In place of the time-honored verities, however, the philosophes had installed a chaos of speculation that offered very little in the way of certitude or solace to the humble.

Rousseau originally entered the battle on the philosophic side, but soon turned the flank of both his enemies and allies. In his *Profession de foi du vicaire savoyard,* which formed part of *Emile,* he assaulted both Christianity and the philosophic enterprise from the ground of the man who was neither orthodox nor skeptical, but ecstatic. Like Saint Teresa or John of the Cross, Rousseau had experienced the divine presence, and his impassioned descriptions of its incomparable value denigrated both conventional religion and philosophic doubt. His impassioned depictions of beatitude enraged both sides of the dispute in equal measure; it was only the great mass of ordinary people who found in him the charismatic leader they had long awaited.

Rousseau commented in his *Lettre à d'Alembert sur les spectacles* that he had once believed it possible to have good morals without religion, "but that is an error from which I have since recovered." For him morality was linked to religious feeling, and he recognized what the Encyclopedists did not wish to see, that for a sizable portion of humanity, the presence of an all-knowing divinity was essential to the maintenance of an ethics.[7] Organized religion, however, was a tainted, unreliable, and deadening force that stood between man and his creator, hindering the immediate union for which he yearned.

The religion which Rousseau presented in the *Profession* and which he defended against the outraged attack of Christophe de Beaumont, archbishop of Paris, began by excluding all organized orthodoxies, all sacred texts, all revelations, and all human authority as sources of truth. In a few brilliant and passionate pages, Rousseau took the philosophes' techniques for discrediting Christianity and raised them to a level of logic, sincerity, and compassion for humanity which his former friends had never achieved. The vicar, however, was speak-

---

[7]Henri Gouhier discusses the theme of "living under the gaze of God," as a means of linking the philosophical speculations of the *Profession de foi* with the affective experience of direct contact with the divinity. *Les Méditations métaphysiques de Jean-Jacques Rousseau* (Paris: Vrin, 1970), p. 93. See also Pierre Burgelin, *La Philosophie de l'existence de Jean-Jacques Rousseau* (Paris: Presses Universitaires de France, 1952), ch. 4.

ing not from the vantage point of doubt, but from that of conviction: "I take as witness the God of peace I adore," he said, "and I tell you that all my research has been sincere, ... it has all been fruitless, and I tell you that as I was foundering in a boundless sea, I retraced my way and I shrank back into my primitive notions. I was never able to believe that God ordered me, on pain of eternal damnation, to be so learned. Thus did I close all the books" (4: 625).

Had Rousseau stopped there, he would have added merely one more eloquent salvo to the century's condemnation of religion's, and especially Christianity's, arrogance and obfuscation. He did not, however, stop there, for he was bent not merely on destroying an old set of beliefs, but on establishing a new one. Emile was to:

> find his true interest in being good, in doing good far away from the eyes of men, and without being forced to do it by laws, in being just between God and himself ... and in carrying virtue in his heart, not only for love of order, which each man always values less than his love for himself, but for love of the author of his being, a love which is combined with that self-love, so that he can finally enjoy the endless happiness that the response of a good conscience and the contemplation of the Supreme Being promise in the life to come. Leave this path and I see nothing but injustice, hypocrisy, and lies among men; private interest which through competitiveness must of necessity outweigh everything else and teach each individual to cover vice with the mask of virtue. [4: 636]

Thus true religion involved a melting of man's love for himself into his love for God. As for the exterior forms of worship, Rousseau insisted that they were largely a matter of indifference; the individual should follow the rites of his fathers.

F.-A. Aulard commented that "Rousseau's thought in the *Vicaire savoyard* is certainly Christian."[8] The reaction of the Sorbonne leaves no doubt that it did not strike theologians of the day as such. Christophe de Beaumont put his finger on the central problem when he stated that Rousseau's plan of education, "far from according itself with Christianity, is not even appropriate for forming citizens or men" because of his denial of original sin (4: 937). Rousseau was absolutely explicit on that point: "The fundamental

[8]*Le Culte de la raison et le culte de l'Etre suprême (1793–1794)* (Paris: Alcan, 1892), p. 260.

principle of all morality, upon which I have reasoned in all my writings and which I developed in [*La Profession de foi*] with all the clarity of which I am capable is that man is a being who is naturally good, loving justice and order; that there is no original perversity in the human heart, and the first movements of nature are always good" (4: 936).

Ronald Grimsley comments: "The orthodox were quite justified in treating Rousseau's religion as Pelagianism, since he allowed no room for original sin and the need for grace through Christ the redeemer; man's natural goodness and freedom allowed him to achieve his own salvation."[9]

Not all critics have taken the same attitude. René Pomeau, for example, says that "Rousseau remains respectfully skeptical, but he adheres to the spirit of the Gospels: to that feeling of the divine, to that love of humanity, which constitute the true revelation of the sacred book. In that sense he believed he had the right to call himself Christian." However, as Pomeau points out, Rousseau's religion excluded "all clerical intervention," miracles, and the necessity of the gospels, and it equivocated on the divinity of Christ.[10] All these reservations mitigated against his inclusion in the ranks of orothodox Christianity, but the two essential distinctions between Rousseau's religion and Christianity were the denial of the fall and the consequent devaluation of the sacraments. Rousseau negated original sin and the entire concept of man as a flawed moral being in need of a divine savior. Without this doctrine Christianity is Christian no more, whatever else it may be. Sergio Cotta situated the nexus of Rosseau's political-religious belief in one principle, "the original innocence of man," and drew the conclusion other critics have often failed to see, that "this principle of man's original innocence is nothing other than the rejection of the Christian notion of the Fall, of original sin."[11]

While Christianity and the Rousseauvian religion have several elements in common, the most striking parallel is the advent of a new sacred victim, come to assume the suffering of the world. "That Rousseau considered Jesus as the founder of natural religion and the remarkable embodiment of its human qualities is . . . revealed by

[9]*Rousseau: The Religious Quest* (Oxford: Clarendon Press, 1968), p. 137.
[10]"Foi et raison de Jean-Jacques," *Europe*, no. 391–92 (Nov.-Dec. 1961), 57–65.
[11]"La Position du problème de la politique chez Rousseau," *JECS*, p. 184.

a curious tendency in his latter years to see himself as a Christ-like figure, for was not Jean-Jacques also—though to a lesser degree perhaps—a remarkable example of the simple, good man persecuted by a wicked world?" (Grimsley, p. 73). This side of Rousseau's religiosity disturbed his former friends far more than conventional Catholicism would have done, for they saw that Rousseau's wish was not to imitate Jesus Christ, but to compete with him, which is an entirely different impulse. Just as Christ had once come to abrogate the law of Moses, Rousseau now came to usher in a new era, one in which the primal guilt of humanity was declared a misapprehension. Thus whereas Christ had offered up his own human person to compensate for man's fall, Rousseau sacrificed himself to the world for the greater truth he contained: man is innocent and needs no personal redeemer. The enemy is not the sin-ridden self but the guilt-provoking other. As Groethuysen put it, "The true dualism is not within us. It is between us and society."[12]

Like the Messiah, Rousseau suffered for the relief he brought humanity. Could it be otherwise? His later works were filled with references to his conviction that his double persecution by both the Christians and the philosophes had divine significance. "Ah," he wrote, "if these gentle Christians could wrench blasphemy from me at the end, what a triumph! With what holy joy they would carry the burning embers to the fire of their zeal, to inflame my pyre!" (3: 742). On the other hand, the news of his sufferings had "filled Europe, the wise are astonished, the good are afflicted; finally everyone understands that I knew better than they this erudite and philosophic century" (1: 1151). He had no doubt that the world stood in need of his message: "I am persuaded that it matters to the human race that my book [the *Confessions*] be respected" (1: 1122).

Rousseau wavered between references to "God" and to the "Supreme Being," and the connotations of these two terms were not identical. Just as Christianity uneasily assimilated the God of Abraham into God the Father of Jesus Christ, leaving more than one disparity to be adjudicated, Rousseau slipped from the Christian deity to something else, an ultimate presence whom Christophe de Beaumont quite correctly perceived as alien to orthodox belief from a number of perspectives. However, Rousseau resolved in a new way the

---

[12]Bernard Groethuysen, *Jean-Jacques Rousseau* (Paris: Gallimard, 1949), p. 291.

intellectual problems which any revealed religion presented; emphasizing the need for affective union with the divinity over the need for logic and clarity, he proclaimed the emotional demands of the good self to be the sole test of truth. In his celebrated letter to Voltaire, he put forth his objections to the anti-Providentialism of the *Poème sur le désastre de Lisbonne.* "It is inhuman to trouble peaceful souls, and to distress men to no purpose, when what one is teaching them is neither certain nor useful," he told Voltaire, and at the end of the epistle, he reiterated the fundamental tenet of his credo: "All the subtleties of metaphysics will not make me doubt for one moment the immortality of the soul or a benevolent Providence. I feel it, I believe it, I want it, I hope for it, I shall defend it until my last breath" (4: 1075).

Beyond the door of death stood another place, for Rousseau; it was not the stratified paradises of Christian theology but the locus of love at last fulfilled. He alluded to his belief in that more real world to come, one where Julie and Saint-Preux might at last melt into one another at peace. Unlike Christianity, however, which held out the promise of paradise to even the most hardened sinner until the very last moment, Rousseau spoke of a different test that would separate the saved from the damned. Good people, those who overcame their selfish desires, went to bliss, while "the souls of the wicked were annihilated at death" (3: 287–88). Perhaps it was an even more startling polarity: the wicked were *always* mere flesh, possessing no immortal soul at all. "Sensual men, bodies without souls," he remarked in *Emile,* and in a draft of the *Rêveries* he commented: "it is true that I do nothing upon the earth, but when I have no more body I still won't do anything, and nevertheless I shall be an excellent being, more full of feeling and life than the most active of mortals" (4: 1166). Thus the good self was the elected soul, it was knowable through its feelings, not its acts, and it would find oneness with God while the men of this world would return to the dust that composed them.

Rousseau's contribution to filling the void left by the denigration of Christianity did not stop with the promise of individual innocence and eventual beatitude. From the good of the isolated self his interest swung to the good of the collectivity. Primitive religion, he held, was a distinct people's relation to its own tribal diety; in this way the body politic worshiped its own supernatural emanation and there could be no contradiction between the man, the citizen, and the believer. Christianity, on the other hand, occupied European peoples with strange near-Eastern dieties having no connection with Western realities, and brought them under the yoke of a foreign leadership which did not correspond to their need for nationalistic unity. In the modern world, if the people are brought together, "it is in temples for a cult which has nothing national about it, which in no way recalls the fatherland . . . in festivals where the people is always despised and always without influence" (*PW*, 2: 430). A *true* state would institute a religion that would worship not some long-dead Jew under the auspices of some dubious Italian, but itself. One of the grave mistakes of history took place when "Jesus came to establish a spiritual kingdom on earth; which, separating the theological system from the political system, had the effect of causing the state to cease to be one and causing the internal divisions which have never ceased to agitate Christian peoples" (3: 462). The good society would restore the circle Christianity had broken and reintegrate man into a state religion: "Whatever fractures social unity is worthless; all institutions which put man in contradiction with himself are worthless" (3: 464). Hence in the legitimate society, based on the General Will, there would be a "purely civil profession of faith whose articles would be fixed by the Sovereign, not exactly as religious dogmas but as feelings of sociability. If somebody, after having publicly recognized these dogmas, behaves as if he did not believe in them, let him be put to death" (3: 468).

In this superior society, people would enjoy religious gatherings as a great sensation of glorious merging with their extended good selves: the fatherland. In the *Lettre à d'Alembert,* Rousseau had expressed his discomfort and contempt for the theatrical presentations of his time, "those exclusive spectacles which confine a small number of people mournfully in caverns of darkness; which hold them fearful and immobile in silence and inaction" (p. 224). Advising the inhabitants of Geneva to forgo such theater in favor of great outdoor gatherings, he told them to "present the spectators as spectacle, make them the actors themselves, see to it that each one sees himself and loves himself in the others in order for all to be better united" (p. 225).

The very syntax Rousseau used reveals the impulse behind these words. Addressing himself to the people of Geneva, he exhorted

ٮem to find their pleasure in the contemplation of their own ;oodness, and then he moved to the causative construction, directing them to "present" the spectators as spectacle, to "make" the audience actors, and to "see to it" that each one sees himself in others. Rousseau spoke to the Genevans as though they were at once the active agents and the passive actors of a celebration which he saw within himself, which they had only to enact in order to share the stimulating swelling of self-love in virtue which he experienced so rapturously. Rejecting the caverns of darkness where vice was represented upon a stage, a true people would meld into one happy being, adoring and admiring itself and its divine principle.

CHAPTER SIX

The Effect Become the Cause

Rousseau's descriptions of the ideal political state were couched in extraordinarily seductive language. He brought to the very margins of consciousness infantile longings for immediacy, fusion, and communion repudiated by the prevailing culture of the Enlightenment, and wrapped them in the flag of moral superiority. He lent legitimacy to the inchoate yearnings of civilized man for return to the undifferentiated self-absorption of early childhood and did so in a voice of awesome moral authority.[1] Yet he hedged his haunting evocations of lost Eden and the chances to regain paradise with reiterated statements of pessimism regarding the possibilities of ever achieving the "good state" in reality. In the *Contrat social* he listed the attributes of the people who might be candidates for moral regeneration, and his list excluded almost everyone:

What people then is appropriate for legislation? The one which, already bound together by some union of origins, of interest, or of convention, has not yet borne the veritable yoke of law; one which has no deeprooted customs or superstitions, one which has no fear of being overwhelmed by sudden invasion, one which, without entering into its

[1] In "L'Art de l'écrivain dans le *Contrat social*," Michel Launay analyzes how Rousseau constructed his work to affect his readership. "The theory of the contract was destined not only to judge reality, but to act upon it, either as a stimulant or as a sedative; . . . simultaneously the blow and the caress; and the caress, as everyone knows, appeases and inflames desire at the same time." *Jean-Jacques Rousseau et son temps*, ed. Michel Launay (Paris: Nizet, 1979), p. 149.

neighbors' quarrels, can resist each of them alone, or help one to fight off another; one in which each member can be known by all, and where no one is forced to charge a man with a greater burden than he can carry, the one which can get along without other peoples and which other peoples can do without. The one which is neither too rich nor too poor and can suffice unto itself, finally the one which unites the consistence of an ancient people with the docility of a new people. All these conditions, it is true, are rarely found together. [3: 390–91]

Thus the people who could be led to "virtue" resembled the individual susceptible to the same improvement: uncorrupted by previous habits, independent of others, sufficient unto itself. Although such ethnic or political entities were rare, Rousseau envisaged one place where an authentic polity might yet be possible. "There is still in Europe one country capable of legislation," he added; "it is the island of Corsica."

Despite the unlikelihood of any real peoples (other than the Corsicans) achieving the good state, Rousseau described the steps necessary to create one. Uniting into one being, the citizens would submerge their individual interests into a common will. Perhaps no other idea of Rousseau's has aroused the controversy this one has. Rousseau's concept of the "General Will" can be best understood, as Robert Derathé demonstrates in his notes to the Pléiade edition, by juxtaposing the relevant passages from both versions of the *Contrat social*, the definitive version and the somewhat different one referred to as the Geneva manuscript. The Geneva manuscript refers to the "common will" as follows: "There is in the State a common force which maintains it, a common will which directs this force, and it is the application of the one to the other which constitutes sovereignty." The idea of a common force is easily deduced from observation of every existing political state; its most obvious manifestations are the military and the police. In the Europe of Rousseau's day these armed units were directed by specific agencies of specific sovereign bodies: agents of the central, municipal, or provincial governments. Their activities frequently contradicted the wishes of many of the citizens. But what was meant by a "common will"? In what way was it possible to speak of a "common will" as analogous to a "common force"? In this sentence Rousseau slid from the concrete, discrete, historical phenomenon to a supposed causative factor that possessed no immediate referent in the real world. The Geneva manuscript provides a clarification of his meaning, which is not explicitly stated in the final version: "As the will always tends to the good of the being who wills it, [since] the private will always has particular interests in mind, and the general will common interests, it follows that the latter is or ought to be the sole true motivating force of the social body."

Thus the human body was again offered as an adequate metaphor for the "body politic." Just as people want their own benefit, the "social body" in which individuals might submerge themselves wants its own benefit, and this desire either is or should be the source of its actions. In the definitive *Contrat social*, Rousseau rather slid by these precise points, to consider whether or not "sovereignty is indivisible," and whether "the general will can be wrong." On this latter point he focused sharply.

The common will was not the same thing as what everybody wants. "There is often a difference between the will of all and the common will" (3: 371). The common will, however, could not err. "It follows that the common will is always right and always tends toward public utility: but it does not follow that public deliberations have the same rectitude. One always wishes for one's own good, but one does not always see it: never is the people corrupted, but frequently it is misguided, and that is the only time when it appears to want what is evil" (3: 371). Thus the "general will" revealed itself as a mystical entity, separate from the people who possessed it, transcending their expressed wishes, which were really only illusions, in favor of a superior fusion in desire, the true reality. The great "body politic," Rousseau's own goodness swelled to form an incorruptible people, could have but one will; in communion with this super volition, individual whims withered.

How was the common will to be formulated and enunciated? Parliamentary procedures would not eventuate in the common will because people had inclinations of their own and formed partial interest groups that obscured the interest of the people as a whole. "It is important therefore in order to state the general will that there exist no partial associations within the state" (3: 372). Since members of all existing societies were bound to a multiplicity of partial associations, such as families, communities, economic, social, and religious groups, it would see impossible for the general will ever to be formulated. At this point in his argument, however, Rousseau invoked a superior being who would resolve the dilemma by speaking for the wishes of the people unable to recognize what they really wanted. "To discover the best rules of society appropriate to the Nations," he proclaimed in a much-disputed passage, "it would take a superior intelligence, who sees all human passions and who does not experience any of them, who would have no connection with our nature and who would know it to the core, whose happiness would be independent of us and yet who would be willing to take care of ours" (3: 381). The Legislator would "institute" a people, a very particular function which Rousseau described in detail:

> The one who dares to attempt to institute a people must feel that he is capable of changing, so to speak, human nature; of transforming each individual, who, by himself, is a perfect and solitary whole, into a part of a greater whole from which this individual receives in some way his life and his being; of altering the constitution of a man to reinforce it.... In a word he must deprive man of his natural strengths in order to give him strengths which are alien to him and which he cannot use without the help of others. The more the natural strengths are dead and destroyed, the more the acquired ones are great and durable, and the more solid and perfect the institution is. [3: 382]

The Legislator would be an exceptional being, not only divorced from the passions of the people he was to institute, but perhaps an outsider among them. "It was the custom in most Greek cities to trust strangers with their establishment. The modern Republics of Italy often imitated that usage; Geneva did the same and profited from doing so" (3: 382).[2]

The Legislator would not be able to *persuade* people, however, because a misled and egotistical people could never understand his

---

[2]Bernard Gagnebin notes: "the appeal of a foreigner to draw up a code of law has happened on several occasions in contemporary history." He mentions the National Convention's thoughts of turning to Immanuel Kant for guidance, Venezuela's requests to Jeremy Bentham, Kemal Ataturk's reliance on the aid of the Swiss professor G. Sauser-Hall, and the international commission which drew up penal codes for Ethiopia. "Le Rôle du Législateur dans les conceptions politiques de Rousseau," *JECS*, p. 280. Raymond Polin, in an appendix to *La Politique de la solitude*, points out that "Rousseau's actual theory presents such peculiar characteristics, his [the Legislator's] very presence is, in some regards, so surprising, that it has misled or discouraged the majority of interpreters. It remains to this day obscure and ambiguous" (p. 221).

sublime views. Thus a further problem presented itself: how could a flawed people be "instituted" to virtue, even if they were ready and had found a Legislator? How could a real people be made to obey their own general will as long as they were unaware of its existence? "In order for a nascent people to be able to appreciate sound political maxims and follow the fundamental rules of *la raison d'Etat,* the effect would have to become the cause, the social spirit which must be the effect of the institution must preside over the institution itself, and men must be before the laws what they must become through the laws" (3: 383).

The effect would have to become the cause: only an already virtuous people could accept and love the state that would make them a virtuous people. This "strange loop," to use Douglas R. Hofstadter's expression for a set which generates another self-inclusive set,[3] could be realized if a people were led to accept "institution" from what it believed to be a divine source. "Here is what has always forced the founding fathers of nations to have recourse to divine intervention, and to give the Gods credit for their own wisdom, in order that the peoples, submissive to the laws of the state as to those of nature . . . obey with liberty and bear with docility the yoke of public felicity" (3: 383).

If the philosophes had been unanimous on one topic, it was their conviction that the complicity religion had consistently displayed in relation to the temporal powers was a scandal. In Voltaire's words: *"The accord of priesthood and empire* is the most monstrous of systems."[4] For Rousseau, however, this free-thinking dogma was remote from the concerns of Jean-Jacques, which were to express the feelings of goodness which so pleasurably welled up inside him in such a way that other people could partake of them too. The wise, dispassionate, benevolent Legislator and the good, ignorant, misled, impassioned people corresponded exactly to Rousseau's own description of himself listening to Fabricius on the road to Vincennes: two entities distinct since the time of his "intellectual and moral reform."[5]

---

[3]A "strange loop" is defined as "an interaction between levels in which the top level reaches back down toward the bottom level and influences it, while at the same time being itself determined by the bottom level." *Gödel, Escher, Bach: An Eternal Golden Braid* (New York: Basic Books, 1979), p. 709.

[4]*Philosophical Dictionary,* trans. Peter Gay (New York: Basic Books, 1962), 2: 433.

[5]English Showalter, having examined Rousseau's own handling of the illumination

As he so eloquently attested in the *Confessions,* at the moment of the reform he "became virtuous, or at least drunk with virtue.... I was really transformed, my friends, my acquaintances no longer recognized me." When he retired from Paris, however, and his exaltation collapsed, he became once more "fearful, accommodating, and timid, in a word the same Jean-Jacques I used to be. If the revolution had only brought me back to myself, everything would have been all right; but unfortunately it went farther and carried me rapidly to the opposite extreme. From that time on, my soul, in motion, has only passed through the point of repose, and its oscillations, always renewed, have never permitted it to remain there" (1: 417).

The two representations of Rousseau, the reasoning intellect superior to "the morals, the maxims, and the prejudices of my century" and the susceptible, confused, sensation-bound Jean-Jacques, both found expression in the couple formed by the Legislator and his people. The Legislator would understand the people's true wishes and voice them, just as the reformed Rousseau could articulate the reality the bewildered Jean-Jacques was incapable of perceiving. Thus there was absolutely no contradiction between obedience and liberty as long as the individual had no awareness of obeying a will foreign to his own, for the Legislator, being the morally impeccable manifestation of Rousseau, was only putting into words what was latent within himself, the authentic body politic.

The "foreignness" of the Legislator corresponded to Rousseau's writings about the self which emerged at the time of the reform, of that self which was "him" and yet was so alien to his previous personality: "What a change! Let someone look for the state the most contrary to my nature in the whole world; he will find that one.

---

of Vincennes, has drawn attention to the fact that Rousseau accorded this supreme moment less importance in the *Confessions* than the phenomenon of memory itself. "It is...startling that he should substitute this digression for the description of his intense emotional and physical reaction to the question proposed by the Dijon academy.... His intuition, however, should be respected, and we must consider memory and forgetfulness a theme perhaps more central to the reform, than the philosophical system born to the road to Vincennes." As Showalter observed, "The illumination itself was a remembrance of a forgotten self." *Madame de Graffigny and Rousseau: Between the Two Discourses* (Oxford: Voltaire Foundation, 1978), p. 104. Judith Shklar emphasized Rousseau's treatment of memory as a pathological faculty linked to an invidious nostalgia: "Memory induces reflection which is crippling, inhibiting and destructive." *Men and Citizens: A Study of Rousseau's Social Theory* (Cambridge: Cambridge University Press, 1969), p. 140.

Let someone recall one of the brief moments of my life when I became another, and ceased being me; again he will find it in the time of which I am speaking" (1: 417). It was that "other" who was to be the Legislator, who would do for the nation what it had done for Rousseau.

Control of the citizens' actions was not the main objective, however, but control of their wishes. The ideal Legislator would "institute" his people so that their volitional lives would be identical with the general will as he uttered it, and this process would result in a state of "virtue." "Do you wish the general will to be accomplished? Make all the private wills connect to it; and since virtue is nothing but the conformity of the private will to the general, to say the same thing in a word, make virtue reign" (3: 252). As at the end of Fabricius' prosopopeia, the mandate Rousseau consistently laid upon the legitimate government was not the task of providing political, economic, or social justice, but the essential charge of "making virtue reign."

"Institutions" were not the same things as laws, nor were they the ingrained habits and traditions that evolved within a given society; rather they were a third value system imposed upon the people: a set of idiosyncratic usages enunciated by a great legislator and somehow incorporated into the mentality of the citizenry. Rousseau's models were Moses, Lycurgus, and Numa. These three had succeeded in "instituting" a people. "The same spirit guided all these ancient Legislators in their institutions," said Rousseau. "All sought to bind the citizen to the fatherland and to each other, and all found those links in particular habits" (3: 958). Thus it was, for example, Moses' injunctions to the Hebrews that made of them a real people, apart from the others, and bound to their tribe by unbreakable chains.

"Institutions" differed from positive laws. They could not be rationally deduced from premises and they constituted imperatives *only for a closed group,* not for humanity as a whole. An "institution," for example, was established by Moses' injunction to the Hebrews: "Thou shalt not wear a garment that is woven of wool and linen together" (Deuteronomy, 22:11), or Lycurgus' order that "no discourse be permitted unless it contain great good sense in few words." Numa Pompilius was "instituting," not governing, the Romans when he proclaimed that "a child of three years was not to be mourned at all; one older, up to ten years, for as many months as it was years old."[6] The Hebrews, the Spartans, and the Republican Romans, in Rousseau's view (and Denise Leduc-Fayette points out: "it is important to emphasize in effect that the antiquity admired by Jean-Jacques was already quasi-fable for the writers whom he cites and through whom he imagines it: Sallust, Cicero...Plutarch"[7]) were "real" peoples, "virtuous peoples," not because of what they accomplished, but because of their complete self-absorption. Such total fusion with the collective ego became the *political* equivalent of the personal inversion that Rousseau labeled "virtue." As in the case of the individual, this virtue had no relationship to performing good acts. Compassion or acts of charity were not associated with political virtue. "Patriotism and humanity are, for example, two virtues incompatible in their energy, especially in a whole people. The legislator who wants both will obtain neither" (3: 706).

Thus the ideal state would cleave to its own unique ways, patterns of social behavior which it had not elected but had received from an alien Legislator, claiming divine inspiration. These peculiar usages would constitute a "yoke of iron" bending people to virtue, now defined as the extension of love of self onto the state. The Legislator, according to Rousseau:

> sought bonds to attach the citizens to the fatherland and to one another, and they found them in particular usages, in religious ceremonies which by their nature were always exclusive and national, in games which kept the citizens assembled often together, in exercises which increased their pride and self-esteem along with their vigor and strength, in spectacles which, by reminding them of their ancestors, their misfortunes, their virtues, and their victories, interested their hearts, inflamed them with lively emulation, and attached them firmly to that fatherland with which they are ceaselessly concerned. [3: 958; "Considérations sur le gouvernement de Pologne"]

In this question of the ideal state of classical antiquity once again Rousseau ended up in opposition to the fundamental thrust of the philosophic movement. Although in the years Diderot was editing the *Encyclopédie* he also had praised Sparta, in a letter to Catherine of

---

[6]See *Plutarch's Lives*, trans. Dryden (New York: Modern Library, n.d.), pp. 64 and 84.

[7]*J.-J. Rousseau et le mythe de l'antiquité* (Paris: Vrin, 1974), p. 144.

Russia some years later he commented: "Lycurgus created armed monks; his legislation was a sublime system of atrocity. He formed the most fearsome ferocious beasts" (*Corr.*, 14: 82).

When Rousseau had occasion to give specific advice to the Poles, he insisted upon this point: that the government must separate the Poles from all the rest, creating a people so distinct that it would have no relation to others. "Provide another direction to the passions of the Poles, you will give their souls a national physiognomy which will distinguish them from other peoples, which will keep them from dissolving into other peoples, from being happy or allying with them." Rousseau recommended that "the Citizens be ceaselessly occupied with the Fatherland, that it be made their most important affair, that it be held incessantly before their eyes" (3: 962). Poles must wear Polish costumes, they must spend their time at public games "where the good motherland enjoys herself watching her children play" (3: 962). Gambling, theater, comedy, and opera must be abolished because they "effeminize men." Instead the Poles should attend many "outdoor spectacles where the ranks are carefully distinguished but where all the people take part" (3: 963). There aristocrats should joust and demonstrate their "natural right to superiority;... the more these exterior signs are neglected the more those who govern become effeminate and corrupt with impunity." Poles should see their leaders in public frequently, "provided that subordination always be maintained and that the [people] never gets confused with [the leaders]" (3: 964).

The cohesiveness of a people demanded cultural purity. "The ruin of the Roman Empire, the invasions of a multitude of barbarians, made a mixture of all the peoples which of necessity destroyed the morals and the customs of each. The crusades, commerce, the discovery of India, navigation, long voyages ... maintained and augmented the disorder" (3: 964). Commerce with outsiders, whether social or financial, could only introduce decay into the healthy body politic. Rousseau wanted to see the power of money reduced as much as possible within the state, because he saw it as the invariable source of moral corruption. If luxury could not be abolished in Poland, however, "let us tolerate military luxury, the luxury of weapons, of horses, but let all feminine finery be held in contempt" (3: 966).

The most important institution for forming the citizenry to virtue, however, was the proper raising of the children: "It is education which must give national strength to the [people's] souls, and direct their opinions and their tastes, so that they become patriots by inclination, by passion, by necessity" (3: 966). It is in this area that Rousseau's thought may be classified as "utopian." "Virtue is the key to the persistence of a utopian way of life," George Kateb noted, "and...in turn, the key to virtue is education in the fullest sense."[8]

"Children should be brought up together in the same way," their education should consist of learning facts about Poland and outdoor gymnastics. The latter program would actually form their character. "Keep the children out of breath, not with boring studies in which they don't understand anything and which they hate simply because they are forced to sit still; but by exercises they enjoy...one must not let them play separately according to their whim, but all together and in public" (3: 968). These recommendations for a state-controlled rearing reflect the views Rousseau expressed in the *Economie politique* and elsewhere, that the responsibility for raising children should be assumed by the government. "The education of children ought all the less be left to the lights and prejudices of their fathers since it is more important to the state than to the fathers. The state remains and the family dissolves." Not only should the state take on the burden of raising children, it ought also to expropriate paternal authority. "The public authority in taking the place of the fathers and assuming their important function, acquires their rights by fulfilling their duties" (3: 260). Children, therefore, were to be raised:

> together in the bosom of equality, if they are imbued with the laws of the state and the maxims of the general will, if they are taught to respect them above everything, if they are surrounded by examples and objects which speak to them ceaselessly of the tender mother who nourishes them, of the love she has for them, of the inestimable benefits they receive from her, and of the return they owe her, let us not doubt that they will learn to love one another like brothers, never to want anything but what the society wants. [3: 261]

Thus Rousseau's reasoning came to close an enormous circle begun with the first two discourses. From his initial premises, that

[8]*Utopia* (New York: Atherton, 1971), p. 12.

man's essential goodness in relation to a protective "mother nature" had been hopelessly and tragically compromised by his fall into society and interdependent relationships, he projected into the future a possible healing of the split. Man could once again become whole by freeing himself from these impure ties and dissolving completely into the "mother state," who would care for him in the same way that prelapserian nature had done. The love of self, called "goodness" in regard to nature, would be transformed into "virtue" when it embraced the state. Man would thus be free from any moral imperative to get enmeshed in personal ties, and even parenthood would no longer threaten to complicate the joys of sexuality. In the second *Discours,* children toddled off into the woods at an early age to be cared for by nature; now they would become wards of the state. In neither case would an individual have to sacrifice his own pleasure or well-being to look after children, as he was expected to do in the corrupt society of eighteenth-century France, where "the state kills them before they are born by making them a burden to their parents" (3: 528). Thus other people would not have to suffer, as Rousseau had done, by being blamed for placing children in a public facility. On the contrary, this act would finally be understood as the deed of a virtuous citizen.

Not only would the conflict between pleasure and parental responsibility be resolved, freeing the individual from the consequences of his sexuality, but the child himself would be brought up, in keeping with the principles of the "morale sensitive," to be effortlessly virtuous. Since Rousseau denied the principle of original sin and knew that essentially, if not existentially, all men were as good as he felt himself to be, children raised in a state that was an extension of Rousseau's virtue could never develop vices. As he said in *Emile:* "it is impossible for them to become rebellious, wicked, lying, or greedy unless the vices which would make them like that were sown in their hearts" (4: 341). He made the same point in his letter to Christophe de Beaumont: "Youth never goes astray by itself: all its errors come from being badly guided" (4: 943).

The political works, seen from this perspective, offer a panorama of human completeness regained which complements the lost wholeness depicted in the early works. Between the past, which visited Rousseau like revelation, and the ideal future he found by "looking into his own heart," lies history—everything that really existed, had been weighed, and had been found wanting.

While Rousseau's advice to the Poles showed a shrewd grasp of the tricky realpolitik any government of that country wedged between Russia and the German states would have to cope with, in the areas where he was free to express a preference for the shape of a society, he argued, just as he had in the *Contrat social,* for a modern Sparta.[9] The same insistence upon the fusion of the citizen into the collectivity, the denigration of the intellectual and artistic, the rejection of eighteenth-century movements toward improving the status of women as a source of moral degeneration, and the value placed upon the self-absorbed isolation of the state that had characterized the *Contrat social* and the *Economie politique* marked the more practical plans for Corsica and Poland.[10]

Rousseau's political theories prescribed a new relationship of man to the state which was based on a longing for an ancient, forgotten oneness. In the same way he proposed a role for women in the life of the city, a role which ran counter to the prevailing culture, but which accorded with a powerful nostalgic vision of the intact male for many of his readers.[11] He broke new ground in his prescriptions for the political status of women, not by extending the rational hypotheses of eighteenth-century philosophical egalitarianism but, on the contrary, by reaching deep into the recesses of his own personality, finding the secret significances of the female to him, and having the

[9]Jean Fabre defended Rousseau's plan for Poland against charges that it was "utopian" in the sense of unrealistic and idealized, arguing that Rousseau's affiliation was more appropriately with the tradition of prophets than of utopian speculators. "Réalité et utopie dans la pensée politique de Rousseau," *AJJR,* 42 (1959–62), 209. On the problem of individual happiness and the overriding consideration of the happiness of the state, see Michèle Ansart-Dourlen, *Dénaturation et violence dans la pensée de J.-J. Rousseau* (Paris: Klincksieck, 1975).

[10]Victor Goldschmidt discusses the problem of consistency in Rousseau's work as a whole, warning against selective, motivated choices of texts: "The coherence of a philosopher does not reside in the harmony of his formulations, taken literally, and chosen, if need be, on purpose to contradict each other.... Rather it lies in what one might term the author's substantial unity." *Anthropolgie et politique,* p. 12.

[11]*French Women and the Age of Enlightenment,* Part 5, presents studies of the philosophes' attitudes toward women: S. Malueg, "Women and the *Encyclopédie*"; P. Kra, "Montesquieu and Women"; G. Russo, "Voltaire and Women"; B. McLaughlin, "Diderot and Women"; and Gita May, "Rousseau's 'Antifeminism' Reconsidered." The political, cultural, and social aspects of women's lives are treated in Parts 1–3.

courage and assurance to announce these meanings to the world, as unfashionably retrogressive as they seemed to his friends among the philosophes. In one of the best known episodes of the *Confessions,* he related how a spanking administered by his teacher, Mlle Lambercier, had linked his ideas of sexual arousal of those of pain. Later in life, unable to bring himself to request such treatment from women, he spoke of finding a "moral substitute": "I became fond of acts of submission; thus I found the means of approaching the object of my desire by confusing the attitude of a suppliant lover with that of a penitent schoolboy" (1: 1157). He commented upon the pleasure he found in the harshness of a woman he desired: "This severity was a hundred times more delicious to me than her favors would have been. It seemed to me that she treated me like a thing that belonged to her, that she received me as property." In a letter to "Sophie" he asked her, "Am I not your thing? Have you not taken possession of me?" (1: 1161). The woman to whom this letter was addressed, Mme d'Houdetot, had not at all impressed Rousseau the first time they met. He recounted falling hopelessly in love with her, however, when she arrived at the Hermitage on horseback, dressed as a man. "Although I hardly cared for that sort of masquerade, I was taken with the romantic air of that particular one, and this time it was love" (1: 439).

Rousseau, as was discussed in Chapter 3, depicted himself as surrendering his will in the presence of a magnetic woman. When he looked at Mme Basile, "my eyes swam, my chest felt heavy, my breathing, from moment to moment more constricted, was difficult for me to control" (1: 74), and while pouring water for Mlle de Breil, "I was taken with such trembling that having filled the glass too full, I spilled part of the water on her plate and even on her" (1: 96). By means of his uncanny capacity to become the characters of his novel, *La Nouvelle Héloïse,* he was able to master this threatening but exciting domination of the alluring woman by identifying with her, and as Julie, he could taste the pleasure of being the female figure who was at once all-powerful and all-good. Jean Rousset, in a few luminous pages of *Forme et signification,* has explored how Rousseau used the epistolary form in order to offer "an uninterrupted contemplation converging on a unique and immobile character": Julie.[12]

[12]P. 92. P. D. Jimack notes: "The creation of Julie...precedes that of her husband, and far from being 'faite pour plaire à l'homme,' it is Wolmar who is made for

When it came to *Emile* and the political works, however, the radiating center of active power was not the magnetic female figure but rather the Preceptor or the Legislator or the entire virtuous Spartan state. In the patriarchal-virtue mode of being, Rousseau displayed an attitude toward women that was markedly different, and in this respect, as in so many others, he parted company with the philosophes.

As Otis Fellows has pointed out: "Social historians... have been giving increased stress to the concept that the eighteenth century in Europe should be designated as a feminist age."[13] The climate of opinion in Rousseau's time was indeed moving toward a reassessment of women's place in society, although, as recent scholarship has shown, not without ambivalence and self-contradiction.[14] Throughout the century, in line with the general devaluation of privilege, caste, and other forms of traditional and irrational subordination, philosophical reasoning was aspiring toward a system of social integration of all human beings upon an equal footing.[15] Dissatisfaction with the frivolous nature of feminine pursuits among the leisured classes led many writers to criticize the kind of education and upbringing women received and to argue for reform. Montesquieu, in an eloquent passage of the *Lettres persanes*, had expressed the point of view which was to characterize one central stand of educated, liberal though through most of the century:

> The dominance we have over them is a real tyranny; they have only let us assume it because they have more gentleness than we, and consequently more humanity and reason. These advantages which surely ought to endow them with superiority, if we had been reasonable, have

---

her.... Emile, in contrast, is a totally male-oriented work." "The Paradox of Sophie and Julie," *Women and Society in Eighteenth-Century France*, eds. Eva Jacobs et al. (London: Athlone, 1979), p. 164.

[13]"Diderot and the Mystery of Women," *Forum* 16 (Winter and Spring 1978 [1980]), 24.

[14]Jean Bloch emphasizes the kind of confusion and ambivalence generated during the eighteenth century between the intellectual conception of equality and the moral concerns regarding family and society. "Women and the Reform of the Nation," *Women and Society in Eighteenth-Century France*, pp. 3–18.

[15]According to David Williams, "By the 1780's feminism had become well integrated into the broader movements for social change." "The Politics of Feminism in the French Enlightenment," *The Varied Pattern: Studies in the Eighteenth Century*, ed. Peter Hughes and David Williams (Toronto: Hakkert, 1971), p. 337.

caused them to lose it, because we are not in the least reasonable. Why should we have a privilege? is it because we are the stronger? But that is a real injustice. We use every sort of means to beat down their courage; if the education were equal the strength would be too.[16]

Montesquieu's attitude epitomized the highest moral attributes of the enlightened "gentleman": recognizing physical differences while denying the validity of ethical or political consequences derived from them; and extending to the "other" the same ideal of justice enjoyed by the self. The Enlightenment's application of the natural law theory of equality was in this passage. D'Alembert, too, spoke critically of the "slavery and the kind of debasement where we have placed women" and urged a more egalitarian education.[17] Diderot, keenly concerned with the fate of women as his own daughter grew to maturity, composed a grimly realistic picture of the feminine condition, which he saw as disadvantaged by both biological processes and social burdens.[18]

In 1783 the Academy of Chalons-sur-Marne had proposed a contest for essays on the fashionable subject "What are the best ways of perfecting the education of women?" Choderlos de Laclos composed a response in which he called for nothing less than revolution, in rhetoric reminiscent of Rousseau's in the *Contrat Social*:

> Women, listen to me. Learn how, born man's companion, you have become his slave, . . . how, degraded more and more by your long habits of slavery, you have come to prefer debasing but convenient vices to the more difficult virtue of a free and respectable being. If, upon the account of your miseries and your losses . . . you burn with the noble desire to regain your advantages, to regain the plenitude of your being, do not let yourselves be abused by deceptive promises, do not wait for help from men, the authors of your misfortunes. Be aware that one comes out of slavery only by means of a great revolution.[19]

Rousseau rode resolutely against this century-long Enlightenment current. In a striking reversal of the stance he took regarding men,[20]

[16]*Lettres persanes* (Paris: Pléiade, 1956), 1: 186.

[17]*Oeuvres philosophiques, historiques, et littéraires* (Paris: Bastien, 1805), 5: 349.

[18]"Sur les Femmes," *Oeuvres complètes*, Assézat, Tourneux (Paris: Garnier, 1875–77), 2: 251.

[19]*Oeuvres complètes* (Paris: Pléiade, 1944), p. 405.

[20]See Richard A. Brooks's "Rousseau's Antifeminism in the *Lettre à d'Alembert* and

he argued that women were *not* socially conditioned for inferiority, but that they really were inferior, and that the virtuous society was the one which reinforced the natural subordination of the female to the male sex. Here, once again, it was Rousseau who had the courage to stand up and say what so many men actually felt but were ashamed to think, and he expressed this fundamental notion not as the quirky fulmination of a crusty reactionary, but as the revelation of a superior moral world for all people.

Rousseau formally differentiated the human species from the rest of creation on the basis of one criterion: freedom. "It is not so much understanding," he specified in the *Second Discours,* "which provides the specific distinction between man and the animals as it is his quality as free agent" (3: 141). The essential attribute, therefore, of a human being, the irreducible core of the species, was its capacity to choose its own acts. In *Emile* he emphasized the supreme value of freedom for the boy. "Nourished in the most absolute liberty, the greatest evil he can imagine is servitude" (4: 536). But just as Emile was raised to be absolutely free, his wife, Sophie, was brought up to be completely dependent. "All education of women must be relative to men, pleasing them, being useful to them, raising them when they are young and caring for them when they are old, advising them, consoling them, making their lives pleasant and agreeable, these have been the duties of women since time began" (4: 703). For this reason the girl must be subjected to constant discipline. "Always justify the burdens you impose upon girls but impose them anyway. Girls must be vigilant and laborious; that is not all, they must be thwarted from an early age...they must be exercised to constraint, so that it costs them nothing to stifle all their fantasies to submit them to the will of others" (4: 709). Further, "dependence is a natural state for women, girls feel themselves made to obey" (4: 710). "Do not allow them a single instant of their lives when they don't know the tether. Accustom them to being interrupted in the middle of their games and brought back to other duties without a murmur.

Emile," *Literature and History in the Age of Ideas,* ed. Charles G. Williams (Columbus: Ohio State University Press, 1975), pp. 202–27. In "Rousseau's 'Antifeminism' Reconsidered," Gita May deals with the fascinating paradox of the overtly misogynous writer adored by women, demonstrating how the identification with Jean-Jacques as victim induced the strongest possible emotional adherence. *French Women and the Age of Enlightenment,* pp. 309–17.

Habit suffices in this, because it only seconds nature" (4: 710).

The girl was not to develop her own judgment, but must learn to obey her father and then her husband. "Not in a state to judge themselves, they must receive the decision of fathers and husbands like that of the Church" (4: 721). She must not be educated prior to her marriage, but be left to her spouse for instruction. Sophie, for example, had read only two books in her life, Barrème's work on household management and a copy of *Télémaque* which Emile's Preceptor had arranged for her to come across "by chance." As for women who claim intellectual distinction, "a female wit (*bel·esprit*) is the scourge of her husband ... all these women with great talents never impress anybody but fools. One always knows who the artist or friend is who holds the pen or brush when they work" (4: 768).

In the *Lettre à d'Alembert* Rousseau expressed himself still more forcibly: "Women in general don't love any art, don't understand any, and have no genius" (p. 207). The Greeks, according to Rousseau, understood the real place for women when they kept them sequestered. "As soon as these young persons were married they were no longer seen in public; closed up in their houses, they limited all their activities to caring for their households and families. Such is the way of life that nature and reason prescribe for the sex; also healthier men are born from those mothers" (4: 705; *Emile*).

This servitude, in which one sex becomes the means while the other becomes the end, was not only useful and natural but morally warranted because of the charm which women exercise over men. "It is just that this sex shares the trouble of the ills it has caused us" (4: 709). So enticing were women, in fact, that if they were to be left unbridled, the result would be catastrophic to the male sex. "With the facility that women have for arousing men sensually, ... tyrannized by them, men would end up their victims, and would all see themselves dragged to their death without ever being able to defend themselves" (4: 694).

Rousseau evoked a virtuous society in which strong, patriarchal males would pursue the affairs of state in dignity, their relations with women severely limited to those of family, and secondary to the more important masculine bonds. The magnetism of women could only serve to distract the virtuous man from his union with his own moral value. In the *Lettre à d'Alembert* he stated:

Let us follow the indication of nature, let us consult the good of society: we will find that the two sexes must get together sometimes, and live separated ordinarily. [Men] react as much or more than [women] to excessively intimate commerce: [women] lose only their morals by it but we lose at the same time our morals and our constitution; because this weaker sex, unable to take up our way of life which is too difficult for them, forces us to take up their way of life, which is too soft for us; and not wishing to suffer separation, unable to become men, women turn us into women. [P. 204]

Thus Rousseau saw relations with women as being a threat to men's very existence. If men were not exhausted to death by female sexuality they were likely to be deprived of their masculinity by the corruptingly sedentary, frivolous quality of female life. In a society clearly segregated along sexual lines, however, "men, among themselves, no longer obliged to lower their ideas to the level of women and to decorate their thoughts with gallantry, can give themselves to grave and serious discourse without fear of ridicule. One dares to speak of fatherland and virtue...one dares to be oneself without bowing to the maxims of some floozy" (p. 207).

In line with the same principles, life at Clarens was to be strictly regulated so that men and women saw very little of one another: "Each one being, so to speak, all for his own sex, the women live quite separated from the men" (2: 451). The Wolmars arranged matters so that commerce between the sexes was strewn with external obstacles. Rousseau thus succeeded in reversing the role of "love slave" which he had depicted as so seductive yet menacing at various intervals in his life. In the name of virtue he postulated a morally superior society, invented and controlled by him, where women would lose the authority and prerogatives they enjoyed in France and be subjected to the will of the masculine sex.

The alluring woman and the enthralled male made up one mythic couple whose presence, alternately summoned and banished, formed the substrate of a great part of *La Nouvelle Héloïse*. Another sexual dyad permeates Rousseau's thought, however, from his very earliest play, *Narcisse*, to one of his last writings, the *Lévite d'Ephraïm:* the couple consisting of only one individual, apprehended through two perspectives, the boy who is mistaken for a woman. In the famous episode at the beginning of the *Confessions* already alluded to, Rousseau recounted how, late at night, he was kissed and hugged by a father who told him how he resembled his dead mother, asking him, between convulsive embraces, "Would I love you as much if you were only my son?" In retrospect, Rousseau took a fond, rather patronizing tone toward these paternal eruptions, referring to his father as "childish." Reversing the childhood role he wrote of having suffered, as author of the *Confessions* he mastered the situation by creating a literary figure, labeled his father, whom he could describe as childish. Yet the theme of the beautiful boy being mistaken for a woman appears repeatedly in his works, and the powerful emotional vibrations surrounding these episodes contrast markedly with the bland condescension of the narrator's voice in the *Confessions*.

The bald story of his parents' life as he set it forth went as follows: For seven years his father, celibate, worked in a Turkish seraglio. Nine months after Isaac Rousseau returned to Geneva and resumed conjugal relations, his wife gave birth to Jean-Jacques and died.

From the double perspective of these two sets of circumstances, it must have seemed evident that sexuality was fraught with dangers for both men and women. The one inviolable rule for a man who lived as watchmaker to a seraglio was to make no advances to the women. The sultan, patriarchy rampant, reserved his erotic paradise for himself, and the punishment for poaching on his preserve was castration or death. For the woman, on the other hand, requited love lead to death directly through the biology of reproduction. These then were the implicit "facts of life" in the Rousseau menage, whatever sentimental embellishments overlay the two stories. Rousseau's self-portrait as a boy vaguely aware of the menacing associations of love, smothered in kisses by a man who viewed him as his lost wife, was reworked under other guises at several periods during his life.

Rousseau's first play, *Narcisse,* was a comedy and therefore supposed to end with a marriage. The figure of the boy, ashamed of his inversion, who was led into a kindly and nonpunitive society by a loving female figure and gave up his autoeroticism for the sake of a socially sanctified relationship, was the first essay at resolving the dilemma of a boy who was taken for a girl, in this instance, by himself.

The piece called *Le Lévite d'Ephraïm* was composed some twenty years later, when Rousseau was in entirely different circumstances.

He was the guest of the Duke and Duchess of Luxembourg at their country estate at Montmorency, but he was aware that he was enjoying their hospitality only provisionally, for his book *Emile* was under fire and there was every possibility a warrant would be issued for his arrest. *Emile,* which was to demonstrate that Rousseau had "the heart of a father" despite his relinquishing of his own children, did not win him the acceptance of his adult male worthiness he had envisaged. On the contrary, its publication elicited a fury of denunciation, ridicule, and menace. He recounted how, nervous, anxious, unable to sleep, he had taken to reading the Bible at night. Early in the morning of June 10, 1762, he was reading the passage called the "Levite of Ephraim" from Judges when he dozed off, still half engrossed in the Old Testament account. It "had a strong effect upon me," he recounted in the *Confessions,* "and I was lost in some kind of a dream when all of a sudden I was jerked up from it by a noise and light" (1: 580). What had awakened him was the arrival of a messenger with word from the Prince de Conti that he, Jean-Jacques, was about to be arrested and had to flee. Conti assured him that if he were gone from Montmorency by the time the officers arrived, he would not be pursued.

The *Lévite d'Ephraïm* was written during his precipitous flight from Montmorency, where his host was no longer able to protect him from an armed crowd determined to drag him away to his punishment. Distressed by the threatening circumstances, Rousseau recounted in the second Preface:

> These sad thoughts followed me in spite of myself and made my voyage disagreeable. I rid myself of them as best I could, there are no thoughts which my heart entertains less willingly than those of ills people may have done me, and I am much more upset by wrongs I have witnessed than by wrongs of which I am the victim. I have decided to throw my daydreams off the scent by concentrating on some subject; [the Levite] came to mind; I found it suitable for my purposes. It offered me a kind of intermediary state between where I was and where I wanted to be. . . . It has a side decent people will appreciate, I am sure, and they will feel that a man who spends his time in such a way when he is being tormented is not a very dangerous enemy. [2: 1207]

Thus the Levite had the very specific function of demonstrating that Rousseau, when attacked, did not fight back but instead turned his attention to daydreams having nothing to do with vengeance. In the first Preface he insisted that the work would always be precious to him because it showed "what I was thinking about during the cruelest moments of my life,...drowning in a sea of misfortune, overwhelmed with ills by my ungrateful and barbarous contemporaries, I escaped only one in spite of them, one which they can have as my vengeance, and that one is hate" (2: 1204).

The work, however, begins with the following exhortation: "Holy rage of virtue, come animate my voice." The story, following Judges, with certain changes, recounted how a young Levite of Ephraim took a woman of Bethlehem as his concubine. Although he could not marry her, he said, "my heart belongs to you; come with me, let us live together, we will be united and free; you will make my happiness and I will make yours." After an idyllic interval together, however, the girl left him to go back to her family. The Levite followed her and demanded her return from her father. At this point Rousseau had the Levite refer to her as "my wife" and her father as "my father-in-law." "Who but I can honor as a wife the one I took as a virgin?" he asked.

That night the Levite and his concubine were forced to stay in the town of Jebus, where they were finally offered hospitality by an elderly man with a young daughter. While they were having dinner, the men of the village came to the door and demanded that the Levite be surrendered to them: "Hand over this young stranger to us," they said, "let his beauty pay us the price of this asylum, and let him expiate his temerity." The old man refused to surrender his guest for the sexual amusement of the townspeople and, instead, offered the men his own daughter. At this point the Levite got to his feet, pushed his host and the girl back into the house, and "taking his own beloved companion, without saying a single word, without lifting his eyes to her, dragged her to the door and threw her among those accursed men. Instantly they surrounded the girl, seized her, tore her apart without pity.... Oh wretches, who destroy your species by the pleasures destined to reproduce it, how is it that this dying beauty did not chill your ferocious desires?"

The Levite found his mistress at the door the next morning only to have her expire in his arms. He had the body brought home, and proceeded to chop it into twelve pieces, which he dispatched to the twelve tribes of Israel. This mute cry for vengeance acted immediately

[128]

upon the whole nation. "There arose in Israel one single cry, but a startling, unanimous one" (2: 1216). The united tribes attacked the Benjamites (in whose territory the atrocity had been committed) and when the battle was over, twenty-six thousand men had been killed, "so that this beautiful country, formerly so full of life, so populated, so fertile, and now devastated by flame and the sword, offered only a horrendous solitude covered with ashes and bones" (2: 1219). Rousseau ended the prose poem with an account of how the tribes arranged for the girls of Silo to be given to the last six hundred Benjamites, in order that their tribe survive in accord with God's will for Israel.

Now this is certainly one of the biblical stories which from a modern perspective seems most alien. As in the description of the destruction of Sodom and Gomorrah (Gen. 19), where two strikingly handsome angels instantly arouse the homosexual lust of the cities' male population, the young Levite is the object of an overwhelming surge of murderous rut. From the standpoint of well-bred eighteenth-century Europe, however, nothing would have seemed as immoral and unchivalrous as offering up first the host's daughter and then the Levite's own beloved as substitute victims for the homicidal orgy. It is curious, therefore, to note that Rousseau comments in the *Confessions,* "I am sure that I have never written anything in my life in which a more touching gentleness of mores was dominant" (1: 586). There are two aspects of this story, from Rousseau's point of view, which represent an ideal moral world. The young man, threatened with being sexually abused as if he were a woman, substituted a female victim for himself and escaped the catastrophe. Nonetheless, it was he, more than she, who was the true victim, and in indicating his offense to his entire nation, he was avenged on an awesome scale without having to take any aggressive steps himself. It sufficed to display the sign of his outrage, the morsels of his mistress's body, in order to arouse all of Israel on his behalf.

The true community, as opposed to the artificial societies of hypocritical egoists to be found in eighteenth-century Europe, would move as one being to avenge the insult done to its member. Instead of the petty bickering and endless wrangling of his contemporaries who did nothing to protect him against his persecutors, patriarchal Israel would have arisen as a single entity and utterly destroyed the depraved throng that had sought to take the man and use him as a girl.

Thus, from one perspective, *Le Lévite d'Ephraïm* joined *Narcisse;* the good society is the one which closes around the sexually ambiguous male figure and opposes his fall into the female role. In *Narcisse,* however, the mood is whimsical and the denouement is marriage; the end of the Levite is mass murder and the Levite himself dead and buried with the bits of his dismembered beloved. The wish for an all-encompassing collectivity had become somber and death-ridden, its role evolved from protector of goodness to avenger.

Desire for violent vengeance flared up at the end of the *Confessions* as well, when Rousseau declared that the one most reprehensible category of evil people, those who denied his virtue, "ought to be strangled" (1: 656). The same fate awaited those citizens of the "virtuous state," Rousseau's goodness expanded, who refused to blend into the great body politic: "The conservation of the state is then incompatible with his; one of the two must perish; and when the guilty one is put to death it is less as a citizen than as an enemy" (3: 257).

This aspect of Rousseau's concept of virtue presents certain problems to those of his admirers who refuse one of its logical consequences. Michel Launay, for example, quotes a note to the "Réponse à Charles Bordes," following the *Premier Discours.* Rousseau had declared, in his defense of the moral superiority of primitive races: "If I were the chief of one of these Negro peoples, I swear that I would have a gallows erected at the country's frontier where I would have hanged without exception the first European who dared to enter it and the first Citizen who attempted to leave." For emphasis Rousseau added the following note: "Perhaps someone will ask what harm a Citizen could do the state by leaving and not coming back? He harms the others by the bad example he provides, he harms himself by the vices he is going in search of. In every way, it is up to the law to prevent him from going, and it is better for him to be hanged than wicked" (3: 90–92). Once again, the good state is the primordial being; evil, whether it attempts to penetrate the good body politic from the outside or tries to alienate itself from the wellspring of moral value by desertion, must be stifled. Failure to do so on so-called "humanitarian grounds" is the real cruelty, for it invites the corruption of goodness. Launay's comment reveals a refusal to accept the deepest convictions of Rousseau: "Rousseau himself would laugh at us, if we did not perceive his malice and for once, his 'paradox,' here: would the dialectic of liberty thus lead us to the Inquisition?"[21]

Malice and paradox were precisely the attributes that Rousseau strived to disavow within himself. The violent and destructive utterances which punctuate all his works, from Fabricius' exhortations to "burn, smash and destroy," to his recommendation of the death penalty for anyone wishing to leave the African nation, or behaving so as to belie the civic religion in the *Contrat social,* to his description of mass murder vengeance in the *Lévite,* cannot be dismissed as aberrant twisted ironies conveying the opposite of what they say. These sudden outbursts of hatred were an integral part of Rousseau's thought, in fact the necessary complement of his interior goodness. He could not, however, accept them as an expression of his own nature, and, for that reason, they remain strangely isolated ejaculations in his otherwise resolutely pacific texts. The abruptly murderous injunctions were not categorized by Rousseau as such. Thus he described the *Lévite,* beginning with an invocation of the "holy rage of virtue" and ending with a massacre, as "depicting the gentlest mores."

By completely divorcing rage from the overtly self-representative texts, Rousseau preserved his image of himself as innocent; statements expressing that wrath were refused recognition or integration. As Thomas Kavanagh notes of the *Lévite*: "This short work...reveals, as a kind of microtext, a structure of denegation centering on victimage and violence which is at the core of a macrotext including not only Rousseau's autobiographical writings, but the major themes of this political works."[22] A parallel mechanism, as we shall see, operated in the discourse of Robespierre and Saint-Just, who wrote as if unaware of the terrifying impact their words and acts had upon others.

Rousseau's thought generated moral polarities. He rejected compromise and mixed solutions to human dilemmas as impure just as he refused to see himself as a morally ambiguous being. The vision of the virtuous self and the virtuous state which he put forth was not to be sullied by the presence of discordant elements, and the death he wished upon those who dissented was, ultimately, a means of

---

[21]"L'Art de l'écrivain dans le *Contrat social,*" p. 147.
[22]Rousseau's *Le Lévite d'Ephraïm,*" ECS, 16 (Winter 1982–83), 148.

protecting the integrity of his own overwhelming insight into what man once was and could be again if all other wills and all other worldviews were subsumed by his.

The rich, the powerful, the intellectuals, and women had all been stripped of their prestige in Rousseau's works, and on their vacated pedestals the "man of virtue" and the "virtuous state" had been enthroned.

CHAPTER SEVEN

Identification with Virtue

France in the decade before the Revolution was poised on the brink not merely of financial insolvency, but, more significant, of moral bankruptcy as well. The church, convicted of venality and hypocrisy by three generations of philosophes, had ceased to order the inner life of the majority of the educated because it failed to command moral respect. The aristocracy, its ancient sources of prestige exhausted, clung to its admittedly unmerited privileges with open greed. The monarchy and Parlement, in their undisguised struggle for power, succeeded mainly in drawing attention to the dubiety of both their claims to be obeyed. It was during this period that the emergence of a new mystical vision of man and society had the opportunity to replace the old. As Ernst Cassirer expressed it: "In all critical moments of man's social life, the rational forces that resist the rise of the old mythical conceptions are no longer sure of themselves. In these moments the time for myth has come again."[1]

Rousseau's myth of virtue emerged in the years before the convocation of the Estates General; in the texts of certain revolutionaries it appears as a model for conceptualizing the self and shaping an ideal state, and as a vehicle for discharging rancor while enhancing self-esteem. The question has repeatedly been raised, however, of how Rousseau's influence made itself felt, since, as Daniel Mornet demonstrated, and Joan McDonald affirmed,[2] the specific political

[1]*The Myth of the State* (New Haven: Yale University Press, 1946), p. 280.
[2]See Chap. 1, note 4.

[133]

works were little read outside of a narrow circle of intellectuals until the events of 1789 suddenly brought them to life.

During the eleven years which separated his death and the convocation of the Estates General, Rousseau's persona outraged many of his former friends and their supporters among the philosophes and the *beau monde*, and at the same time enthralled the generation coming of age during that decade.

Rousseau himself had frequently expressed irritation at the feckless hero-worship his texts had inspired in some of the greatest names in France. His correspondence with the Comte de Ste-Aldegonde, who was to side with the Jacobins during the Revolution, illustrates how powerfully the figure of virtuous man gripped some noble imaginations. Ste-Aldegonde, inspired by Rousseau to become a vegetarian, had a pregnant wife and a pregnant mistress, an actress. He wrote to Rousseau, apparently announcing his intention to raise his wife's child in a state of nature in accordance with Rousseau's precepts. Rousseau's answer reveals how little in reality he wished to act as moral mentor on an individual basis to those who used his concept of virtue for their own ends. "You tell me you are a fanatic about virtue. I admit you're a fanatic but it must be a most peculiar virtue if you think you are going to find it among actresses," he replied. "If you insist on wishing to carry out this extravagant experiment you describe and turn your child into a brute, his tender mother will die of grief, the child will end up being put away, the father will become the horror of decent people, and as for me, I am determined never to answer him or see him again" (*C.c.*, 39: 222–23). Ste-Aldegonde's answering letter was nearly hysterical: "If I ever hid a single one of my thoughts from you I would consider myself the most infamous of mortals," he told Rousseau. He wished to be *tried* by "a sage, my judge, my father (permit me this sweet name), it is before his tribunal that I wish to appear" (*C.c.*, 39: 226).

Madeleine Simons traced the extraordinary impact of Rousseau's texts on the young Ignace de Sauttersheim, who was only one of numerous young men who came to Môtiers to be near "Emile's preceptor." She points out that as Sauttersheim wrote to Rousseau, "the young man told the story of his life in sentences which seemed to imitate the first book of the *Confessions*. There were, it is true, similarities between the situation of the master and of the disciple:

the death of the mother, the father's remarriage, the latter's indifference."[3]

Rousseau's self-representation in the autobiographical writings elicited counterimages; he provided a formula for expressing the self which invited identification. Those, mainly intellectuals, who rejected the seductive appeal to be one with Jean-Jacques frequently reacted with anger or contempt. As Raymond Trousson remarked on his posthumous reputation: "Two currents of opinion distinguished themselves clearly enough. One is hostile, denigrating, but it scarcely extends beyond the world of letters; the other, which is constantly manifested, deep and powerful, animates the majority. Rousseau the master of sensitive souls, the teacher of virtue, persecuted, dying poor and abandoned at Ermenonville was not—could not be—this wicked man, this ingrate: his work adorned him with a halo."[4]

Aside from the intense personal adoration he had inspired in a number of young people, Rousseau soon after his death became the object of an authentic popular cult, celebrated by the great and the humble alike. As early as 1780 the *Correspondance secrète* of Métra (or Mettra) commented: "All religions have their pilgrimages; philosophy has its own. Already half of France has transported itself to Ermenonville to visit the little island devoted to him...the Queen and all the Princes and Princesses of the Court went there themselves last week."[5] The immense change already effected in France which this anecdote illustrates is quite extraordinary. The notion of a queen of France embarking on a "pilgrimage" to visit the grave of an overtly if inconsistently antimonarchical writer would have been unthinkable under any Louis but the last.

The following year a collection of tunes called *Les Consolations des misères de ma vie ou Recueil d'airs, romances et duos par Jean-Jacques Rousseau* was published and its proceeds donated to the Enfants trouvés in the name of Thérèse. The list of subscribers included

---

[3]*Amitié et passion: Rousseau et Sauttersheim* (Geneva: Droz, 1972), p. xx. Simons quotes Rousseau as commenting: "He told everybody and let me know too that he had come to Neufchâtel only because of me, in order that his youth be led to virtue by knowing me" (p. 16).

[4]*Rousseau et sa fortune littéraire*, p. 53.

[5]London: John Adamson, 1786–90, 18 vols. In *Jean-Jacques Rousseau raconté par les gazettes de son temps (9 juin, 1762–21 décembre, 1790)*, ed. P.-P. Plan (Paris: Mercure de France, 1912), p. 227.

Marie-Antoinette, the Princesse de Lamballe, the Duchesse de Choiseul, Melchior Grimm, and Benjamin Franklin. For the less opulent there were other ways in which adoration for Rousseau was expressed, and popularizations of his thought were made widely available. The *Journal de Paris,* under the editorship of three men close to Rousseau, Olivier de Corancez, Jean Romilly, and Louis d'Ussieux, was the central organ for publishing previously unedited fragments of his work and for, in François Moreau's words, a "veritable press campaign" to serve his memory.[6]

Through the decade a series of plays were written in tribute to the philosopher; they were mainly brief and ephemeral pieces, lacking literary pretensions and ranging from middlebrow drama to the level of the fair or carnival spectacle. Some of these dramas, like *The Shades Assembled at the Elysian Fields: Melo-Drama in Two Acts,*[7] and *The Childhood of Jean-Jacques,*[8] were so primitive as to approximate the medieval mystery play, with Rousseau in the role of the martyred saint.

Act I of *The Shades Assembled* featured Saint-Preux, Julie, a "mother who nursed her son, a little boy, and a mother who did not breastfeed." Act II brought Emile and Sophie onto the stage accompanied by Fanaticism, who attempted to set fire to the famous little thicket in which Julie and Saint-Preux exchanged their first kiss. Fortunately Immortality appeared to instruct her sister, Truth, "that genius and virtue are purified on earth by persecutions and that one can find justice only among the dead." The play ended with characters from Rousseau's works and the Sage himself singing songs from the *Devin du village.*

The *Childhood of Jean-Jacques* presented Rousseau, as a boy, and his father. The curtain rose upon the child asleep in a chair, his father still reading to him from Plutarch as the sun rose. "You are getting

[6]"Les Inédits de Rousseau et la campagne de presse de 1778," *DHS,* 12 (1980), 411–25.

[7]Houssaye, *Gazette de littérature* (Paris) June 2, 1787.

[8]François-Guillaume Andrieux, *L'Enfance de Jean-Jacques Rousseau, comédie en un acte, melée de musique* (Paris: chez Madaran, 1794). For a list of popular plays, ballads, engravings of scenes from his works, and other literary and iconographic homages to Rousseau, see "Le Rayonnement de Rousseau jusqu'à la fin de la Révolution," Catalog of exposition at the Bibliothèque nationale *Jean-Jacques Rousseau* (Paris: BN, 1962), pp. 101–23. Many rare examples of ephemera relating to Rousseau are to be found in the Ernest Hunter Wright special collection of Butler Library, Columbia University.

to be a big boy, now," said the father, "I'll soon be thirteen," replied Jean-Jacques. Father and son broke into a duet, set to the music of "J'ai perdu mon serviteur," which began: "Thus I lost her while being born / Your spouse and my tender mother" (p. 11). The young hero distinguished himself by pulling a rival out of the water in a scene reminiscent of Julie's rescue of her child, and the show concluded with a "joyous celebration" in which Rousseau sang his love to Sophie while the other characters intoned "Vitam impendere vero" in the background.

These numerous garbled homages served up a mythic Rousseau, who combined the miracle-child quality of the folk hero, the martyrdom of the Christian saint, and his own peculiar persona of the aggressively radical moralist. Whatever nuances and reserves Rousseau may have actually expressed in his writings, they did not survive to render this popular image of him any less of a great cartoon figure in primary colors. Through these crude dramatic performances, a Jean-Jacques Rousseau became known or at least accessible to large segments of the population who were untouched by the more rarified literary currents of the day. These plays continued through the Revolution, new ones appearing every year. No other eighteenth-century man of letters enjoyed any such postmortem celebration.

It was his moral superiority and the moral superiority one could enjoy by adoring him which were important, not any specific doctrine he had put forth. Jean Roussel comments on the peculiar quality of identification which certain individuals experienced in their reading of Rousseau: "Because of this encounter, they believe they discovered themselves; an original communication established itself, leading the initiate into a personal adventure in common with the author."[9]

Numerous works appeared during the decade which elaborated the view that Jean-Jacques Rousseau was uniquely "virtuous" because he loved himself and that the rest of civilized humanity was largely decadent. François Chas published a lengthy series entitled *Impartial Philosophical Reflections upon Jean-Jacques Rousseau and Mme de Warens*, in which he explicitly labeled Rousseau's liaison with Mme de Warens, his abandonment of his children, and his self-involvement as so many signs of his moral supremacy: "the author proves that the

[9]"Le Phénomène d'identification dans la lecture de Rousseau," *DHS*, 14 (1982), p. 6.

feeling of self makes one necessarily proud, especially when one sees how far away one is from the wicked and the fools who almost entirely compose our perverse and incurable societies."[10]

At first merely one of a number of postulates rejecting the values of the *ancien régime* based on the writings of eighteenth-century thinkers, Rousseau's concept of virtue gained ascendance both in the spoken and the written word, initially under the aegis of the Girondins, and then under Jacobin auspices from the period beginning with the Legislative Assembly until Thermidor. Rousseau, along with Voltaire, Diderot, Mably, Montesquieu, and the Encyclopedists in general, was admired by large classes of Frenchmen. The particular strand of devotion to Rousseau's virtue, however, differed in both kind and intensity from the respect paid to other intellectuals, and was to take distinctive shape in the mentality of certain revolutionary leaders.

Bernardin de Saint-Pierre said: "I've known libertines who got married, young people who gave up eating meat, who slept on the hard floor, women who announced publicly that they owed him their very being. Several pushed themselves to become Héloises. [His] maxims have risen to the throne itself; queens have breastfed their infants" (pp. 18–19). Louis Dauphin, Louis XVI's father, was said to have been deeply moved by *Emile* and to have raised his sons according to precepts he found in Rousseau, including the one urging instruction in manual crafts, which was responsible for Louis's training as a locksmith.[11]

Roger Barny has studied the circle of "ideologues from the petty nobility" who had been associated with Rousseau during his lifetime, and who at the beginning of the Revolution laid claim to him as their very own. He described the group "glitteringly represented by the Comte d'Antraigues and by other 'friends' of Jean-Jacques such as d'Esherny and Dampmartin, who drape themselves with the prestige not only of the work but of their affective bonds with the man, and claim to be the only authorized interpreters of it." According to

[10]Geneva, 1786, and Paris: Royer, 1786, p. 281. Chas's *Eloge de J.-J. Rousseau* won a prize at the Toulouse Academy's *Jeux floraux* in 1787. Bernardin de Saint-Pierre, Rousseau's friend and original hagiographer, was not responsible for the promulgation of the legend since his *Vie et ouvrages de Jean-Jacques Rousseau* was published in distorted form only many years later by Aimé Martin, in 1836, and in a faithful edition in 1907, edited by Maurice Souriau.

[11]This is according to the Abbé Soldini's "Essai sur la vie de Monsigneur Louis Dauphin, mort à Fontainebleau le 20 de décembre en 1765" (BN Fr. 13784).

Barny, the aristocrats made a shambles of Rousseau's ideas, "entirely deconstructing his work," and turning it into "a vast junk shop where one can find whatever gadget is called for by the political circumstances."[12]

To the extent that the royal family or members of the aristocracy had internalized Rousseau's concept of virtue, it could only serve to undermine a social or functional self-representation which was already weakened by external attack from the left. For the two major bourgeois political organizations in the early years of the Revolution, however, the Gironde and the Jacobins, Rousseau's conception of virtue offered a galvanizing and integrating force, providing its adepts with the audacity to denounce and ultimately destroy the prestige of the hierarchy of blood. For both groups, too, it provided the bases for intense personal political binding to a small nucleus of "elevated souls." For both groups, finally, it furnished a model for attributing absolute evil to opposing parties, for refusing to envisage compromise with any persons with whom the group was not identified, and for viewing death as the rational alternative to failure of virtue.

It has been observed that in economic and social thinking, the Girondins were the heirs of the physiocrats rather than of Rousseau. According to Marcel Dorigny: "Girondin Rousseauism seems to have been much more on the ethical or religious level for certain persons; the social content of the work of Rousseau was thus deliberately discarded."[13] "Ethical" and "religious" seem too abstract, however, to describe the significance of Rousseau for Mme Roland, her friend and eventual lover Buzot, Vergniaud, and Brissot. All these figures described the tremendous enhancement of self-esteem they experienced upon reading Rousseau, and how this new vision of their own beings led them to assume certain postures with regard to the political situation. It was less a particular set of postulates which the Girondins stood for than the exaltation of virtue in theatrical opposition to all that was corrupt.

Gita May has portrayed the young Manon Phlipon, before her marriage to Roland, as being deeply identified with the Julie of *La Nouvelle Héloïse*. "She is so profoundly impregnated with the senti-

---

[12]"Les Aristocrates et Jean-Jacques Rousseau dans la Révolution," *AHRF,* 50 (1978), 534–68.

[13]"Les Girondins et Jean-Jacques Rousseau," *AHRF,* 50 (1978), 569.

ments, with the moral atmosphere of the book that she *lives* it and undergoes it like a real experience." Mme Roland's correspondence reveals her over and over assuming the persona of Julie or of Jean-Jacques himself, expropriating, rather than approving, Rousseauvian virtuous exaltation. She described her sensations at mass when she was a girl: "I experienced an extreme devotion at mass; but my own kind of devotion. Removed from everything around me, distracted, moved, I said to my Divinity: 'Oh beautiful, touching, unchanging virtue, you will always be my treasure and my joy.' . . . I leave the definitions to the theologians: I love, I adore what makes me happy with the happiness of others, what I conceive, what I feel." She commented later about *La Nouvelle Héloïse:* "It makes me contented with myself and teaches me to tolerate myself." Gita May remarks, "Mme Roland will model herself upon Julie de Wolmar."[14]

The Rolands made a journey to Switzerland in July and August of 1787, visiting sites enshrined in the Rousseau canon and even former friends of the Sage like Champagneux, the mayor of Bourgoin, who had witnessed Rousseau's wedding to Thérèse. As a married woman, Mme Roland expanded her image of herself as a Rousseauvian character to include her husband. "I just devoured *Julie,*" she wrote to Roland, "as if it were not the fourth or fifth time . . . it seems to me that we would have lived very well with all those personages and that they would have found us as much to their taste as they are to ours" (May, p. 175). This statement conveys marvelously well the unprecedented quality of what Rousseau had to give his readers: a world of moral superiority in which they could participate as equals with fictional characters who were, very thinly disguised, projected epiphenomena of the beloved author's own being. For a time the Rolands thought of buying a large property in the country and setting up a sort of communal life to be modeled on the menage at Clarens. With the Revolution, however, and Roland's sudden appointment as minister of the interior in March, 1792, a different set of roles claimed them.

Intellectually Mme Roland claimed to share with Rousseau the conviction of women's innate inferiority and the necessity of their complete subservience to the male figure. She presided as hostess over a salon frequented by politically ambitious men rather than

[14]May, *De Jean-Jacques Rousseau à Mme Roland* (Geneva: Droz, 1964), pp. 145–46, 125.

influencing politics through direct action in her own name. One of the first habitués of her afternoons was Robespierre, with whom, as Gita May points out, she had much in common both ideologically and temperamentally (p. 191). It was she who labeled Robespierre the "Incorruptible." Her husband was called the "virtuous Roland." Her salon did not house these two summits of moral preeminence for long. Robespierre broke away from their social circle and began a campaign of denigration of the "so-called virtue of Roland," in his publication, *Lettres à ses commettans,* admonishing his readers that "we must never forget we are a spectacle before all the peoples and we deliberate in the presence of the universe" (5: 268). He was to speak harshly of a "feminine triumvirate" consisting of Mme Roland, Mme Robert (Kéralio), and Mme Condorcet.

The eventual fall of the Gironde is traditionally narrated as a countertext of *La Nouvelle Héloïse,* a pathetic story of Mme Roland's final incarnation of Julie de Wolmar: her passion for the Girondin deputy Buzot, her refusal to yield to her love, and her insistence on confessing the whole dilemma to her husband. The subsequent demoralization of Roland hastened the collapse of the movement which he, at least in theory, led. "For Mme Roland, as for her literary models, the need to conform to an interior ideal of virtue became so imperious that it ended up by triumphing over the aspiration toward happiness and even the instinct for self-preservation" (May, p. 213).

Buzot, her political ally as well as her great love, wrote of his *own* early years in terms which underlined his solitude, his virtue, and his attachment to Rousseau.

> My youth was almost wild; . . . never did libertinage stain my heart with its impure breath; debauchery horrified me, and up to an advanced age never had a licentious word soiled my lips. However, I early knew misfortune, and I remained more than ever attached to virtue, whose consolations were my only refuge. With what charms I still recall that period of my life which can never return, when during the day I silently wandered the mountains and the woods of the town reading with delight some work of Rousseau or Plutarch, or recalling to my memory the most precious ideas of their morality and their philosophy.[15]

[15] François-Nicolas Buzot, *Mémoires sur la Révolution française* (Paris: Pichon & Didier, 1828), p. 24. Jaurès comments: "He had mistaken the obscure sufferings of his vanity

For Mme Roland as Rousseauvian heroine, the wedding with virtue meant the division of the world into the virtuous, with whom she belonged, and the vicious, whom she set out to destroy. Michelet commented:

> Mme Roland, it must be said, had arrived in her hatred of Danton and Robespierre at a degree of irritation astonishing to find in such a stout soul. She had scarcely any vices except those of virtue; I call by that name the tendency that austere souls have not only to condemn those whom they call bad but to hate them; and moreover to divide the world exactly in half, in attributing all the evil to one side and all the good to the other. That is what was to be seen in the virtuous circle of M. and Mme Roland.[16]

The most active and influential member of the Gironde, perhaps even more important than the Rolands and Buzot, was J.-P. Brissot de Warville. Brissot, whose anguished career as an embittered pamphleteer and police spy under the *ancien régime* has been so well analyzed by Robert Darnton,[17] described a fervent faith in Rousseau's virtue in a work of 1782:

> Rousseau deserved to become the model for all the centuries....I am not unaware of the various judgments made of the *Confessions*. I know that people depicted him as a cheat, as a slanderer. The most moderate said he was a madman. I have the misfortune to adore this madman, and I share this misfortune with a throng of sensitive and virtuous souls. It is not in the least for his style, it is for his virtue. He made me love it, and it would be a great prodigy if a scoundrel made virtue loved. But were they to add to the horrors told about Rousseau a thousand other details still more atrocious, more infamous, I would not change my opinion, I would believe my inner feelings; I would rather believe the whole universe, testifying against him, was populated with perjurers, than believe Jean-Jacques criminal.[18]

---

for the revolt of his pride. This sickly obsession with the self explodes in his *Mémoires*. Mediocre disciple of Jean-Jacques, he inherited from him a dangerous disposition toward self-exaltation in solitude, toward nourishing himself, with bitterness, on his own virtue" (5: 180).

[16]Michelet, *Histoire de la Révolution française* (Paris: Pléiade, 1952), 1: 1269.

[17] "A Spy in Grub Street," *The Literary Underground of the Old Regime* (Cambridge: Harvard University Press, 1982), pp. 41–70.

[18]Brissot, *De la vérité ou méditations sur les moyens de parvenir à la vérité dans toutes les connaissances humaines* (Paris: Desauges, 1782), pp. 31–32.

Brissot conveys the flavor of the Rousseau worship that seized hold of certain individuals during the decade following his death, a kind of intoxicated adherence not to this doctrine or that theory, but to the virtue of the man himself, seen as a matter of supreme importance, coupled with a profound belief that access to truth concerning his virtue was a matter of "inner feelings."

In 1786 the Academy of Toulouse announced a competition (one of their famous *Jeux floraux*) for an elogy of Jean-Jacques Rousseau. No prize was awarded that year, but in 1787 there were two, one of which went to Bertrand Barère de Vieuzac, who, as simply Barère, was to be a colleague of Robespierre on the Committee of Public Safety. Barère praised Rousseau for deriving his oratorical mastery over the public from his virtue. "His enthusiasm for virtue will be his eloquence," he said, and "it is thus that men of genius were philosophers." He exhorted women to peruse *La Nouvelle Héloïse* and to repeat after him that in the novel "the dominance of an honest soul is omnipresent. Everywhere it is the enthusiasm of Virtue. Oh Jean-Jacques," he apostrophized, "every virtuous and sensitive being will recognize thee for his master and model." Barère, the future government leader, adored in Rousseau the moralist, not the political theorist. "The characteristic which strikes us essentially in this analysis" comments Daniel Ligou, "is the almost total absence of allusions to the political work of Rousseau."[19]

Mme de Staël, the daughter of Louis XVI's finance minister Jacques Necker, in a work devoted to Rousseau written on the eve of the Revolution, emphasized the rare natural genius of "the one who knew how to make a passion of virtue, who consecrated eloquence to morality," and who inspired "just feelings of hatred for vice and love for virtue!"[20]

---

[19]"Bertrand Berère et Jean-Jacques Rousseau," *Jean-Jacques Rousseau (1712–1778)*, Société des Etudes Robespierristes (Gap: Louis-Jean, 1962), pp. 61–74. Barère's address appeared in the *Recueil des Jeux floraux (1784–1788)* (Toulouse, 1788). See Leo Gershoy, *Bertrand Barère: A Reluctant Terrorist* (Princeton: Princeton University Press, 1961). Grimm commented in his *Correspondance littéraire* of September 1789: "the subject of the new Eloquence Prize proposed by the (French) Academy for next year was the elogy of Jean-Jacques Rousseau. What will the shades of d'Alembert and Voltaire say?" (Paris: Buisson, 1813), 16: 253.

[20]*Lettres sur les ouvrages et le caractère de J.-J. Rousseau* (1788), pp. 4, 8: Barny 6063. In *L'Idéal moral chez Rousseau, Mme de Staël et Amiel*, I. Benrubi discusses the almost total identification of Mme de Staël's political thought with that of her master. "Mme de

In his analysis of the bond between Rousseau and his readers, Robert Darnton illustrates the totality of the immersion in Rousseau's works which so many people experienced, and from which they learned new ways of conceptualizing themselves: "Jean-Jacques opened up his soul to those who could read him right, and his readers felt their own souls elevated above the imperfections of their ordinary existence."[21]

The second part of Rousseau's *Confessions* appeared in the fall of 1789, eleven years after his death, at the beginning of the revolutionaries' efforts to undo the abuses of feudal France and establish new bases of sovereignty. The publication seemed to have accentuated feelings of empathy with Rousseau as a "man of virtue" who had reordered the system of values in France somehow through his own person. An anonymous publication, *Jean-Jacques ou le Réveil-Matin de la Nation française* (BN Lb 39 6823), insisted that it was through his writings that the nation had learned: "Virtue makes rank, and the most just man is also the greatest" (p. 174).

Louis-Sébastien Mercier, in a work entitled *De J-J. Rousseau, considéré comme l'un des premiers auteurs de la Révolution,*[22] published in June 1791, set forth the doctrine that what Rousseau had taught the French was the principle of "public virtue," upon which the Revolution was founded. "Rousseau saw that societies can exist only by means of *public virtue;* he begged for it; he posed the basis of his theory and the sublime art of ruling great societies on *public virtue*" (1: 159). "The theory of Rousseau...developed with certitude the principle of *public virtue;* that was the sure, real, necessary principle....It was demonstrated, according to history, that this *virtue* could never have access to thrones" (1: 161). According to Mercier, the National Assembly had risen above the corrupt thought of the *ancien régime* to align the nation with Rousseau's "public virtue." "The free and proud genius of the National Assembly adopting, despite satrapism and despotism, *public virtue,* placed itself above vulgar minds" (1: 167). For Mercier, "public virtue" was an aggressive weapon which permitted those who possessed it to destroy the corrupt. He opposed

---

Staël's political attitude may be characterized by saying that it is of profoundly Rousseauistic inspiration." *AJJR,* 27 (1938), 177.

[21] *The Great Cat Massacre,* p. 249.

[22] Paris: Buisson, 1791; Barny 6034–35.

it particularly to the feudal concept of honor.[23] The Assembly "depended on the *public virtue* of Rousseau and not on the chimera of Honor" (1: 168), he commented, and with "Rousseau's strength, ...the Assembly victoriously struck down all the enemies of *public virtue*" (1: 169). He analyzed a new vocabulary which Rousseau had given the nation, and which permitted it to conceptualize its destiny properly. The term "patriotic virtue, that is the complement of all enlightenment and all the types of courage" (1: 191).

In addition to his insistence on the primacy of Rousseau's public virtue, however, Mercier separated him from the other philosophes and described him as playing the central role in events whereas the influence of the others was on the wane:

> From the day when death overtook those sovereigns of the empire of literature [the philosophes], the star of their reputation has seemed to tarnish and lose its luster for posterity, whose reign, for them, has already begun. Among those pillars which in France supported the temple of genius, one alone remains elevated to its entire height, and on that pillar there is no one who does not read, or who does not engrave with us the name of J.-J. Rousseau. [Between Voltaire and Rousseau]...the glory of the poet seems to have declined while that of the moral writer had only extended itself. [1: 1–2]

The reason for the elevation accorded by the French people of Rousseau, in Mercier's view, was that he was religious and moral; "man and his creator were never the object of his pleasantries, this miserable resource was made for a Voltaire" (1: 27). "What placed J.-J. Rousseau above all the writers of his century was that his eloquence had a moral character" (1: 19).

Pierre-Louis Ginguené (or Guinguené), poet, journalist, and eventually ambassador to Turin, described the reason that led him to publish his *Lettres sur les Confessions de J.-J. Rousseau:*[24] "They were

[23]In *Le Duel sous l'ancien régime* (Paris: Presses de la Renaissance, 1982), Micheline Cuénin offers a historical examination of the social, political, and psychological consequences of the duel, based upon the concept of "honor." John Pappas has demonstrated how this ideal, already weakened by the abuses of some of its adherents as well as the changing climate of French society, was systematically undermined by the philosophes' attempt to transform it from a concept of self-aggrandizement to one of ethical responsibility. "La Campagne des philosophes contre l'honneur," *SVEC*, 205 (1982), 41.

[24]Paris: Barois, 1791; Barny, 6038.

written when the second part of the *Confessions* had just appeared. Some friends urged me to seize the moment when the memory of the one who is the subject of the letters has, in some way, become sacred." The moment of which he spoke was December 21, 1791; the Assembly had voted to erect a statue of Rousseau and awarded a pension to Thérèse Levasseur, and indeed it was during this period that adherence to certain aspects of Rousseau's depiction of the world and of himself began to assume a preponderant role in political discourse.

Ginguené described the particular persona of Rousseau which was beginning to be imbued with intense significance for certain revolutionaries. Like Mercier, he pitted his hero against Voltaire: "Persecuted for the most beautiful of his works, the author of the *Contrat social,* of *Héloïse,* and of *Emile* joined the interest in his misfortunes with the interest in his genius and his virtue. Europe, in reading him, had learned to doubt neither any more" (p. 9). Ginguené went on to detail the quarrels that had separated Rousseau from the philosophes, blaming, in every instance, the latter and especially Voltaire for having attacked Rousseau because of his virtue. He concluded his remarks by suggesting that while Voltaire deserved a statue to be inscribed "to the destroyer of superstition," Rousseau's should carry the words "to the founder of liberty."

In a revised and abridged edition of this work the following year, which included a review of Mercier's book, Ginguené commented: "It must be admitted that since the death of Rousseau, and long before the Revolution had added a great title to his memory, there had been declared in his favor a sort of fanaticism, pushed to the most exaggerated intolerance." Ginguené was not overstating the case, for in the writings of a number of Rousseau's disciples were allusions to a conviction that their master's existence had divine significance. Grimm had noted ironically in his *Correspondance littéraire* that "Jean-Jacques has no admirers, he has worshipers" (8: 462). The Encyclopedists, Grimm included, had systematically and successfully worked to undermine the old sacerdotal prestige of the Catholic church and helped to set the stage for its disestablishment; what they had not understood, however, was that they were breaking specific icons, not the back of mystical adulation. Rousseau's disciple Alexandre Deleyre wrote to a fellow devotee in 1778, "let us be friends in

Rousseau, as the Christians are in Jesus Christ."[25] Mme de Charrière remarked that in her acquaintance with him, "I believed that I saw him assimilating himself with Jesus Christ."[26]

Jean Starobinski has characterized the way the literary self-representation of Rousseau came to fill a spiritual vacuum for many people as the power of Christianity declined: "a vague anonymous hope, lived in the dense tissue of collective experience, perceived as a group aspiration at the same time as a personal appeal.... [Rousseau represented] the ideal model of the stigmatized savior."[27] As we shall see, this mystical vision of Rousseau as the new Redeemer cast light on the discourse of his most important followers, Robespierre and Saint-Just, as well.

One point must be kept in mind if one is to understand the history of Rousseau's virtue in the years that followed his death. Not everyone who admired Rousseau's works or even who considered himself a disciple was interested in Rousseau's virtue. Large numbers of Girondists, Jacobins, even monarchists and aristocrats, expressed or professed respect for a whole array of opinions they believed they had found in Rousseau without paying any special attention to the question of his virtue either as a personal attribute or a theory of polity. Some, indeed, even took explicit exception to that aspect of his work.

An enlightening example of an important disciple of Rousseau who was resolutely indifferent to his virtue was the Abbé Claude Fauchet. Fauchet, founder with Nicolas [de] Bonneville of a crypto-masonic organization called the Cercle social, had been inspired by an idea he had found in chapter 7, book 4 of the *Contrat social,* where Rousseau had emphasized the role of public opinion in maintaining morality.[28] Fauchet decided to found a publication, to be called the *Bouche de Fer* (the mouth of iron), by which public opinion would be pronounced, for "the people need an Iron Mouth to express their ideas. After having long contemplated the political works of Jean-

[25]Quoted by Trousson, p. 177.

[26]*C.c.*, 20: 341.

[27]*La Transparence et l'obstacle*, p. 433.

[28]For a brief biography of Fauchet and an analysis of his debt to Rousseau, see Ruth Graham, "The Revolutionary Bishop and the *Philosophes,*" *ECS*, 16 (Winter-Spring 1983), 117–40. Also see McDonald, pp. 76–81, and Décembre-Alonnier, *Dictionnaire de la Révolution française* (Paris: Administration, 1866–68), 1: 743–44.

Jacques and of Mably, excellent citizens, always persecuted, always slandered ... [I decided] to establish an Iron Mouth in every department."[29]

He set up an iron mailbox in the rue du Théâtre français (de la Nation) with an open "mouth" into which any and all persons, regardless of their opinions, might drop comments, questions, or criticisms, which would then be published. Fauchet declared his dominant idea in the first issues: "everything must derive from a single principle," he claimed, but that principle was not virtue, but *love*. "Banish hatred from the face of the earth and let only love reign there. Thus we will weigh, in the infallible balance of universal love, Rousseau's *Contrat social,* in order to know the true legislation that is appropriate to all men" (October 1790, p. 116).

Fauchet declared that the quarrel between Rousseau and the philosophes should be forgotten, that there should exist "no partisan spirit of any kind." Instead, each item of the *Contrat social* should be weighed against the "universal love of the *'peuple franc'*" and accepted or rejected without prejudice. He came to the conclusion that three principles passed this test: "Man is born free, man is governed for his own advantage, and might does not make right" (October 1790, p. 17). However, according to Fauchet, Rousseau erred atrociously in saying that man was not by nature sociable. "He was wrong to say that the family dissolved when its members became adults. Man is ruled by *love*." Fauchet requested that the Assembly vote on the articles he had proposed as well as one more: "Man is a loving creature, made to associate with his fellow beings" (October 1790, p. 183).

The *Bouche de Fer,* which appeared between January 1790 and July 1791, frequently published or paraphrased maxims from Rousseau, such as "Form the citizens and you will have everything" (October 1790, p. 24). Also included were contributions from Condorcet, an eulogy of Voltaire by Charles Villette,[30] numerous articles concerning the status of women, and letters from a variety of persons

---

[29]*La Bouche de Fer,* ed. Claude Fauchet and Nicolas [de] Bonneville, Oct. 1790, p. 10. BN 8° LC 2. 317.

[30]Charles Villette, a *maréchal général des logis* under the old regime although reputedly a coward, had endeared himself to Voltaire, who had arranged for the debauched marquis to marry Mlle de Varicourt. It was at his house that Voltaire died. Villette's revolutionary career was marked by the same equivocations which distinguished him under the monarchy.

agreeing with or taking issue with Rousseau's thought. Thus a mother who signed herself: "The Friend of Children" described how she was raising her son according to the regimen prescribed in *Emile:* she and little Felix played together all day long and she didn't care a fig about propriety. "His day dress is his night gown," she confessed, but despite the seeming insouciance of his upbringing, "Felix never does anything except what I want, and he doesn't suspect a thing" (October 1790, p. 151).

On the other hand, a Jew who signed himself Moïse wrote to protest against the poll tax (the *marc d'argent*), which "would have excluded Jesus Christ and Jean-Jacques," but even more pointedly against schemes of education which proposed to "relieve" parents of the burden of child-rearing and hand children over to the state: "You call relief the cruelest sacrifice a tyrant could demand of his victim, the rupture of a bond which holds society together! Oh Rousseau! I do not pardon you for having forged ahead in a sacrifice to which so many fathers would prefer death. With all your reputation, you are not worth the most common of them" (October 1790, p. 348).[31]

The free-wheeling, eccentric *Bouche de Fer* suspended publication after a year and a half, and Fauchet, elected Constitutional Bishop, was executed in 1793.

The Abbé Grégoire also admired Rousseau and borrowed from his writings without seeming to understand what Rousseau had said about virtue. He explained, for example, that in his view Rousseau had demonstrated how the arts and sciences *improved* the individual, and "what he said about individuals applies absolutely to nations, perfecting the arts is the conserving principle of liberty."[32]

Lucius Junius Frey in his *Philosophie sociale dédiée au peuple français,* wrote that "Rousseau provoked and determined the Revolution."[33]

[31]Du Pont's comments on the *Contrat social,* as quoted in "Rousseau jugé par Du Pont de Nemours," in which Jean Perkins discusses the relations between Rousseau and the physiocrat, make it clear that he too refused to accept the antifamily premise of the *Premier Discours:* "Man is born and lives naturally in the family because being susceptible to the pleasures of love at all times the male and the female have no reason to separate once they are joined, and, on the contrary, are impelled by their very lively and natural attraction to prolong the liaison and to help each other reciprocally with all their ability." *AJJR* 39 (1972–77), 184.

[32]*Rapport sur l'établissement d'un conservatoire des arts et des métiers.* Paris: Imprimerie nationale, 8 vendémiaire, III [Sept. 29, 1794].

[33]Paris: Froullé, 1793, p. 5. Barny, 6040.

However, he specifically took issue with the notion that Spartan virtue was a desirable goal for the state. In fact, he accused Rousseau of having followed Lycurgus in erroneously believing that virtue could be inculcated in a people without their awareness, calling such a program "tyranny" rather than liberty. Lycurgus confounded equality with liberty, and Rousseau failed to rectify this point, which is what "gave such a vague and unlimited idea to the word *virtue,* which, properly speaking, is only a synonym for *morality*" (p. 20).

For a writer such as Charles François Lenormant,[34] on the other hand, what was interesting about Rousseau was not his virtue but the case for conservatism which could be pieced together by a judicious editing of his work. Joan McDonald concluded, in her study of Rousseau's influence on the Revolution up to 1791, that

> both revolutionaries and aristocrats appealed to the authority of Rousseau in the first place not because of his political writings, but because the Rousseauistic myth had become an integral part of the common intellectual background of the educated classes. [After 1791] There continued to be an official association between the group in power and the cult of Rousseau on the one hand, while on the other, individuals still continued to appeal to Rousseau's authority both to support and to oppose the ruling faction. For example, Robespierre has probably been credited with having been inspired by Rousseau's works more than any other revolutionary leader. Both he and Saint-Just were admirers of Rousseau, and the members of the Committee of Public Safety frequently quoted Rousseau's name. [Pp. 170–71]

In the following chapters I wish to demonstrate how the peculiar nature of the cult of Rousseau's virtue to which Robespierre, Saint-Just, and their colleagues on the Committee of Public Safety dedicated themselves in their speeches, pamphlets, letters, and other writings functioned as the source of a profoundly powerful identification, providing them with rhetorical ascendancy over other revolutionaries on the one hand, and, on the other, contributing to shaping the

---

[34]*Jean-Jacques Rousseau aristocrate* (Paris: N.p., 1790); Barny 6029. For a study of how counterrevolutionaries used Rousseau's work in support of reactionary positions, see Gordon H. McNeil, "The Anti-Revolutionary Rousseau," *American Historical Review,* 58 (1933), 808–23; and Roger Barny, "Les Aristocrates et Jean-Jacques Rousseau dans la Révolution," *AHRF,* 50 (1978), 534–68.

enunciation of policy between the beginning of the Legislative Assembly in 1791 and Thermidor.

Saint-Just and Robespierre differed from the rest of the revolutionaries, and their relation to the Revolution was of another order from that of all the rest. Each of these two men, so unlike in many ways, described making himself into a new man by means of virtue and offered this exemplary being to the nation as a constant object of admiration, of pity, and of fear. The three elements were woven together in the emotions both elicited from their constituencies, and it is interesting to observe how both men moved instinctively in their discourse to a position where one of the three affective states would be aroused. Fusing with the "people," in its goodness, moving apart from the "people" to describe its pathos to the deputies, acting upon it as its "legislator," remerging with it to avenge its wrongs, Saint-Just and Robespierre were personages in a *chanson de geste,* ever on stage, seemingly completely consubstantial with the figures they enacted. Unlike a Danton, or a Brissot, or a Desmoulins, known to abandon the heroic posture from time to time to be crude, foolish, or simply human in public, Saint-Just and Robespierre were never described as relinquishing the image they had created of themselves. Whereas other politicians could use Rousseau's name, could look up a few passages for a speech, could remember some of the phrases, Robespierre and Saint-Just did not bolster their arguments with Rousseau's virtue, they possessed it. The words, the affective links between ideas, the easy melting and crystallizing of identity with the "people" against its enemies, these sources of strength were inside them, not outside. What Jean-Jacques Gross said about Saint-Just applies equally to Robespierre: "That code of conduct which raises republican virtue as the rule, necessarily introduces a style. The man who wishes to make himself obeyed, respected and loved, must incarnate republicanism."[35]

Robespierre and Saint-Just, like Rousseau, did not merely preach virtue, they made it an object of display. Their persons, like that of their mentor, were shown in order to fascinate, not in the old, evil way of the monarchy, but in the new republican way, by the irresistible appeal of virtue. Lying directly adjacent to the virtue, and possible only because of its alliance with it, was violence. The two

[35]"Saint-Just en Mission," *ACSJ,* p. 57.

attributes were inseparable, but the third leg of the triangle was the one which, in some way, ensured a momentary stability to the other two. Theatrical Saint-Just and Robespierre, virtuous, terrifying, were in reality victims, and their status as martyrs was an indispensable part of their divinely appointed fate, as it had been of Rousseau's.

CHAPTER EIGHT

Robespierre and Saint-Just

The significance of Maximilien Robespierre's political career has been the subject of nearly two hundred years of frequently acrimonious debate.[1] As Georges Rudé has pointed out, however, most serious observers have agreed about at least one thing: "he was a man of unshakable principles." Rudé defined those basic tenets of Robespierre's thought as follows: "the end of politics must be the embodiment of morality in government; that morality, or goodness or 'virtue', emanates from the people and from the people alone; and, therefore, it is the people's will, and not that of their fallible and corruptible rulers, that must be sovereign and prevail."

Rudé then went on to pose the questions that such declarations evoke: "But what is 'virtue'; what is 'sovereignty'; and who indeed are 'the people'?"

To Robespierre virtue is essentially that which contributes to the public good: love of country and the subjection of the private to the public

---

[1]In the *Répertoire de l'histoire de la Révolution française*, Gérard Walter provides a complete bibliography of material relating to Robespierre before 1940 (Paris: BN, 1941), pp. 457–74. The introduction to J. M. Thompson's *Robespierre* offers a scholarly analysis of the sources of information about Robespierre and a chronological assessment of historical evaluations of his political role from the time of the Revolution until 1935 (New York: Howard Fertig, 1968), 1: xv–liv. In the *Actes du Colloque Robespierre* (Paris: Société des Études Robespierristes, 1967), appear two series of historiographical articles: "Robespierre vu par ses contemporains," and "Robespierre dans l'historiographie internationale," of which Jacques Godechot's "L'Historiographie française de Robespierre" (pp. 167–90) is especially valuable.

interest. To promote public good . . . sovereignty must be undivided and exercised by the people as a whole. Yet some people, he believed, were more trustworthy as depositories of virtue and therefore more fit to exercise sovereignty than others. And the main purpose of the Revolution, as Robespierre conceived it, must be to create a republic of such socially independent citizens, exercising a common sovereignty and restored by good government to their natural and inalienable rights of personal freedom, political equality and the pursuit of happiness.[2]

Rudé charted the cardinal points of Robespierre's public discourse: "virtue," "sovereignty," and "the people." He states that in Robespierre's intellectual development "the greatest debt of all he owed to Rousseau" (p. 96). In his history of Robespierre's political activities, however, he has tended to reduce the role of these conceptions to a large degree or to bring their definitions more closely in line with the mainstream of revolutionary thinking. Where Robespierre's speeches have struck observers as peculiarly innappropriate, as somehow grounded in an alien worldview, Rudé has tried to normalize their meaning, to neutralize the oddly galvanizing effect of certain passages, to fit Robespierre into the mold of a reality-oriented politician. Yet, if we examine how Robespierre used the words "sovereignty," "people," and above all, "virtue," in the volumes of his collected works representing his speeches before the assemblies and the Jacobins, his correspondence, and his contributions to journals, a coherent vision emerges, and it is one of a figure engaged in an intense, heroic effort to render real and concrete and exaltation of virtue which he had found in Rousseau.[3]

---

[2] *Robespierre: Portrait of a Revolutionary Democrat* (New York: Viking, 1975), pp. 95–96.

[3] "Robespierre's doctrine of the state," says his English biographer J. M. Thompson, "upon which everything else rests, is clearly based on Rousseau's" (2: 47). In the words of J. L. Carr, it was not only ideology but personal identity that he found in Rousseau, and Robespierre's "identification [with Rousseau] was in fact almost total." *Robespierre* (London: Constable, 1972), p. 119. According to Gérard Walter, Robespierre recognized himself as "the spiritual son of the author of the *Confessions*." *Robespierre* (Paris: Gallimard, 1961), 1: 25. Jean Jaurès referred to him as "the younger brother of the Savoyard vicar" (3: 7). Georges Rudé commented: "There was a Rousseauistic quality in his choice of imagery and turn of phrase, in his manner of thinking and way of life; and no other revolutionary leader identified so closely with Rousseau as he did in both word and deed" (p. 97).

Walter concludes: "the capital event which decided the psychological orientation of Robespierre seems to have been that Sunday walk in the forest which he took as a young student in the forest of Montmorency, during which he was privileged to

Alfred Cobban also credited "Rousseauistic inspiration" for Robespierre's basic conceptions, which he enumerated as follows:

> The constant relating of political to ethical ends, the definition of utilitarianism in terms of morality, the emotional deism expressed later in the Cult of the Supreme Being, faith in the natural goodness of the people, the assertion of the sovereignty of the people and the General Will, emphasis on the idea of equality, suspicion of the rich and powerful, combination of the idea of sovereignty with separation of functions in government, supremacy of the legislative power, hostility to representation...above all, there was a Rousseauistic quality in his mind.[4]

Cobban, however, noted that for all these similarities and references to Rousseau in his speeches and writings, Robespierre hardly mentioned the *Contrat social* and "it is remarkable also that there is no evidence in Robespierre of any acquaintance with the political writings of Rousseau other than the *Contrat social*" (p. 152).

Cobban claims that "the interest in the career and ideas of Robespierre for the historian, and particularly the historian of political ideas, lies in their value as illustrating the theoretical and practical difficulties involved in the application of the principle of democratic sovereignty" (p. 190). While this may be true when his career and ideas are interpreted externally—that is, from the vantage point of the historical development of representative institutions— "popular sovereignty" for Robespierre, Saint-Just, and some of their colleagues figures only as an ancillary issue to the essential problem of the state, which they explicitly labeled "virtue," not democracy. When the same idea and career are viewed from within the rather alien context of that set of semantic postulates, different values emerge, of no less interest to the historian of ideas.

Besides Robespierre's eight volumes of political texts, a number of parallel and complementary documents produced by such figures as

---

contemplate the august features of Jean-Jacques Rousseau. His mind was made up: like Rousseau he declared himself ready to purchase [posterity's] gratitude...at the price of a premature death" (*Robespierre*, 2: 138). For further evaluations of Robespierre's adherence to Rousseau, see Albert Soboul's "J.-J. Rousseau et le jacobinisme," *JECS*, pp. 405–24, and R. Schatz, *J.-J. Rousseaus Einfluss auf Robespierre* (Borna-Leipzig: Noske, 1906).

[4]*Aspects of the French Revolution*, pp. 151–52.

Jean-Paul Marat, Jacques-Nicolas Billaud-Varenne, Georges Couthon, Philippe Le Bas, Gheslain Lebon, and Anacharsis Cloots bore witness to the commitment to "making virtue reign." During a few crucial years this florid production of texts dedicated to "Rousseauvian virtue" seems to have corresponded to a deeply felt need in France; that moment past, the nation went on to other business as did most of the political figures who had taken it up for opportunistic reasons. But for the self-representations Robespierre and Saint-Just created there was no other business, and when the "reign of virtue" ceased to speak to the vitals of a significant part of the French population, their time had come to an end. In the following chapters we will examine not the political careers of the leaders of the Jacobins, but the expression of their dominant idea as it was tested in the arena of the French Revolution.

Robespierre was born in Arras four months after his parents' marriage. His father abandoned him when he was eight years old, shortly after his mother had died in childbirth. "His family circumstances," Norman Hampson suggests, "were oddly reminiscent of those of Rousseau."[5] It is possible that these similarities between his background and Rousseau's contributed to the intense feelings of identification he experienced in reading the *Confessions*.

In his "Dedication to Jean-Jacques Rousseau"[6] he addressed himself to Rousseau as follows:

> Divine man, you taught me to know myself: while I was still young you made me appreciate the dignity of my nature and reflect upon the great principles of the social order. The old edifice is crumbling: the portico

---

[5]*Will and Circumstance: Montesquieu, Rousseau, and the French Revolution* (Norman: University of Oklahoma Press, 1983), p. 129.

[6]The circumstances of the writing of this piece and its purpose are unknown. An autograph copy exists, however, which demonstrates its authenticity and is reproduced in the otherwise apocryphal *Mémoires authentiques de Maximilien Robespierre* (Paris: Moreau-Rosier, 1830). J. M. Thompson, following H. Buffenoir, *Les Portraits de Robespierre* (Paris: Leroux, 1910), p. 176, states that "internal evidence suggests [it] dates from 1791" (*Robespierre*, 1: 9). Walter, however, takes issue with this dating, placing the passage "during the first months of 1789" because it does not "generally accord with the spirit of these lines, which essentially envisage the future" (*Robespierre*, 2: 396). I tend to agree with Buffenoir and Thompson because the notion of having already "placed his stone" on the new edifice constructed after despotism has been abolished would seem more appropriate at the end of the Constituant Assembly than before the meeting of the Estates General.

of a new edifice is rising upon its ruins, and, thanks to you, I have brought my stone to it. Receive my homage; as weak as it is, it must please you: I have never flattered the living. I saw you in your last days, and this memory is for me the source of proud joy, I contemplated your august features; I saw in them the imprint of the dark grief to which the injustices of men had condemned you. From that moment on I understood all the pains of a noble life devoted to the cult of truth. They did not frighten me. The consciousness of having wanted the good of his fellow beings is the recompense of the virtuous man; then comes the gratitude of the peoples who surround his memory with the honors due to him... even when he purchases them at the price of a premature death.

Called upon to play a role in the midst of the greatest events which have ever agitated the world, witness to the death of despotism and the awakening of real sovereignty; on the verge of seeing break forth the storms building up on all sides, storms the results of which no human intelligence can predict, I owe to myself, I shall soon owe my fellow citizens, an accounting of my thoughts and of my acts. Your example is there, before my eyes, your admirable *Confessions,* that free and courageous emanation of the purest soul, will go on to posterity less as a model of art than as a prodigy of virtue. I wish to follow your venerable footsteps, even if I were to leave only a name which fails to interest the centuries to come: happy if, in the perilous career that an unprecedented revolution just opened before us, I remain constantly faithful to the inspirations I found in your texts!

This Dedication is quoted in its entirety because several important aspects of Robespierre's Rousseauvian self-representation emerge from it. He calls Rousseau "divine," and this attribution of superhuman quality is no mere hyperbole on Robespierre's part, for, as we have seen, he was not alone in assigning a supernatural significance to the career of his mentor. What he gleaned from his study of Rousseau, it is to be noted, was not originally a political theory or a set of principles regarding the state; what he learned was to know himself. The significance of the revelation is clear: through Rousseau he learned "to appreciate the value" of his nature and it was that appreciation which led him to "reflect upon the great principles of the social order." Thus, politics, for Robespierre as he described himself, began with the discovery of his own worth, and from that vantage point of heightened self-approbation he was able to understand the fundamentals of society. It was not the political writings

M: ROBBESPIERRE,

From an original Picture by Bouteville.

Engrav'd for C. Lowndes and I. Parsons No 21 Paternoster Row Sep. 10. 1794.

Maximilien Robespierre. Engraving 1794, from a drawing.
(Courtesy of the Bibliothèque nationale, Paris)

that brought Robespierre to his recognition, it was the *Confessions*, and the aspect of the *Confessions* that was meaningful to him was the virtue he discovered there. Robespierre, like Rousseau, alluded to his conviction of his own inner goodness: "I have never known jealousy except by hearsay. Never will a vile sentiment approach my heart" (5: 115).[7] Assured of his own goodness, he displayed himself in his role as legislator of the nation. "The first thing the legislator must know," he said, "is that *le peuple* is good" (5: 19).

Thus Robespierre began, in a metaphysical rather than chronological sense, with Rousseau's two postulates: a statement of belief in his own goodness, dependent in some way on that of Rousseau, and an affirmation of belief in the goodness of *le peuple*. "I tell you that I have understood this great moral and political truth announced by Jean-Jacques, that men never sincerely love anyone who does not love them, that *le peuple* alone is good, just, and magnanimous and that corruption and tyranny are the exclusive appanage of those who disdain *le peuple*" (8: 308). Contempt for the people was an attribute of evil whereas love for the people was a sign of goodness. "Vile egoists," Robespierre wrote in the *Défenseur de la Constitution*, "insist on slandering the people, they attempt to degrade the people, they slaughter the people when they can . . . they render divine homage to the people's executioners." Thus the "people's enemies" were vicious; the "people," however, was "closer to nature and less depraved" (4: 116). (In French, as opposed to English, the word "peuple" is singular, and this attribute facilitates conceptualizing the people as if they consitituted one single being, rather than a group of individuals. In order to respect that nuance, I shall use the French word "peuple" in the appropriate quotations rather than the English "people," which does not carry identical connotations.)

It must be understood that the "people" was not any specific person or group of persons. On the contrary, particular human beings were by definition not the "people." This aspect of Robespierre's lexicon has occasioned confusion, with attempts being made to determine whether "the people" meant the poor alone, or the petty bourgeois, or some other externally identifiable group. "Le peuple"

---

[7] Jacques-Vincent Delacroix uttered a comment about Robespierre which echoed the opinion of many of his admirers: he was "the most eloquent man of the Revolution because he is the most virtuous. Virtue alone is truly eloquent." *Robespierre vu par ses contemporains*, ed. Louis Jacob (Paris: Colin, 1938), p. 108.

in his discourses, however, was a single figure of goodness with which it was possible to fuse in imagination. "I understand by that word all the French," he said. To the extent that someone distinguished himself from that figure, he was not "the people" any more. "The morality which has disappeared in most individuals can be found only in the mass of people and in the general interest" (6: 281; June 11, 1790). As François Furet pointed out, this question of the actual identity of the "people" was at the heart of much of the philosophical and political problem raised by the collapse of the *ancien régime*. "Which group, which assembly, which meeting, which consensus is the depositary for the word of the people? It is around this deadly question that the modalities of action and the distribution of power organize themselves."[8] "Individuals" and "the people" were antithetical terms: "*Le peuple* is always worth more than the individuals," Robespierre proclaimed (5: 209). To the extent that his own goodness was extended outward, it included humanity, the people, and "all Frenchmen," indiscriminately. "Man is good," he said, "leaving the hands of nature; whoever denies this principle must not think of instituting man" (5: 207).

Robespierre identified with the great undifferentiated body of "the people," and when he was accused of leading them astray he responded angrily: "You dare to accuse me of wishing to mislead and flatter the people. How could I! I am neither the courtier, nor the moderator, nor the defender of the people; I am (the) people myself! (Je suis peuple moi-même!)" (8: 311). The people, however, was also the sovereign. There was no separate body ruling a passive citizenry; in Robespierre's text, the nation and the legislature, the agent and the patient were one. This was the difficulty with revolutionary governments; "they saw the people only as subject and never as sovereign." To remedy this the National Convention should adopt:

> purer and more democratic principles. It will adopt them, no doubt, and the portrait of the Legislator traced by the most eloquent of our philosophers must not frighten us: "It would take a superior intelligence, which sees all the passions and experiences none of them; which, aiming for a distant glory in the progress of time, could work in one century and enjoy in another. It would take Gods to give laws to men" (J.-J. Rousseau, *Le Contrat social*, VII). [5: 19]

[8]*Penser la Révolution française* (Paris: Gallimard, 1978), p. 49.

Robespierre recognized and enunciated the same "strange loop" Rousseau had identified: that in order to create a state of virtue, people would have already to be virtuous. "In order to form our political institutions," he said, "we would have to have the morals that those institutions must someday give us" (5: 20). Robespierre, then, defined his role in the Assembly and later in the Convention, not as that of a "representative" or as a "spokesman," but as a Legislator, in the same sense that Rousseau had intended.

"The first thing the legislator must know," he said, "is that *le peuple* is good: the first feeling he must experience is the need to avenge the people's insults and give the people back all its dignity" (5: 19). Thus love for the "people," on the one hand, was wed to a program of reprisals against the "people's" enemies, and the primary need of *le peuple* was a sense of its own worth, always refuted by those who willfully separated themselves from it. "If you wish to be happy and free," Robespierre wrote, "*le peuple* must believe in its own virtue" (5: 118). It was that very belief which formed the Republic, not some group of elected representatives or legal formulas. "Republic is not a vain word; it is the character of the citizens, it is virtue, that is, love of the Fatherland" (6: 285).

Thus Robespierre was not talking about a political organization in the ordinary sense, he was invoking a state of emotional fusion between his good self and the emanation of that self which he called "the people," or "the Republic" or "the Fatherland." "The soul of the republic is virtue," he said, "that is to say love of the fatherland, the magnanimous devotion which merges all private interests in the general interest" (5: 17).

Robespierre's political fortunes were linked with those of the Mountain, which he defined as:

> a part of the room in the Constituant Assembly where, from the beginning of the Revolution, sat the small number of deputies who defended the cause of the people to the end with the most consistency and fidelity. It is known that the opposite side, called the right side, was always occupied by men of a diametrically opposite character.... Solon of Athens had observed that his country contained three classes of inhabitants whose characters were different: those of the mountain, who were lively, courageous, and born of the republic, those of the plain, who were quieter and more moderate, those of the seashore who were harder and inclined toward aristocracy. I blame Solon for having made

bad laws to please those two classes of half-breed Athenians; he should have brought them all together to the principles of liberty and to the eternal laws of reason and justice, engraved in the hearts of all men. Solon was a "feuillant," who fondled all the parties [5: 197–98].

Like Rousseau, Robespierre extolled the rigorous Spartan constitution over the corruption he found in Athens, and described his role as Legislator, together with his fellow Montagnards, as creating a state which would make all citizens "men of the mountain." Democracy did not signify the compromises arrived at by a motley amalgam of alien individuals and groups, but rather the one pure will of the truly virtuous people whose spokesman was Robespierre.

"Virtue," said J. M. Thompson, "was Saint-Just's point of contact with Robespierre."[9] Saint-Just's brief revolutionary career, beginning with his election to the National Convention in September 1792, until his execution on 10 thermidor, year II, was inseparably bound to that of Robespierre, with whom he shared mastery of a common moral vision derived from Rousseau.[10] Like Robespierre, Saint-Just presented

[9]*Leaders of the French Revolution* (Oxford: Blackwell, 1963), p. 191. In his introduction to Jean-Jacques Gross's scholarly study of Saint-Just's career on mission to the armies, Albert Soboul sums up postrevolutionary attitudes toward Saint-Just: "What has not been written about Saint-Just! Among the historians alone; for Michelet he symbolized the 'Archangel of Death,' for Taine he was 'living glory.' Saint-Just aroused even more interest among writers and poets than among historians. For Lamartine, he incarnated 'the dream of Dracon's Republic'; for Sainte-Beuve he was 'a young man, atrocious and theatrical,' for Barrès he was a 'light in the tomb.' And again, for some he was 'a bloodthirsty tiger,' for others 'a well-groomed monster.'" *Saint-Just: Sa politique et ses missions* (Paris: BN, 1976), p. 7. Gross's work on Saint-Just at the front goes far to demystify the quasi-legendary young Jacobin. Yet, as Soboul's quotation suggests, it was his consciously created theatrical persona which impressed itself so deeply upon the imaginations of his own and of future generations. Albert Camus, in *L'Homme révolté* evoked better than anyone the mythic quality Saint-Just assumed, calling him the "Anti-Sade." Nonetheless, according to Camus, the two admirers of Rousseau "legitimized terrorism, an individual one of the libertine, a governmental state to the priest of virtue" (Paris: Gallimard, 1951), p. 154.

Norman Hampson in *Will and Circumstance,* explicates many of Saint-Just's texts in terms of his debt first to Montesquieu and then to Rousseau. Hampson quotes numerous passages in which Saint-Just adduces *vertu* as the true goal of the state, and although Hampson leaves the word in French, indicating its polysemic status, he does not investigate the term itself.

[10] Henri Peyre comments: "We know how the echo of [Rousseau's] doctrines will resound in the noble formulas of Saint-Just, who was perhaps the revolutionary most deeply steeped in Rousseau's thought." "The Influence of Eighteenth-Century Ideas on the French Revolution," *Historical and Critical Essays* (Lincoln: University of Nebraska Press, 1968), p. 81.

himself as a man free from any taint of evil: "certainly," he remarked, "no one ever hoped that I would lend my pure hands to inequity" (2: 480). In a work entitled *L'Esprit de la Révolution et de la constitution en France,* which Saint-Just published in 1791, before being elected to office, he described the Revolution from the point of view of virtue: "So many men have spoken of this revolution, and most of them have said nothing. I do not know that anyone, until now, has put himself to searching, deep in his heart, for virtue in order to know what he deserves from liberty. I do not claim to accuse anyone; each man does well to think what he thinks, but whoever speaks or writes owes an accounting of his virtue to the city" (1: 251). Saint-Just described how he had evaluated the first assemblies: "as a member of the sovereign I wanted to know if I was free." He concluded that he had found reason to believe that in the new laws "I would be obeying only my virtue" (1: 251).

Thus, from the very beginning, Saint-Just depicted his role as that of the man of virtue who would find in the new government not negotiations or coalitions between the various elements which constituted France, but his own inner value externalized to become the law of the land.[11] At the conclusion of the work he commented on the decision to erect a monument to Rousseau. "France finally just honored Jean-Jacques Rousseau with a statue. Ah, why is this great man dead?" The National Assembly, he said, had a mission, which it:

> would not exercise like Lycurgus, Mohammed, and Jesus Christ, in the name of heaven; heaven was no longer in men's hearts, they needed another lure more in conformity with human interest. As virtue is still a marvel among arrogant and corrupt mortals, ... everyone became intoxicated with the rights of man, and philosophy and pride found no fewer disciples than the immortal gods. However, under the simple name of national assembly, the legislator, speaking to men only of themselves, struck them with a holy vertigo and made them happy. [1: 341]

Rousseau's dream of virtue, therefore, was the touchstone of the new republic, replacing the Christian heaven that had served the

[11]R. R. Palmer notes: "[Saint-Just] believed absolutely in his own virtue. So did Robespierre and others, for in no trait were the French revolutionaries so alike as in their moral self-approval. The doctrine of the *Social contract,* with these moral overtones, became the theory of the Terror." *Twelve Who Ruled* (Princeton: Princeton University Press, 1941), p. 77.

monarchy long and well. Unlike the priestly caste of the *ancien régime*, however, the legislator would not speak to men about God, but about themselves, causing immediate bliss for all rather than describing the possibility of beatitude for some.

Saint-Just, like Robespierre and Rousseau, stated as axiomatic the innate goodness of man or the "people." "Each *peuple* is right for virtue," he said, and only those who wish to tyrannize over others see wickedness as natural to the human race. "I combat this pretext used by tyrants, of the natural violence of man, in order to dominate him" (1: 421). Man is what his government makes him, morally speaking. "The virtue of Lacedemonia was in the heart of Lycurgus." "Our corruption under the monarchy was in the heart of all the kings, corruption is not natural to peoples" (1: 423).

Saint-Just never wavered from his statement that "le peuple" was good, although sometimes "too simple, too pure, too poor" (1: 395). As object, the people's goodness was its passive nature: " 'le peuple,' is good and credulous, because the people is without ambition and without intrigue" (1: 392).

The word "people" could then signify, as Annie Geoffroy demonstrated, not any *existing* human beings, but "an ideal political unity," and as she pointed out, this single body was characterized by poverty and passivity.[12] *Le peuple* spoke through Saint-Just; it was he who found the laconic pronouncements that expressed its goodness and its concomitant pathos.

Le peuple, however, was capable of an alternate manifestation, in which it played the role of protagonist in its struggle with "the enemies of the people." Saint-Just described *le peuple* in its active phase as the "revolutionary man," whom he envisaged in the following terms:

A revolutionary man is inflexible, but he is sensible, he is frugal; he is simple without advertising false modesty; he is the irreconcilable enemy of all lies, all indulgence, all affectation. As his aim is to see the Revolution triumph, he never criticizes it, but he condemns its enemies without enveloping them with the Revolution; he does not exaggerate it, but he enlightens it, and jealous of its purity, he watches himself when he speaks of it, out of respect for it; he claims less to be the equal of authority, which is the law, than the equal of men, and above all of the

12"Le 'Peuple' selon Saint-Just," *AHRF,* no. 191 (Jan.-Mar. 1968), 138.

unfortunate.... The revolutionary man pursues the guilty and defends innocence in the courtroom; he tells the truth in order that it instruct, not for it to do damage; he knows that in order for the Revolution to affirm itself, people must be as good as they used to be wicked; his probity is not an intellectual *finesse*, but a quality of the heart. Marat was kind at home, he threatened only traitors. J.-J. Rousseau was a revolutionary and certainly was not insolent: I conclude from this that a revolutionary man is a hero of good sense and probity. [2: 372 (26 germinal, year II)]

Saint-Just's thought was so close to Rousseau's and it was expressed so elliptically that it would often be incomprehensible without that referent. Frequently, however, on certain questions, he assumed an ultra-Rousseauvian posture and he did so in the name of virtue. In this way he consistently went beyond Rousseau in the pursuit of a Rousseauvian argument by denying one of the balancing considerations which his mentor invoked. Thus, in the paragraph cited above, Saint-Just refused the "legislator" supernatural powers, in defiance of Rousseau's suggestion in Book 2, chapter 7 of the *Contrat social,* but he did so to bolster the importance of *virtue* and it alone as the standard of society. Similarly, Rousseau had accepted, with reservations, the principle of capital punishment in the *Contrat social.* In his *Esprit de la Révolution,* Saint-Just refuted Rousseau on the grounds that a truly good government would create a citizenry *so good* that it would be incapable of serious crime, so that a capital offense would, in reality, condemn the government, not the offender.

Whatever veneration the authority of J.-J. Rousseau imposes, I do not pardon you, oh great man, for having justified the death penalty....Before consenting to death the contract must consent to be altered, because crime is but the result of that alteration; now, how does the contract come to be corrupt? By the abuse of laws which permit the passions to awaken and open the door to slavery. Arm yourself against the corruption of laws, if you arm yourself against crime you are taking the fact for the right.... The social treaty, Rousseau says, aims to conserve the contractants; now, they are conserved by virtue and not by force. [1: 315]

By means of this logic, Saint-Just showed that the only possible crime was the act committed against *le peuple* and its virtue. Since it was the government, under any form of polity, which was defined as opposed to *le peuple,* only individuals with political power could ever be guilty.

In his role as a member of the Committee of Public Safety, Saint-Just has been accused of switching sides on the question of the death penalty. As we shall see, however, he came to prove the necessity for capital punishment by means of exactly the same argument he had used against it: the "corruption of laws" was the enemy needing to be punished, not individual criminals, who were victims of a corrupt state. Man was born good, and in an ideal state "the sovereign consists of all the hearts yearning for virtue" (2: 509). This definition of the "sovereign" (*le souverain*) as a collective sentimental mystery, distinct from "sovereignty" (*la souveraineté*), the exercise of the "common will," follows Rousseau. Two aspects of the same phenomenon, the good people fuse together to form a sovereign state of virtue which exercises its sovereignty by creating good people. In this way the good state was defined as virtue, and the state which was not good was wickedness itself. "The monarchy," said Saint-Just (8 ventôse, II), "is not a king, it is crime; the Republic is not a senate, it is virtue" (2: 234).

That Saint-Just spoke in terms of the familiar tenets of morality his generation had absorbed from Rousseau in no way made him unusual. Where Saint-Just was innovative, however, and what lent tremendous power to his oratory, was the distinct persona he assumed in relation to the "people" and the government. Although he spoke first as a representative to the National Convention and later as a member of the Committee of Public Safety, he always took the position that he spoke for a single, undifferentiated body called the people, or the fatherland, which was surrounded by enemies, principal among whom was the government itself. This was his most disconcerting and effective rhetorical weapon in the constant political infighting that marked the failure of the Convention to achieve stable functioning. Rousseau had aligned himself with nature, with antique virtue, and with the simple goodness of the humble artisan in order to humiliate those whose claim to influence was based on birth, money, or achievement. Now, in a representative government, Saint-Just took the same attitude toward his fellow deputies, other elected officials, and the entire bureaucratic organization of the state.

The anger that sometimes emerged in Rousseau's writing as for example, at the end of the *Confessions* when he declared that any reader who didn't respect the author "deserves to be strangled," was closely linked, for Saint-Just, with the idea of his own role in bringing the people to their own goodness. Two passages, one from the beginning of his career and one from the day before the end, serve to illustrate this connection.

In a letter to an associate, Daubigny, Saint-Just expressed his feelings about being too young for election to the Legislative Assembly. It was July 1792, he was twenty-four years old, and he had just published his *Esprit de la Révolution*. He had apparently been to Paris, had an unsatisfactory meeting with Camille Desmoulins, and returned to Noyon.

> It is unfortunate that I cannot stay in Paris. I feel that I have it in me to leave my mark on this century. Go see Desmoulins, embrace him for me and tell him that he will never see me again, that I esteem his patriotism but I despise him, because I have seen through his soul. . . . He does not in the least possess the audacity of magnanimous virtue. Adieu, I am above misfortune. I shall endure everything, but I will tell the truth. My palm will rise, however, and perhaps it will put you in the shade. Wrench out my heart and eat it; you will become what you are not, great! O Gods! must Brutus languish forgotten by Rome! My mind is made up however; if Brutus does not kill others, he will kill himself. [1: 349]

This passage is of especial interest not only because it demonstrates the rage which charged assertions of moral superiority with tremendous energies, but also because of the conclusion: failure to destroy "others" necessitated destruction of the self.

Usually reticent to a remarkable degree about personal matters, even in his private notes, Saint-Just commented once more on his role in a set of fragments entitled "Sur les institutions Républicaines": "The day when I become convinced that it is impossible to give the French people morals which will be gentle, energetic, sensitive, and inexorable toward tyranny and injustice, I shall stab myself" (2: 504).

A rhetorical position which placed the speaker outside the framework of the representative organization to which he belonged, which permitted him to assume a posture of alienation through identification with "the people" in virtue, and which was based upon a declaration to kill either the opposition or himself, these were the elements which Saint-Just brought to the National Convention and with which he rapidly established himself as revolutionary legislator capable of influencing opinion.

CHAPTER NINE

The Trial of the King

It was during the trial of Louis XVI that Saint-Just forged the special moral vocabulary which he and so many of his generation had absorbed from Rousseau into an instrument of oratorical power. The reader will recall the conflicts that threatened France and the Revolution in the summer of 1792. The Constitution of 1791 had become a cumbersome legal fiction, impossible to respect, extremely difficult to undo. After the king's aborted flight to Varennes in June 1791, the fact that France remained a monarchy at all enraged the left, while those still attached to the crown found the notion of a captive kind insufferable. The government, since April under the Girondist leadership of Roland, Mme Roland, and a coterie of close friends, issued pronouncements in which lofty moral superiority toward both the king and the Jacobins was coupled with verbal incitements to violence on behalf of virtue. Much of the early rhetorical shift toward a bloody moral polarization of political life must be attributed to the Gironde. Mme Roland was, in Gita May's words, "one of the first to advocate methods of intimidation and repression against all suspicious elements."[1]

The Legislative Assembly, led by the bourgeois but bellicose Gironde, had lost authority. The presence of *sans-culottes* from the Paris sections, lining the corridors leading to the Assembly hall and within the hall itself, functioned to shape the discourse pronounced at the

---

[1]*Madame Roland and the Age of Revolution* (New York: Columbia University Press, 1970), p. 164.

podium. The sections were at once an audience to whom words were addressed, a symbolic chorus enacting the role of the *peuple* of whom the orators were speaking, and ultimately the judges and guarantors of the Assembly's legitimacy. This triple function structured the dynamics of political oratory for speakers of every political persuasion.

Robespierre, no longer part of the government, was devoting his energies to the Paris Commune which, on August 10, invaded the Tuileries in search of the "tyrant Capet." Louis, the queen, and their children crossed the Tuileries on foot and took refuge in the Assembly itself. The Commune succeeded in having the king and the royal family incarcerated in the Temple.

According to Jean Jaurès, "The last phase of the Legislative's authority was a subordinate one. But would the Commune limit its power to Paris?" It quickly became apparent that the Parisian patriots had no such intention; the Commune sent "commissars" to the eighty-three departments, and "that was the Paris Commune's seizure of all of France" (4: 174).

The Commune suspended liberty of the press, arrested and imprisoned known monarchists as well as a number of obscure individuals, and closed convents and monasteries. Philippe Buonarroti characterized that period in the following terms: "To the value of the conceptions of Jean-Jacques [the men of August 10] added the boldness of applying them to a society of twenty-five million men" (Jaurès, 3: 77).

In Jaurès' words, however, "it was Robespierre who by means of the Commune was the true mayor of Paris" (4: 189). By the end of August a sort of reaction seemed to be setting in, and members of the Legislative began to express their disapproval of the continuing usurpation of the elected body's authority by the insurgent group.

On September 2 the more radical sections, excited by the successes of their direct action, both encouraging and encouraged by popular fear of foreign invasion, sounded the tocsin. *Sans-culottes* broke into the prisons and executed the prisoners, including a number of suspect priests who were said to be in league with enemies of the nation. Eleven hundred persons were killed in Paris in four days.

The way in which the massacres were described throws light on the workings of the emerging dominant morality. Those who participated in the assassinations and those who directed them were not to be considered immoral. On the contrary, they expressed hurt at being criticized. A member of the surveillance committee, Antoine-François Sergent, who had signed the order to "judge all the prisoners of the Abbaye," complained only four days later that the assassins were being accused of stealing the deceased's belongings. He reacted by wishing to reassure the assassins that their virtue was appreciated. "M. Sergent told about the odious means employed to slander the people, . . . he proposed that to make a man virtuous, it is necessary to appear to believe in his virtue, he demanded that the General Council [of the Commune] put forth a proclamation which, by making the people feel its virtue, would make them fear to tarnish it."[2] Sergent's request underlines how essential it was for many revolutionaries to experience themselves and their actions as legitimized by a widely accepted morality. The people could rise to the assassination of conspirators with pride; to label them petty thieves was to destroy their self-esteem and reduce them once again to rabble.

Restif de la Bretonne, that intrepid observer of life in revolutionary Paris, expressed a feeling which underlies much of the ambivalence toward the massacres. In a truly democratic state, in the absence of a transcendental theory, was the group impulse not always right? If the masses, incarnating the people, felt inclined to kill the representatives of a discredited religion or political system, who was to blame them? "No," he commented in the *Nuits révolutionnaires*, "no, I do not pity them, those fanatical priests, they have done too much harm to the fatherland. The minority is always guilty, I repeat, even if it is morally in the right."[3] The notion that "the minority is always guilty" and hence subject to execution was in the air during the election (as the massacres were taking place) of the National Convention and had its effect upon the results of that selection process.

By September 20, the Assembly had been replaced by the new ruling body. It included no overt royalists, the Paris delegation was entirely Jacobin, the Republic was proclaimed, and a whole new political and moral frame of reference had come into existence. The Convention quickly revealed, however, the same three-way split characteristic of all the Revolution's governing bodies, which Robespierre

[2]BR, 18: 266.
[3]*Les Nuits révolutionnaires*, ed. François Funck-Brentano (Paris: Fayard, 1915), pp. 108–9.

described. Girondins elected entirely by the provinces, now displayed ambivalence toward extralegal violence, advocating it in the case of the king, but protesting it when threatened themselves. Despite Brissot's cry; "No peace with the Bourbons!" the Girondins' policy seemed inconsistent; as Albert Soboul commented, their stance as war party, on the one hand, was incompatible with their "policy of social reaction."[4] Thus weakened, they were pushed to the right by the numerically inferior Mountain, spiritually in touch with the Commune on the left. In between was the uncommitted Plain.

This then, was the context in which the question of judging the king arose: the Commune was pressing the Convention to relinquish its royal prey to popular justice. The Mountain had decided to champion the cause of his prosecution. Deliberately associating itself with the Commune, the Mountain now faced an unfocused but embittered oppositional majority. The legislative body settled into a complicated debate on the unprecedented constitutional problems of prosecuting a king, a dispute that the majority of delegates did not seem eager to see end. Some members of the legislative body, still reeling from the implications of the prison massacres and Robespierre's threats against the Gironde, found the notion of expressing solidarity with the *septembriseurs* by means of an official political execution frightening. The legal grounds for the Convention to accuse and try Louis were uncertain. The constitution had specifically labeled the king inviolable; for the Convention both to accuse the dethroned monarch and then to judge him was venturing onto the shaky ground of unprecedented jurisprudence. The uneasy majority, however, had one essential maneuver at its disposal: it could stall for time indefinitely by introducing a series of obfuscating diversions.

In the midst of this factional jousting sat Saint-Just, at last twenty-five years old and elected to take his seat at the Convention as delegate from l'Aisne. On November 13 he rose to deliver his maiden speech, one which set Louis's fate in the new moral framework and in some way established the speaker's moral authority over the assembled deputies. In his address of December 27 on the same topic, he completed his brilliant dialectical conquest of the Convention.[5]

---

[4] *Le Procès de Louis XVI* (Paris: Julliard, 1966), p. 24.
[5] Françoise Fortunat offers a subtle analysis of Saint-Just's highly individualistic mode of linguistic usage, commenting that "it was not a question of echoing a real

No other revolutionary leader was able to pose the vital questions of France's destiny on such an exalted plane and maintain the tone. After his trenchant formulations of the issues, other orators sounded verbose and compromised, as if mere humanity were incapable of rising to the realm inhabited by the leader who bore the evocative name of Saint-Just.[6]

The simple but deadly argument which Saint-Just elaborated before the Convention was based on the logical extension of meanings Rousseau had attached to the word "innocence" and the word "guilt," but denuded, as was Saint-Just's habit, of the qualifications with which Rousseau hedged the terms. "Innocence," in Saint-Just's Rousseauvian vocabulary, was an essential attribute of the "people," while "guilt" was the inescapable lot of the "people's enemies." Saint-Just was impatient at the Conventionals' difficulty in grasping the vital distinction. "Defenders of the king," he asked, "what do you want for him? If he is innocent, *le peuple* is guilty" (1: 396; December 27, 1792).

As Saint-Just spoke, groups of *sans-culottes*, armed with pikes, were wandering freely in the *Manège*, punctuating the speaker's words with enthusiastic applause. Saint-Just had discovered a potent technique for leading the Convention. Rather than objecting to the "manifestations of popular will" organized by the Commune, he explicated them before the delegates, so that they could be more responsive to the people's wishes. "*Le peuple*," he told his colleagues, "is innocent and good." Saint-Just did not presume to speak for the "poor people"; rather that body was speaking through him.

In the course of these two speeches, Saint-Just took a major ontological step; he disassociated himself from the government and identified himself completely with the carefully defined entity he called the people. Until his execution some twenty months later,

---

praxis but rather of transforming reality or at least the will to transform, to regenerate." "L'Amitié et le droit selon Saint-Just," *AHRF,* 54 (1982), 182.

[6]Eugene Curtis remarked: "Having won his spurs by his striking utterances in connection with the king's trial, he became the spearhead of his party in the great drives against the Girondins, the Hébertists and the Dantonists. The decision to overthrow these groups was of course a party and not an individual decision, but Saint-Just was in each case put forward to give the *coup de grâce*. It is clear that they regarded him as the best speaker for this type of work." *Saint-Just, Colleague of Robespierre* (New York: Octagon, 1973 [1st pub. 1935]), p. 341.

although with Robespierre, he came to dominate the Committee of Public Safety and through it the operations of the government, he presented himself as a powerless emanation of the axiomatically pure people. He did not speak as a representative of a separate body called the government. He frequently alluded to his conviction that "a people has but one dangerous enemy: its government" (2: 76).

Jean-Paul Gross comments, in regard to the kind of aura surrounding Saint-Just, that "it is not as 'archangel of death,' but as talented young politician that Saint-Just first made himself known to his contemporaries."[7] While it is true that the Saint-Just of the Committee of Public Safety and of the missions to the army became a mythical figure of his own making, the essential operative elements of the legend were all in place at the time of the trial: the peculiarly trenchant speech with its metaphysical oppositions between goodness and evil, life and death; the skillful use of implicit menace, in this instance, the grandstands filled with *sans-culottes* recalling fresh memories of the September massacres. At the front, Gross points out, Saint-Just used exemplary instant executions to achieve the same electrifying results.

Saint-Just explained that the French had been frivolous and depraved before the Revolution, but since the people had become sovereign, the reign of egotism was over. Now the wishes of the people could immediately become law, provided that the Convention itself was not treacherous, and an era of justice would be born. The iniquitous past was over, its order of value reversed: "an unfortunate is superior to the goverment and the powers of the earth; he must speak to them as a master" (2: 514).

Thus Saint-Just developed the possibilities of Rousseau abrogation of original sin; the "republic of virtue" offered the humble what Christianity never did: power over the great *in the present,* not some theoretical preference over them in the world to come. If the "government and the powers of the earth" were not sufficiently responsive, "*arm the people,* the people must reign" (1: 356).

The king and the government were separated from the "people" and to the extent that they actively ruled they were culpable. To reign was to impose a will upon a people distinct from its own, to direct its activities toward some mediated goal, to mark distinctions

[7]"Saint-Just en Mission," *ACSJ*, p. 42.

between men. A legitimate leader would lose himself in the people, he would merge with the fatherland, and, far from crossing the will of the sovereign people, he would express it, putting into words the inchoate volation of the masses which he discovered by looking into his own heart. Saint-Just explained that traitors often tried to fool the people with complicated intellectual arguments. As for himself, however, "I know only *just* and *unjust;* these words are understood by all consciences. All definitions must submit to the conscience: the mind is a sophist which leads virtue to the scaffold" (2: 495).

A reigning monarch was irrevocably separated from a people, and its innate purity. Saint-Just's celebrated aphorism, "no one can reign innocently," condemned Louis as the negation of the innocent people, and hence essentially guilty. His rhetoric cut through the complex legal knots the Convention was busily tying in its efforts to avoid pronouncing on Louis's fate. Contemptuously dismissing the squabbling over technicalities, Saint-Just declared the king a being apart, for whom the laws applying to the people were invalid. He then reasoned from Louis's separation to the necessity of his execution: "Since the French *peuple* has demonstrated its will [by invading the Tuileries], everything outside the sovereign is the enemy.... Between the people and its enemies there is nothing in common but the blade" (2: 76). Louis, the "enemy of the people," was a different species from the French people, he was *outside* the city, a "barbarian" (1: 372). The rules that applied to the citizenry were not to be taken into consideration for the outsider. In all of France he was the exceptional one, no appeals to justice could be accepted from him. "Louis," said Saint-Just, "is a stranger in our midst" (1: 370).

Camille Desmoulins, the clever and frequently impudent journalist whose role it was for a time to express the same ideas as Saint-Just and Robespierre in cruder form, commented: "You know very well that to the Republican all men are equal. I am mistaken, you know very well that there is only one man whom the true Republican cannot regard as a man [but] a two-legged cannibal, and that enemy beast is a king."[8]

Saint-Just spoke from a still world of absolutes, he denied process as he denied compromise. Events could reveal the nature of certain persons, they could "lift the mask," or "rend the veil," but they could

---

[8]In Robespierre, *Lettres à ses commettans*, 5: 213.

not be used to judge moral attributes. Just as the people was innocent in Saint-Just's world of existential stasis, the king was guilty, not of this crime or that, but of having been king. It was not the specific acts of treason with which Louis XVI was charged that interested Saint-Just in the least; it was the culpable nature of his being. The handsome, self-possessed, young delegate urged his colleagues to close the gap between themselves and the people by acting directly upon the person of the king, by becoming not only Louis's prosecutor and judge but his executioner as well. "Someday they will be astonished that in the eighteenth century people were less advanced than in Caesar's time: then the tyrant was immolated in the middle of the senate with no more formality than twenty-three strokes of a dagger, and no other law than Roman liberty" (1: 366).

Saint-Just squeezed the Convention between his strangely abstract logic on the one hand, and on the other, his exegesis of the noisy throng in the galleries, evoking the picture of a Commune poised once more to run amok. The delegates, in their extended debates, had been reaching for some sort of compromise formulation among the half-dozen positions to be taken on the question of Louis XVI. Saint-Just denounced conciliation and reduced the delegates to two choices: "I see no middle ground," he told them. "This man must reign or die" (1: 368). The tacit corollary of this maxim, that the delegates themselves might die if the king reigned, was underscored by the restless crowds outside the *Manège* and in the grandstands, imposing their presence on the deputies. Albert Soboul comments: "That the Convention deliberated under the menacing gaze of the galleries, there can be no doubt. What is more, by their applause, or their murmurs, they intervened in the debates."[9]

Some of the bolder representatives complained of the ominous mobs at their elbows. Saint-Just answered them by praising the openness of the trial: "kings used to prosecute virtue in the dark; us, we judge kings before the universe! Our deliberations are public so that no one accuses us of unseemly behavior" (1: 386). When Saint-Just said "we," the referent was not "we representatives." The "we" of whom he spoke was himself, at the podium, and the "people" in the gallery. His colleagues in the Convention were a distant "they," or "those who...," as in a statement from his note-

[9]*Le Procès de Louis XVI*, p. 196.

book after the trial and execution of the Gironde delegates: "Those who govern must be frightened, *le peuple* is never to be frightened" (2: 530).

In Saint-Just's pursuit of the guilty Louis XVI, he had to combat the implicit accusation that the Mountain, using the *sans-culottes* as a weapon, was plotting coward's revenge on a defeated man, rather than planning an act of republican morality. The king had been a virtual prisoner for more than a year, during which time it was said that he and his family were reviled and threatened. Moreover, there were certain ambiguities attached to his actions in office, if not to his general ineptitude. From various accounts Michelet assembled a picture of how Louis appeared on December 11, as his formal arraignment was about to begin: he was "a man like so many others, he seemed like a bourgeois, living off his investments, a family man; he had a simple air about him, a bit near-sighted, his skin already pale from prison; he was sensing death."[10]

The lonely figure of the former king, amid the vociferous throng, aroused some compassion. Louis, the ineffectual, the worried, the fat, utterly lacking the legendary Bourbon panache, seemed to some observers less like a tyrant than a martyr. Proposals were aired to pardon him as a gesture of the generosity of a great Republic,[11] and Saint-Just was challenged to wrest moral superiority from the middle and harness it to the guillotine. To do this he had to overcome the obstacle of Louis's pathos. To vote, in cold blood, to decapitate a man whose actions were open to so many interpretations was difficult for many of the delegates. The task was rendered still more delicate by the fact that they were, by and large, imbued with Rousseau's belief in the moral significance of pity. Man's instinctive, nonintellectual sympathy for the sufferer, to Rousseau, was nature's basic virtue. "What is generosity, clemency, humanity, if not pity applied to the

---

[10]*Histoire de la Révolution française*, 2: 79.

[11]Claude Fauchet commented a few days after the king's execution on the feeling that France had irrevocably demeaned the Revolution by the trial and execution of Louis XVI: "It is not the death of the tyrant which breaks my heart, although a sensitive man is grievously affected by any death which is not ordered by nature or useful to society; the sadness which will follow me to the grave is that my fatherland tarnished its revolution by a fatal act of cruelty, a solemn murder." Fauchet also claimed that the legislators were under constant threat "from brigands" (*Journal des Amis*, Jan. 26, 1793). Also see "Sur le décret de mort contre le ci-devant roi et son exécution," BR, 23: 303.

weak, the guilty, the human species in general?" Rousseau had asked (3: 155). The men of the Convention knew that spontaneous sympathy for the sufferer was the sign of a superior soul. How then could this large assembly vote the death of Louis and still experience itself as one with the "innocent people"?

The answer Saint-Just found in his mentor was that pity was aroused naturally, and hence legitimately, only by the poor, the humble, and the good. As for the wicked, "the pity they inspire is never very keen," Rousseau had pointed out (2: 713). For Rousseau, the only authentic pity was that aroused by suffering innocence; to sympathize with the guilty was to sacrifice the people for the sake of one individual, since "pity for the wicked is a great cruelty toward men" (4: 548).

In his *Lettres à ses commettans* Robespierre put forth Rousseau's argument that pity was the natural principle underlying clemency, and used it to condemn Louis XVI. The king, by violating the "political pact," had entered a state of nature and had to obey its law. But what was the law of nature?

> It imposes a double duty upon men; the first is that of seeing to their own conservation, from which derives the right to punish all those who attack their liberty or their security; the second is to help our oppressed fellow men, from which, again, is derived the right to punish those who oppress them. Because next to the penchant which leads us to defend our existence, nature has placed the imperious feeling of compassion, which is but an emanation of the first penchant. [5: 58]

Rousseau's dual-instinct theory is recognizable here; compassion in only an "emanation" of the impulse toward self-protection, and the self empathizes with the one he perceives to be the victim. Thus, Robespierre insisted, one must not ask the question: "Is it necessary to inflict punishment upon Louis, dethroned, powerless, abandoned at this hour?" (4: 59). The real question was: "Have not all nations until now been granted the right to strike tyrants down, and has not the admiration of the centuries put such courageous acts on the level of the most sublime characteristics of virtue?" (4: 58).

Saint-Just, whose discourses were in philosophic harmony with Robespierre's, denounced pity for Louis as aristocratic wickedness toward the people. Counterrevolutionaries "try to stir up pity, soon they will buy some tears, they will do anything to touch our sympathies, to corrupt us" (1: 372). The spontaneous sympathy natural to the people was being exploited by the enemy, who used it against them: "This humanity they talk to you about is cruelty toward the people; this pardon they are looking to suggest is the death sentence of liberty" (1: 396).

Since Louis was a priori guilty because of his separation from the "people," Saint-Just showed that his actions were irrelevant to his trial. Whatever Louis did was *by definition* intended to harm the people. Acts of kindness toward his subjects only demonstrated that he was a hypocrite as well as a tyrant. That Louis used to distribute alms to the poor—by late eighteenth-century standards an act of exemplary virtue—only betrayed his corrupt essence. Saint-Just point-ed out how Louis's charity could be but a sham, one so vile as to cast a shadow on virtue itself. "Louis insulted virtue," he said, "to whom will it ever appear innocent again?" (1: 392).[12]

Distinguishing act from intention, Saint-Just reserved moral judg-ments exclusively for the latter. Intention alone was the criterion of guilt or innocence, and intentions, one's own or other people's, were known by reference to the "public conscience," moral analogue of the "general will." The public conscience was "composed of the people's inclination toward the general good. Respect the mind, but rely on the heart" (2: 374). Those delegates whose hearts were attuned to the public conscience would realize that Louis was an unusually cruel tyrant precisely because he behaved so well. His reign was "the first under the sun, in recorded history, [where] the system of the king's tyranny was sweetness and the appearance of goodness; everywhere he put himself in the place of the fatherland and tried to alienate affection belonging only to it" (1: 391).

Saint-Just demonstrated that the king's only authentic existence was as the people's enemy. The people fused to form one innocent body, the fatherland, menced by its archetypal Nemesis incarnate in Louis XVI. Saint-Just described the day of August 10, when Louis sought refuge in the Assembly itself. Rather than seeing him as a fugitive from a mob, Saint-Just reversed the situation so that it was

[12]Le Père Duchesne vulgarised Saint-Just's chillingly elegant pronouncement as follows: "From the priests...Louis XVI learned the art of fooling men and hiding a gangrenous heart and a soul of clay under the mask of virtue....His wife and the little bugger are still alive, you will have no peace until they are destroyed," BR, 23: 313.

the king who brutalized the body politic: "He forced his way into the bowels of the Fatherland with blows of his sword," said Saint-Just, "in order to hide himself inside" (1: 395).

Saint-Just's rhetoric transcended itself in this passage: the body of the fatherland, passive and patient in its innocence, had been violated by the aggression of the hated stranger. The galleries, according to Michelet's rather romantic account, were effectively aroused by Saint-Just's eloquence: "they felt the hand of a master and trembled with joy" (2: 79). Saint-Just drew the necessary conclusions from his argument; the Convention had to choose between a corrupt sentimental pity for the king as man, and its duty to punish a being whose very essence was tyranny. "The Fatherland is in your midst," he said, "choose between it and the king, between the exercise of the people's justice and the exercise of your personal weakness" (1: 399).

It is interesting to note how the king's defense attorney, De Seze, attempted to answer the charges brought against the prisoner: "Here is my response," he said, "I read in Jean-Jacques Rousseau these words: 'Neither the law which condemns nor the judge who sentences can abide by the general will because the general will cannot, as general will, pronounce upon either a man or an act.' Thus spoke Louis before the bar, thus spoke Rousseau, instructing the peoples about liberty" (Jaurès, 4: 284).

Despite the appeal of Rousseau's authority, of 749 delegates, 387 voted to behead Louis. The age of despotism was over, France was about to embark upon an era of peace and unity. "With the kings," said Saint-Just, "all systems of violence have been destroyed" (2: 360).

The trial and execution of Louis XVI are of interest from a variety of perspectives. The question of whether he was legally guilty, or whether the actions of the Convention were appropriate, of what results the verdict had for the future of the Revolution have been disputed since the trial began. What is significant from the point of view of this book, however, is the nature of the argument put forth most effectively by Saint-Just and the way this model of justice was to gain ascendancy over previous standards in the months to come. The essential quality of the accused, as evaluated by the hearts of pure patriots, would come to be the criterion of guilt or innocence, and behavior would not only be discounted, but labeled a subversive consideration. Cobban comments: "The trial and execution of the King proved to be the first of a long series of political trials and condemnations, in the course of which all ideas of judicial impartiality vanish."[13] The very expression, "judicial impartiality," implies a set of cold, intellectualized, procedure-ridden attitudes which the republic of virtue wished to replace with a more emotionally immediate and hence morally superior method of justice.

[13]*Aspects of the French Revolution,* p. 171.

CHAPTER TEN

The ·Widening Circle;
The Narrowing Way

From the declaration of the Republic on September 21, 1792, until the fall of the Committee of Public Safety on 9 thermidor, an II (July 27, 1794), the "republic of virtue" generated two seemingly antithetical discursive motions: at once an ever-widening spiral of social and political theoretical writings, stimulated by the necessity of creating a new constitution, and at the same time a narrowing definition of which inhabitants of France were worthy of being called "the people."

It was as if the fall of Louis XVI released great surges of authorial energy that had remained in check as long as the dynasty was still, however marginally, on the throne. France crossed the threshold into a new world with the removal of Louis, one where the people, at last, were sovereign, and the old forces of evil inherent in the monarchy were abolished. Henceforth France's history would be narrated by its elected representative body as conscious and rational author, never again by the convoluted whims of its numerous privileged ranks. "The people" had become both the collective hero and the narrator of a new history. With the seed of evil destroyed, however, evidence of continuing wickedness required constant refining of the definition of "the people."

The new constitution, which was presented on June 24, 1793, but never put into practice, was accompanied by Robespierre's version of the "Rights of Man and of Citizens," by a civil code, and by projects to establish a system of education. It was the society as a whole, the

Jacobins had learned from Rousseau, which formed men, and efforts to lead them to virtue without destroying monarchical social structures and replacing them with republican ones were bound to fail. The question of education, therefore, underlay all other concerns.

Jacques-Nicolas Billaud-Varenne, deputy from Paris to the National Convention, member of the Committee of Public Safety, and friend of Robespierre until the eve of Thermidor, composed the *Eléments du républicanisme*,[1] which consisted largely of paraphrases of the *Contrat social* and elaborations of Rousseau's arguments. "A heart jaded from the cradle by vicious institutions," he said, "believes in nothing, it doesn't even believe in the possibility of virtue, which it labels pride or stupidity" (p. 9). The revolutionaries had to face up to their responsibility to "raise men to virtue." "You will lose the younger generation," Billard-Varenne warned, "by abandoning it to parents with prejudices and ignorance who give it the defective tint which they have themselves. Therefore, let the fatherland take hold of children who are born for it alone and let it begin by plunging them into the Styx, like Achilles" (p. 57). "Once, however, public modesty is reestablished in all hearts, from then on the citizens will learn to esteem each other as men, and to cherish each other as brothers" (p. 10).

Billaud-Varenne praised the educational efficacy of Sparta, which he termed a "magnanimous nation." "There is the obvious effect of the return to virtue, and this example demonstrates that the transition from depraved morals to austere morals can take place, and more easiy and more rapidly than the perversion of an honest heart. How could anyone have questioned that man was born with an irresistible disposition toward searching for and cherishing virtue?" (p. 38).

In debates on the question of educating the citizenry to virtue, the validity of Jean-Jacques Rousseau's great texts was at issue. Condorcet,

[1]Paris: chez citoyen, l'an I; BN microfiche 6106. Gérard Walter describes Billaud-Varenne as the "mind and the soul of the conspiracy of 9 thermidor." Walter recounts how Billaud-Varenne rose from obscurity, as late as 1791, to membership in the Committee of Public Safety on the strength of his rhetoric. He displayed mastery of the same Rousseauvian political lexicon which Robespierre and Saint-Just were able to command. His rationale for executions under the Terror, for example, followed the organicist model that Rousseau had shaped so memorably: "it is time to restore robust health to the body politic at the expense of its gangrenous members." Quoted in Walter, *La Conjuration du neuf thermidor* (Paris: Gallimard, 1974), p. 73.

The revolutionary calendar, surmounted by a panorama of the "Holy Mountain," under the watchful eye of Surveillance and flanked by portraits of the martyred Le Pelletier de Saint Fargeau and Marat. (Courtesy of the Bibliothèque nationale, Paris)

[184]

the celebrated mathematician, friend and disciple of the Encyclopedists, had prepared a detailed plan for the reformation of education
under the Legislative Assembly, one which, in its broad scope and
democratic aspirations, offered a basis for pedagogical legislation on
liberal, Encyclopedist lines,[2] Durand-Maillane, deputy from Bouches-
du-Rhône, attacked it as promoting the materialism, immorality, and
atheism of the philosophes rather than following the wisdom of
Rousseau, who had shown the unfortunate effects of the intellectual
life upon virtue. Jacob Dupont, deputy from Indre-et-Loire and
admirer of the Encyclopedists, denounced both Durand-Maillane
and Rousseau for equating ignorance with virtue:

> Durand-Maillane has dared to repeat, even after August 10, the soph-
> isms and the paradoxes of the Genevan philosopher who [said] that the
> sciences and the arts corrupt morals: I ask Durand-Maillane, in the
> presence of Brutus' image and that of Jean-Jacques himself, who armed
> the brave men of Marseilles against the kings and royalty? Was it the
> prejudices and ignorance of the sixteenth century or the philosophy
> and the enlightenment at the end of the eighteenth century? What is
> this so-called corruption of morals, then, so much exaggerated that
> according to our critics one would have to think that virtue and probity
> would soon be exiled from the land of liberty? I will confess that
> Durand-Maillane's assertions seemed most strange to me, when he
> wanted to circumscribe within certain limits man's reason, or, following
> the example of the despot, give one direction rather than another to the
> thought and the hand of man, whereas, under the republican regime,
> man's thoughts and man's hand can go in all directions and take all
> possible forms in widening his domain.

As for teaching religion in the public schools, Dupont was absolutely
opposed: "Nature and reason," he said, "these are the gods of man"
(Jaurès, 8: 10–12).

Dupont's liberal, open-ended idea of education, inherited from

---

[2]*Mémoires sur l'éducation publique*, ed. Gabriel Compayre (Paris: Hachette, 1883). For
a discussion of Condorcet's report on public instruction, see F. de la Fontainerie,
French Liberalism and Education in the Eighteenth Century (New York: Franklin, 1971).
Renée Waldinger discusses education and its relation to human progress in "Condorcet:
The Problematic Nature of Progress," *Condorcet Studies I*, ed. Leonora Cohen Resenfield
(Atlantic Highlands, N.J.: Humanities Press, 1984), pp. 117–29. In the same volume
see also M. Albertone: "Enlightenment and Revolution: The Evolution of Condorcet's
Ideas on Education," pp. 131–44.

the philosophes, did not correspond to the Jacobin vision of an interventionist training which would totally regenerate mankind and lead it to certain predetermined ends. It was the educational project of Michel Le Pelletier de Saint-Fargeau, former great noble elected to the Convention from the department of Yonne, which was to receive Jacobin endorsement and would eventually, after the assassination of Le Pelletier, be reformulated for presentation by Robespierre to the Convention.[3] The project called for all children to be taken from their parents and raised by the state, free of charge, from the age of five until twelve for boys, and eleven for girls, "all children, without distinction and without exception, will be raised in common at the expense of the Republic and all, under the holy law of equality, will receive the same clothing, the same nourishment, the same instruction, the same care."

Le Pelletier, like Rousseau, saw in education the real source of national character, and believed that as long as children continued to be raised at home, they would develop as egotistical individuals with family ties, rather than as citizens completely devoted to the state. The attachment to family life had to be broken; "thus will be formed a new race, laborious, regulated, disciplined, one which an impenetrable barrier will separate from the impure contact with our obsolete species."

Obligatory state boarding schools not only would separate the children of the rich from their corrupt families; they would benefit the poor as well. Just as Rousseau had described population growth leading to the degradation of primitive man, Le Pelletier saw the growth of the family as a source of its corruption among the poor. "The birth of a child is an accident," he said, and sometimes parents were consoled at the death of their child by the thought that "it is

[3]I am following the modernized spelling used by Gérard Walter rather than the alternate, Lepeletier, used in some texts. Michel's brother, Félix Le Pelletier de Saint-Fargeau, anxious to defend the project against charges of being "Utopian," demonstrated more fraternal sentiment than education himself: "A utopia! that's how they tried to denigrate the lofty thoughts of Plato and Thomas More: shades of my brother, be consoled!" (Jaurès, 8: 27). Gérard Walter (*Robespierre*, 2: 487) quotes a curious passage from the comments of Félix concerning Robespierre's acquisition of the manuscript which implies that Robespierre took the project away from Félix and presented it as his own, which might account for the odd blend of adherence to and rejection of Le Pelletier's ideas. On the other hand, Félix's post-thermidorian memory may not be reliable.

one less burden." "Useful and unfortunate citizens," he wrote, "perhaps soon this burden will cease to be one; perhaps, returned to financial ease and the delicious impulses of nature, you will be able to give children to the fatherland without regret" (Jaurès, 8:25).

Robespierre, presenting this project before the Convention, commented: "Man is good, coming from the hands of nature: whoever denies this must not think of educating man" (5: 207). Hence, "if nature created man good, it is back to nature that we must bring him." It was in that perspective that the legislators were to consider Le Pelletier's proposals. The new government of France would do for the citizen what nature did for primitive man: permit him to couple without needing to concern himself with the upbringing of his offspring. Thus sexuality would be divorced from responsibility, in the name not of vice, as under the *ancien régime,* but of virtue, for the children would be raised to a higher level of morality simply by being separated from their parents and experiencing equality. "Treated all the same, nourished all the same, dressed all the same, taught all the same, these young students will know equality not as a specious theory but as continually effective practice." Le Pelletier then applied himself to the practical application of such a program, including such details as diet (wine and meat must be excluded), and ways of making it financially feasible for the hard-pressed revolutionary government.

Le Pelletier's program, as opposed to Condorcet's plan, would represent a real break with the family patterns of the past. The child raised according to his scenario would have a fundamentally different experience of life from that of his parents and would have a relationship to the state that the older generation could never know. The problem of morally tainted stock passing its stigma on to the future would be solved. As the Girondin leader Ducos expressed it in December 1792, "Using Plutarch's words, as long as you have not molded on the same form of virtue all the children of the Republic, it is in vain that your laws proclaim the holy law of equality" (Jaurès, 8: 32).

Le Pelletier's ideas, however, regulated the life of the child only from five years until eleven or twelve. How was the Republic to mold the citizenry to virtue the rest of the time? In his *Institutions républicaines,* Saint-Just addressed himself to this question. These fragments were apparently produced over a five-year span, from the early days of the Revolution up to the very eve of Thermidor, since they contain references to situations that events of the Terror superseded, as well as remarks which must have had reference to the Terror. The bulk of the manuscript, however, appears to have been written in the winter of 1792–93. Composed during odd moments of a period of extreme tension, while Saint-Just was shouldering tremendous responsibilities as a member of the Committee of Public Safety and as a representative on mission, the *Institutions républicaines* narrate a sort of Utopian daydream, a "pays des chimères," a lost Eden to be refound, interpolated with phrases that might be entries in an intimate journal. Thus the depiction of an ideal world is strikingly punctuated by anguished references to the actual situation.

Saint-Just's peculiarly terse syntax, what Albert Camus called his *"style guillotine,"* was not peripheral to his vision of France but was an integral part of it. He put forth his ideas in a series of somber aphorisms, as if the words caused him pain. Saint-Just, like Rousseau, labeled verbosity the curse of the ruling class, the symbol of the vices of the *ancien régime.* The monarchy, "effeminately" garrulous, displayed its corruption in gushes of words. The male republic of virtue would utter only sibylline pronouncements. What Rousseau had said about the difference between Sparta and Athens applied to the distinction between the monarchy and the republic: "Ever made to conquer, [the Spartans] crushed their enemies in every sort of war, and the blabbering Athenians feared their words as much as their bodies" (4: 362). The ideal republican would use speech like a sword. As Roland Barthes has remarked: "The Revolutionary script was like the entelechy of the Revolutionary legend: it intimidated and imposed civic consecration of bloodshed."[4]

The laws themselves had to embody a lapidary ideal; "It is impossible," said Saint-Just, "to govern without laconism. Long laws are public calamities. There must be few laws." As for the verbal playfulness of the *ancien régime,* which Rousseau had so often denounced, Saint-Just recognized that "he who makes jokes while at the head of state tends toward tyranny" (2: 504). To make a joke while in a position of power implies the existence of a hiatus between the thought and the word, a moment of nonengagement between the speaker and his listeners. But the object of the Revolution, as it

---

[4]*Le Degré zéro de l'écriture* (Paris: Seuil, 1953), p. 20.

emerges from the writings of Saint-Just, had been precisely the elimination of all distinctions between the ruler and the ruled; in fact, the elimination of all separate consciousness.

The stark language of the *Institutions*, marked by the present tense, short phrases with few dependent clauses, and a paucity of adjectives and conjunctions, was the stylistic manifestation of the Plutarchian political aesthetic that Rousseau had done so much to popularize. Saint-Just's style, a striking example of this aesthetic, by the fact of its very existence reproached the specious vacuity of the aristocratic ideal.

Saint-Just used the word "institutions" as Rousseau had defined it in the political writings and the *Lettre à d'Alembert*: a group of idiosyncratic habits, traditions, and prohibitions enunciated by a "legislator" and in some unspecified way incorporated into the mental life of the people, thus setting it apart from all others.[5] Saint-Just, seeing himself as the next great "legislator," pronounced the "institutions" as statements of fact, as descriptions of real life in a dream world, as though that world already existed.[6]

The picture of Saint-Just's perfect republic which emerges from the *Institutions* bore little resemblance to eighteenth-century France.

---

[5]M. Abensour, in an article "Les Institutions, le législateur et le peuple," *ACSJ*, states that "Saint-Just conceives the project of a total revolution. Republican ideology is a real cement which, by means of institutions, penetrates the ensemble of real connections between men and thus all levels of the social totality." Abensour concludes: "We are thus a long way from ... Rousseau. The institution is not merely the oblique way, it is not to be confused with manipulation, it does not play upon emotion and pleasure, it is founded upon setting the example and values" (p. 282). In addition, he comments: "It is ... within the problem of the relations between legislator and people that Saint-Just formulates the notion of institution.—And above all, it is by this notion that he attempts to escape from this area and its constraints, and to break its magic circle" (p. 241). This, however, seems compatible with Rousseau's prescriptions concerning the primacy of "institutions" over laws, and it is difficult to understand in what way Saint-Just's concept is "a long way from Rousseau," except in the fine details of what sorts of "institutions" would be appropriate to which peoples.

[6]Saint-Just remarked: "The most tender heart aided by the most lively imagination scarcely conceives the first society so great has been the alteration in the human spirit." François Theuriot comments: "We must not let ourselves be fooled by the word 'heart.' The alliance of this word with the verb *conceive* shows very well, on the contrary, that it is a question of knowledge and not the domain of sentiment." "Saint-Just, esprit et conscience publique," *AHRF*, no. 191 (1968), 121. But Theuriot is ignoring one of the basic principles of the republic of virtue: knowledge and sentiment are not separate faculties, as under the corrupt old regime, but are inextricably wed in the heart of the good patriot.

It was rather like a stage-setting for a stylized tableau, inspired by Plutarch and Rousseau in his Spartan manifestation. It was a landscape dominated by the arresting moral posture, where Cornelia reigned at last undisputed and only the Gracchi had rights to the city. The atmosphere was one of austere exaltation, at once lofty and menacing, a France contemptuous of Caesar and intoxicated with Brutus. It was a world bathed in mysterious divine presence, in which the concerns of everyday reality would have seemed irrelevant if not tasteless. Most of the fragments dealt with the morality of the people; economic and political questions were treated secondarily and strictly from a moral perspective.

Three areas were accorded special importance: education, the office of censor of morals, and the question of adoption and inheritance. The last appears to have been a matter of great personal concern to the orphaned Saint-Just.

The description of education began with the "institutionalization" of breastfeeding, that practice which, since Rousseau, had become so intimately linked with the virtue of the whole family.[7] "Children belong to their mother until the age of five, if she has nursed them, and to the republic after that, until death. The mother who has not nursed her baby ceases to be a mother in the eyes of the fatherland" (2: 516–17). Thus Saint-Just's state would ensure a proper republican beginning to the citizen's life by reinforcing nature's will with the force of national sentiment, or perhaps of law. Unlike Le Pelletier, Saint-Just would not turn the child back to the family at eleven or twelve, but would surrender him to the republic for life. He provided no other details of the children's upbringing until the age of five, when they were to be segregated by sex, the boys being sent to "schools in the country" for their common education. There they were to dress in cloth, sleep eight hours a night on mats, eat only roots, fruits, legumes, dairy products, and bread, and drink only water. They might not be petted or struck. They would learn to read, write, and swim. Above all, they must learn to be still. "Chil-

---

[7]Cissie Fairchilds points out while attitudes toward the family had undergone marked change in the decade preceding the Revolution, in the 1780s "the fashion for maternal nursing was most prevalent in the upper levels of society." *Domestic Enemies: Servants and Their Masters in Old Regime France* (Baltimore: The Johns Hopkins University Press, 1984), p. 215.

dren are raised," said Saint-Just, "to love silence and to hold chatterers in contempt. They are trained for laconism" (2: 517).

"From age ten to sixteen, the education of children is military and agricultural." Saint-Just described adolescents as being grouped into bands of sixty, "for the study of cavalry maneuvers and all tactical exercises." Besides performing these military efforts, they would be "distributed to farmers, at harvest time." From sixteen until twenty-one, boys were to undergo specialized training in farming, manufacturing, or the navy. During this period they might wear a special outfit, the "costume of the arts," provided they had "swum across a river before the eyes of the people, the day of the youth festival." From twenty-one until twenty-five, they were part of the national militia.

The education of girls, however, was dismissed summarily in two sentences. "Girls are raised in the maternal home," Saint-Just specified; further, "on holidays a virgin over the age of ten may not appear in public without her mother, father, or tutor."

One emotional tie was institutionalized to permeate this otherwise abstemious society: masculine friendship. Friendship, the nonbiological tie, neither dictated by the family nor linked to procreation, was elevated to the level of a national principle.[8] "Every man twenty-five years old," Saint-Just stated, "is obliged to declare in the temple who his friends are. This declaration must be renewed every year during the month of ventôse. If a man abandons his friend, he must explain his reasons before the people, in the temples.... If he refuses, he is banished" (2: 519). Saint-Just, like Rousseau, envisaged friendship as an underlying impulsion toward virtue; friends were put side by side in combat; a Theban band, they wore mourning for each other. If one committed a crime, the other was banished. As for "the one who says he does not believe in friendship, or has no friend, he is banished" (2: 519). Thus the state was to give legal preeminence to a male-couple bond while the importance of family structures was lessened.

Saint-Just looked to banishment to resolve the problem of the individual who rejected his "institutions." His republic rarely punished

[8]See Fortunat, "L'Amitié et le droit selon Saint-Just," for an analysis of how Saint-Just's concept of friendship was related to his program for "regenerating humanity."

evil-doers; instead it purged itself of those who refused to accept its virtue. The idler was banished, as were the official "convicted of leading a bad life" and the desecrator of tombs. In this way evil was constantly flushed from the body politic, leaving it cleansed of impurities. The same thinking led Saint-Just to purge the foreigner, for it was he who introduced corruption into France. It was the alien, who, "from vicissitude to vicissitude has led us to his ends," and who, Saint-Just said elsewhere, "troubles our repose." According to Saint-Just, it is "the foreign influence which forms traitors, or has the Gracchi killed, causes crime to be honored and virtue proscribed" (2: 509). The good state would expel all elements which resisted the fusion in virtue with the body politic.

The second key institution of the republic of virtue would be a class of "censors" or "magistrates to provide the example of morals." Saint-Just described this institution in two fragments. "In every revolution," he wrote, "it is necessary to have a dictator to save the State by force, or censors to save it by virtue" (2: 530). The censors would be chosen from the men who had reached the age of sixty: "Men who have always led blameless lives will wear a white sash at the age of sixty. They will present themselves for this purpose in the temple on the day of the festival of old age, to be judged by their fellow citizens. If no one accuses them, they will take the white sash. Respect for old age is a cult in our society" (2: 526).

These "men of the white sash" were charged with performing various services in the community; for example, "they kept incense burning in the temple." Their principal function, however, was supervising the morals of public officials, army officers, and elected representatives. They were to rid high office of corruption. These awesome figures pursued their ends in a Saint-Justian silence: "It is forbidden for censors to speak in public" (2: 531).

Saint-Just's *Institutions* stand halfway between literature and political rhetoric. After Thermidor a project for a decree was found among his papers, one proposing the establishment of a class of censors. Saint-Just restated the arguments he had put forth in the *Institutions* but now declared: "The Committee of Public Safety has charged me with presenting the following decree" (2: 538). He then went on to dictate the terms of an actual law, establishing censors in each district in France. "This censorship is exercised upon the government," he stipulated, "and cannot be exercised upon the incorruptible people." The articles of the decrees are either para-phrases of the *Institutions* or word-for-word transpositions. Only the matter of white-sashed sexagenarians is omitted. It is not possible to ascertain, at this point, whether the Committee of Public Safety had charged Saint-Just with such a decree or whether it belonged to the private world of his imagination.

On July 13, 1793, a few months after Saint-Just had probably written most of his *Institutions*, Robespierre presented the Convention with his version of Le Pelletier's plan for education. He began by declaring the importance of the subject. "The National Convention owes three monuments to history," he declared, "the Constitution, the code of civil laws, and public education." It is to be noted that none of these three objects had been achieved under the old regime, the first being traditional rather than transcribed, the second being particular rather than general, and the third being the concern of the church and not of the state. "Let us give them the perfection of which they are susceptible!" he continued. "For the glory of conquests and victories is sometimes ephemeral, but beautiful institutions remain and they immortalize nations." Thus, once more, education was seen as an "institution," in its particular Rousseauvian sense, with all the overtones of creating a way of life that would be the envy of the ages. In reference to Le Pelletier's plan, Robespierre remarked: "I confess that what has been said up until now does not correspond to the idea I have formed for myself of a complete plan for education. I have dared to conceive vaster thoughts; and considering to what point the human species is degraded by the vice of our former social system, I am convinced of the necessity of operating a total regeneration, and, if I may express myself in this way, of creating a new people."

Robespierre's Rousseauvian argument has two interesting characteristics here: both origins and ends are absolutes. Robespierre does not present himself as wishing to consolidate the ideas of Le Pelletier, to be part of an on-going group enterprise concerned with national education; he is impelled to negate Le Pelletier's text in order to substitute, in toto, his own. His aims, too, are not reform or improvement of existent humanity but the creation of a "new people."

He addresses the distinction between "education" and "instruction." The latter, concerned with intellectual achievements, was adequately dealt with by Le Pelletier, in Robespierre's opinion, and in any case was of secondary importance. "Education," on the other hand, "must be common to everyone and universally beneficial. [The Committee] has entirely neglected it." Before the question of instruction, Robespierre placed priority upon the necessity for "institution": "For my part, I believed we had to lay foundations for the institution of the public before instruction. The latter profits a few people, the former is for the good of all. Instruction propagates useful knowledge, institutions create and propagate necessary habits" (10: 31). Thus Robespierre, while modifying Le Pelletier's script, incorporated it into a bold new program for France, one designed to move from the page into the lives of the people, destroying the "aristocratic" mentality inherent in family life and substituting for it a new consciousness, one derived from institutions generating a virtuous race.

The National Convention met as usual on January 21, 1793, the day that Louis XVI was executed and the day after Michel Le Pelletier had been assassinated. News of the two killings contrasted in disquieting ways, from the perspective of the republic of virtue. Saint-Just, Robespierre, and Marat had repeatedly issued warning notices that acts of government were by their very nature suspect, and that popular sovereignty was best expressed by the spontaneous uprising of the people against disloyal deputies. Marat, whose publications pushed each credo to its limit, had just stated that while popular sovereignty was the sacred principle of the Republic, "there is only one case where the people can exercise the act of sovereignty, in applying it to the Declaration of Rights" by declaring that all laws "the people" judged not in accord with it would be met by armed resistance.[9]

In that light, the ceremonial execution of Louis XVI by the government and the spontaneous assassination of Le Pelletier by an enraged citizen seemed to reverse the proper order of things. An effort was needed to relocate the radiating center of virtue firmly back in the Mountain. The Convention, meeting on January 21, rather than seeming triumphant at having destroyed the monarchy, was, according to the *Moniteur*, seized with an epidemic of suspicion. As the session began: "Rovère and Chabot denounced Chambon.

---

[9]"Opinion de Marat sur l'appel au peuple," *L'Ami du Peuple*, January 18, 1793, reprinted p. 268.

Jeanbon Saint-André denounced a poster of Valadi's. Garran denounced a poster exhorting the people to save Louis. Goupilleau announced that he was almost executed in a cafe. Carrier denounced Thibaut." Pétion, presiding, at length attempted to stem the flood of accusations. He said it was a pity that the deputies "only greeted each other with a suspicious air and that trust was banished from the assembly" (BR 23: 5). He was interrupted and the denunciations and counterthreats continued.

Marat, who had written of his wish that Louis's death, "far from troubling the peace of the state, would serve only to affirm it" (*OM*, p. 271), published a disillusioned text after he witnessed the uproar at the assembly. "Vain hope! The very evening of the victim's inhumation, [disputes] broke out with fury over the nomination of a new president.... Men don't change their hearts... so it is not a matter of living in peace with them, but of declaring an eternal war upon them" (*OM*, p. 273).

Newspaper accounts from the weeks following Louis's execution indicate that it neither unified nor purified France. Roland was accused of treason and Buzot complained that the Committee of General Security was arresting too many people on vague grounds. The Abbaye was again filled with prisoners. "It is very important that the individual liberty of the citizens be respected," Buzot said, "and the Committee of General Security harms it every day. Nobody dares to speak his piece frankly anymore, everyone is afraid of being sent to the Abbaye where memories of September 2 [an allusion to the massacres] await him" (BR 23: 404). His words were greeted with "violent muttering."

Robespierre held that "the punishment of the tyrant made the principles of equality real. Since then a great number of those who used to blaspheme against the republic have been reduced to rendering homage to it, as hypocrisy renders homage to virtue, by adopting its forms and stammering its language" (5: 304).

Jacobin language had undergone a narrowing corresponding to Jacobin orthodoxy. The speeches and publications of the following months show an ever-shrinking vocabulary repeating, with hypnotic regularity, certain key words: "virtue," "people," "pure," and "mass," were contrasted with "vice," "enemies," "corrupt," and "individuals." I have not attempted to find synonyms for these words in translating because the sparse lexicon is an integral element of revolutionary Rousseauvian virtue.[10] A more varied, supple style might be more palatable to the modern reader but it would betray the profound significance of Jacobin discourse, its exact correspondence with feelings of political virtue, not elegance or aesthetic felicity. Robespierre refused to be satisfied that the wicked had ceased to pose a threat, however, even when they spoke the prescribed language.

> All the vices engendered by tyranny have not disappeared with the tyrant; the corrupt minority of the nation struggles against the wholesome majority, not without advantages because they are the most educated, the most scheming, the cleverest in the art of speaking and swaying the public.... They favor with all their power the rich egotists and the enemies of equality. Liberty would have long been established among us if individuals were as pure as the mass of the nation. [5: 304–5]

Robespierre presented the virtuous people as the reality of France, and it was his duty to speak for it and to denounce its enemies. During the trial of the king he had described "the people," as that entity appeared to him; never a throng of individuals, it constituted but one single, uncorrupted being. "Look at *le peuple*, when they speak to him of his rights and his interests, see if he is not grave and attentive. See how afflicted he seems, when he notices that his delegates are deliberating on public safety with scandalous levity" (5: 128 [December 14, 1792]).

In February 1793, however, Robespierre declared that the "enemies of the people" were disguising themselves as the "people." Shortages of food and other basic necessities occasioned riots and looting of grocers' and butchers' shops. In an effort to appease the hungry, proposals were made to restrict hoarding, to regulate prices and trade, and even to limit the legal significance of property.[11] Robespierre expressed opposition to direct measures of reducing

[10]Barthes comments on a paradox of revolutionary discourse: "This writing, which shows all the signs of inflation, was nonetheless exact. Never has language been at the same time more unlikely and less false." *Degré zéro de l'écriture*, p. 20.

[11]Restrictions on the rights of property discussed by Robespierre at this time were, according to Albert Soboul, less an expression of ideology than a response to specific emergencies: "These Rousseauistic themes were brought forward by Robespierre in the spring of 1793, under the pressure of events: 'the force of things,' Saint-Just will say, let us call it the logic of facts, the necessities of war, the imperatives of revolutionary defense, and not an abstract ideological view." "Jean-Jacques Rousseau et le jacobinisme," *JECS*, p. 420.

the drastic disparity between the rich and the poor, on the grounds that it was precisely this gap which ensured the superior virtue of the impecunious classes:

> It is much more important to make poverty honorable than to proscribe opulence. Fabricius' thatched cottage has nothing to envy in Crassus' palace. For my part, I would rather be the son of Aristides, raised at the expense of the Republic, than the heir apparent of Xerxes, born in the filth of royal courts, to occupy a throne decorated with the degradation of peoples and glittering with public misery. [April 23, 1793]

He made it clear that the poor did not wish to own "the treasures of Crassus. For pure and elevated souls there are more precious goods than those. The riches which lead to so much corruption are more harmful to those who possess them than to those who are deprived of them" (4: 117).

According to the *Moniteur*, inflation and shortages were rampant. The government seemed loath to take strong measures to protect the poor, who were suffering acutely from high prices, the scarcity of basic provisons, and the irritating systems of distribution which involved endless waiting before the baker's and the grocer's. Olwen Hufton states categorically that "ultimately when death and diseases came in 1794 all the poor were to be affected by the total failure of French Revolutionary legislation on poor relief."[12] Fights erupted in the working-class neighborhoods of Saint-Antoine, Saint-Marceau, and Saint-Martin, where throngs of men and women broke into shops and took merchandise, often leaving behind, as was customary, what they considered to be a fair price for the items commandeered.

In Robespierre's texts, these uprisings were subject to conflicting interpretations. Since he had consistently stated that *le peuple* were always pure, "closer to nature and less depraved than the vile egotists" (4: 116), he could not reconcile with his beliefs the notion that they would break into grocery stores. The people with whom Robespierre described himself as identified so compellingly took the Bastille, they took the king from the Tuileries, they even, in their justifiable rage, took the prisoners from the Abbaye and killed them.

---

[12]"Women in Revolution," *French Society and the Revolution*, ed. Douglas Johnson (Cambridge: Cambridge University Press, 1976), p. 155.

They did not take sugar and coffee. The solution to the problem had to be that those who snatched foreign luxury items from the stores were not *le peuple*. This was the conclusion Robespierre advanced:

> What is there in common between the people of Paris and a mob of women, led by valets of the aristocracy, by disguised valets; a gathering the fine *sans-culottes* took absolutely no part in, in which the citizens of the Saint-Antoine and Saint-Marceau *faubourgs* had no part whatsoever? Is it the people, it is patriots who dared to cry "Long live Louis XVII [the imprisoned Dauphin], the hell with the Jacobins, the hell with the Mountain and the Paris deputies"? Overturn the Bastille, destroy royalty, conquer tyrants and destroy traitors, that's what patriots do, those are the exploits of the people of Paris: everything else belongs to the people's enemies. [5: 344 (April 6, 1793)]

For the first time Robespierre's text denounced crowds of working-class Parisians, or those alleged to be so described.[13] The virtuous people whose every impulse Robespierre said he discovered by looking into his own heart was now defined as distinct from those who looted shops. "The people can put up with hunger," he commented, "but not with crime; *le peuple* is able to sacrifice everything except its virtues" (10: 560).

Robespierre stated that he, like the people, like Rousseau, was fated to suffer for his virtue. Persecution was inextricably wed to exemplary goodness, as in the case of his mentor. "Oh thou, true and sublime friend of humanity, who was persecuted by envy, intrigue and despotism," he apostrophized, "immortal Jean-Jacques" (4: 123). Callier (commissioner of national accounting) wrote to him (25 prairial, year II), telling him that his enemies were attempting to prove that "Robespierre was not always in agreement with himself. The enemies of Jean-Jacques did the same thing," Callier reminded Robespierre, "and they went so far as to slander the first apostle of the rights of man" (4: 131).

[13]Soboul saw the moment of disengagement between the idealized "people" of the Jacobins and the *sans-culotte* societies as being a critical juncture for the Revolution. "To understand the evolution of revolutionary institutions, one cannot overemphasize the importance of this attitude on Robespierre's part. For the first time the incompatibility of the essentially Jacobin revolutionary government and *sans-culotte* democracy was affirmed. It did not suffice to restrict the activity of the societies more and more. To force then to dissolve, they had to be discredited." *Mouvement populaire et gouvernement révolutionnaire en l'an II [1793–1794]* (Paris: Flammarion, 1973), pp. 424–25.

Virtue increasingly manifested itself in Robespierre's texts along an axis that swung from suffering violence to inflicting it on those steeped in evil. These two modes of goodness, one passive, the other active, were opposite sides of the same coin. "I have come to the point of suspecting that the true heroes are not those who triumph," he wrote in his *Lettres à ses commettans* (5: 156), "but those who suffer." "It is only too true that intrigue never forgives frankness...that persecution will always be the seal which will mark pure and tested virtue in the eyes of the centuries to come" (4: 68).

Jacques-René Hébert, who as Père Duchesne vulgarized to the point of caricature certain aspects of the Rousseauvian thought of the Jacobins, expressed the same line of reasoning in characteristically crude form: "Good citizens must expect persecution, f.... The more virtuous a man is, the more enemies he has. F..., the people as a whole is always pure, it may be misled, but its intentions are good."[14]

Albert Mathiez devoted a chapter of *Autour de Robespierre* to a correspondent named François-Victor Aigoin whose letters illustrate the curious double-edged virtue which he professed to share with his mentor. On the one hand, Aigoin, who had named his son after Robespierre and asked the Incorruptible to tell him all his thoughts and "even his dreams," insisted that Robespierre answer his frequent and rather demanding letters on the grounds that he deserved to be loved because he was unhappy. "Would it be that you care for me less?" he asked, after a long silence, "I cannot believe that for I am not happy."[15] Unhappy virtue was recognized as a form of entitlement among disciples of Rousseauvian virtue and it specifically allowed the destruction of vice. "Virtue may do anything in order to triumph over vice," Aigoin assured Robespierre, "the slave is allowed to do anything in order to kill tyranny" (p. 69).

Hence the difficulties Robespierre encountered in creating an adequate textual representation of the economic demands of the Paris working people, for instance. To satisfy the poor would have been to ruin them, for a contented people, enjoying the indulgent pleasures of consumerism, drinking coffee with sugar, would no

---

[14]*Le Père Duchesne, 1790–1794*, ed. Albert Soboul, 10 vols. (Paris: EDHIS, 1969), 3: 353.

[15]*Autour de Robespierre* (Paris: Payot, 1926), p. 75.

longer be the "suffering animal" with whom it was happiness to identify, and would no longer be justifiably violent.

Tenaciously, in every text, Robespierre showed himself in constant touch with the goodness of France, of the people, a goodness which he said he found in his own heart. He was able to compare that inalterable model with the corrupt specimens of real humanity he encountered every day. "Liberty would have been long since affirmed among us if individuals were as pure as the mass of the nation" (5: 304), he had noted as early as 1790, and this anomaly continued to exist. France was not melting into one pure cohesion of cells in a virtuous body politic. On the contrary, numerous insurrections against the Revolution had broken out in various parts of France, the Vendée had risen, Lyons was ceding from the Revolution, Toulon had surrendered to the English, and even in Paris every other day was marked by skirmishes in the streets. Rather than recommending efforts to effect compromise formations between these warring groups, Robespierre urged the movement toward purification.

Already in 1792 Robespierre had explained the basic conceptual framework of the Terror: in the beginning, he said "the nation divided into two parties, the royalists and the defenders of the people's cause." After destroying the royalists, however, "the so-called patriots divided into...two classes: the bad citizens and the men of good faith" (5: 17). This antithetical pattern marked Robespierre's discourse until Thermidor. Each purification left France still divided between the pure citizens and the wicked ones, the latter ever disguising themselves under new masks. Thus it became clear, in the spring of 1793, that the Convention would have to be cleansed of the deputies from the Gironde, either by expulsion or execution. Buonarroti, who claimed to be a disciple of Robespierre, described the efforts to unseat the legally elected representatives of the Gironde as necessary to establish flawless morality. Philippe Buonarotti wrote: "At that time, the most powerful enemy remaining to combat was immorality and the greatest, the only means they had to establish the true Republic solidly was the purity and the virtue of the National Convention. Thus it was to preserve that purity and that virtue and above all the opinion that people should have had of them that those who presided over the destiny of France had to devote themselves."[16]

[16]Quoted in Mathiez, *Autour de Robespierre*, p. 240.

As we have seen, however, those who were loosely associated under the label "Gironde" had also exhibited pretensions of their own to virtue. Roland had long been referred to as "the virtuous" Roland because of his reputation for integrity in financial matters. This was not at all the definition of virtue which Robespierre and his colleagues approved. "The so-called 'virtue' of Roland," said Robespierre, "is far from that impetuous passion which smoulders in the breasts of true patriots." Vergniaud, on May 10, rose to denounce the particular definition of virtue which was being used to denigrate him and his friends. He attacked what he called the "Spartan virtue" of the Jacobins, which, he claimed, was leading them ever deeper into violence. "By chasing after an ideal perfection, a chimeric virtue," he said, "you are acting like beasts" (Jaurès, 8: 125).

Armed men from the sections of Paris entered the National Convention of May 31, and the representatives of the nation voted to expel twenty-two members of the Gironde. This expulsion was written about in Jacobin journals in a specific way: the virtuous people of France had rid themselves of a foreign substance within the body politic, just as they had when they executed Louis XVI, the "alien in our midst." It was impossible for the "free Frenchman" to quarrel with himself. Clearly, what looked like *internal* dispute had to be understood as *external* attack. "We have no civil war," the *Journal de la Montagne* proclaimed, "what we have to support is the *foreign* war. Dissidents identify with enemies of the state. The free Frenchman can have no internal dissensions" (Jaurès, 8: 196).

In July 1793, Marat, "the people's friend," was stabbed by Charlotte Corday. Again, as in the murder of Le Pelletier, the assassination was associated with discordant vibrations. Marat was himself a disciple of Rousseau.[17] The motto of his journal, *L'Ami du Peuple*, "vitam impendere vero," to dedicate one's life to the truth, was Rousseau's own, and he too depicted himself as constantly persecuted for his virtue, hounded underground like an animal for his goodness. As for his incitements to murder, they were always in the name of virtue. His self-representation, like those of Robespierre and Saint-Just, was never guilty of egoism, enjoyment, or avarice. He

---

[17]In *Jean-Paul Marat* (1927; New York: Blom, 1966), Louis Gottschalk discusses Marat's debt to Rousseau (p. 18) and points out that Marat was the author of two novels, *Les Aventures du jeune Comte Palowski* and *Les Lettres polonaises*, which were imitations of *La Nouvelle Héloïse*.

was stunned at being accused of venality: "I am perhaps the only author since Jean-Jacques who must be excluded from such a suspicion," he said (*OM*, p. 44). He claimed he was glad to be called a "splenetic madman" because that was "the invective with which the Encyclopedist charlatans gratified the author of the *Contrat social*" (*OM*, p. 231).

After his assassination, his embalmed heart was suspended over the lectern at the Jacobin Club, and he became the object of a cult as a "martyr of virtue." On the other hand, in counterrevolutionary circles, Charlotte Corday herself was portrayed as the incarnation of avenging morality, heroically dispatching, in the name of virtue, the one who had urged the assassination of others, in the same cause. André Chénier, shortly before he was executed, composed an ode to Charlotte Corday in which he praised her: "One less scoundrel crawls in the mud. Virtue applauds you," and further, "Oh virtue, the dagger, only hope of the earth, is your sacred arm...."[18] Thus the word "virtue" was becoming more and more intimately associated with martyrdom, on the one hand, and on the other, with assassination.

Robespierre joined the Committee of Public Safety on July 27, 1793, and commented on the continuing penetration of the good nation by evil: "Called to the Committee of Public Safety against my inclination, I saw things there I would never have dared suspect. I saw on the one hand patriotic members who sought in vain the good of their country, and on the other hand, traitors who plotted within the very heart of the Convention, against the interests of the country" (10: 65 [August 11, 1793]). In the same week the Convention decreed that "colleges and faculties of theology, medicine, arts, and law are suppressed on the entire surface of the Republic" (*Moniteur*, August 8). On September 5 the Convention voted Terror the "Order of the Day." The Committee of Public Safety ordered the Théâtre de la Nation (formerly the Comédie française) to be closed and had all the actors arrested.

In some notes of Robespierre's dating from that September, he reflected upon events and men: "What is the point?" he asked. "The execution of the Constitution of favor of the people. Who will be our

---

[18]"...un scélérat de moins rampe dans cette fange. / La vertu t'applaudit. De sa mâle louange / Entends, belle héroine, entends l'auguste voix. / O vertu, le poignard, seul espoir de la terre / Est ton arme sacrée..." *Oeuvres complètes* (Paris: Pléiade, 1958), p. 180.

enemies? Vicious men and the rich. We must proscribe mercenary authors who lead the people astray" (Jaurès, 8: 258).

Thus in September 1793, at the end of the Republic's first year, "le peuple" had come to be defined by Jacobin leadership as the totality of inhabitants of France less the royal family, monarchists, aristocrats, vicious men and the wealthy, actors and mercenary writers. Another vast category, however, was about to disappear from the ranks of the people: women.

CHAPTER ELEVEN

The Sex Made to Obey

In October 1793 a document written by Jean-Baptiste-André Amar and promulgated by the Committee of General Security finally determined whether women were to be considered part of the French people under the Jacobin Republic. The question had found expression in a number of texts from the beginning of the Revolution. The very act of drawing up *cahiers des doléances* to be presented at the gathering of the Estates General demanded conscious definitions of authorship and of subject. Whose grievances were legitimate? Those of all segments of the population or only masculine ones? In whose name were they to be voiced?

Of the regular *cahiers des doléances*, according to Elizabeth Racz, thirty-three recommended educational reforms for women.[1] Ruth Graham has studied the numerous pamphlets written by women in imitation of the authorized *cahiers*. "The women's *cahiers* were unofficial but the very name reminded readers that women were excluded from the Estates-General. France in 1789 was in acute, economic distress; society was turned upside down and the women advocated one cure: Rousseau's regeneration of *moeurs* or morality."[2]

One such document, addressed to the king, expresses a female

---

[1]"The Women's Rights Movement of the French Revolution," *Science and Society*, 16 (1951), 153. See Samia I. Spencer, "Women and Education," in *French Women and the Age of Enlightenment*, for a discussion of traditional education and the eighteenth-century debate over reform.

[2]"Rousseau's Sexism Revolutionized," *Women in the 18th Century and Other Essays*, ed. Paul Fritz and Richard Morton (Toronto and Sarasota: Hakkert, 1976), p. 128.

ambition to be considered serious citizens with a moral mission in society. Distinguishing themselves from prostitutes, for whom they recommended workhouses and "marks of identification," and requesting a minimal education, the authors stated their wishes:

> We ask to come out of this state of ignorance, to be able to give our children a sound and reasonable education so as to make of them subjects worthy of serving you. We will teach them to cherish the beautiful name of Frenchmen; we will transmit to them the love we have for Your Majesty, for we are willing to leave valor and genius to men, but we will challenge them over the dangerous and precious gift of sensitivity; we defy them to love you better than we; they run to Versailles, most of them for their interests, and when we, Sire, see you there, with difficulty and with pounding hearts, and are able to gaze for an instant upon your August Person, tears flow from our eyes. The idea of Majesty, of Sovereign, vanishes, and we see in you only a tender Father, for whom we would sacrifice our lives a thousand times.[3]

This self-portrayal of woman as an adoring, submissive complement to a benevolent patriarch was rapidly replaced by a more combative female posture. Other unofficial *cahiers* were put together by women who, more in touch with the emerging political restructuring of France, stated that the exclusively male composition of the primary assemblies was undemocratic. Thus, in a brochure, dated March 5, 1789, entitled "Doléances des Femmes françaises," was stated the following objection to the Estates General: "The notion that the organization of this respectable assembly of the Estates General, as it is presented to us, can really represent the entire Nation, while more than half the Nation is excluded; that, gentlemen, is a problem, and a problem injurious to our sex."[4]

[3]*Women in Revolutionary Paris, 1789–1795*, ed. Darline G. Levy, Harriet Applewhite, and Mary Johnson (Urbana: University of Illinois Press, 1979), pp. 20–21. The amorous tone of this quotation recalls Joel Schwartz's comment about the nature of "love of King": "One could say that the aspiring tyrant simply radicalizes and universalizes the sentiment underlying the behavior of the serenading lover (while failing to reciprocate the love he seeks)." *The Sexual Politics of J.-J. Rousseau*, p. 31. In "Women, Democracy, and Revolution in Paris, 1789–1794," Applewhite and Levy emphasize the impact Parisian women's groups had on advancing the concept of popular sovereignty, even though their hopes to participate in French political life were dashed first under the Jacobins and eventually under the Napoleonic code. *French Women and the Age of Enlightenment*, pp. 64–79.

[4]Pamphlet at the Archives nationales, Paris.

Jane Abray discusses other such pamphlets, including a *Cahier des doléances et réclamations des femmes* by Madame B. B. The author asked "whether man could continue to make women the victims of their pride and injustice at a time when the common people were entering into their political rights and when even the blacks were to be free. She insisted that just as a noble could not represent a commoner in the Assembly, so a man could not represent a woman."[5] Although occasional gender-conscious belligerence emerged in these documents, as Ruth Graham points out "most of the cahiers were written by middle-class women, influenced by Rousseau's views on education and the family."[6]

The authors of *Women in Revolutionary Paris, 1789–1795* distinguished between educated women's "social, economic, and political demands that were radical even at a time of unlimited enthusiasm for reform" and, at the other end of the scale, the periodic insurgencies of common women over subsistence issues (pp. 3–12). The Revolution, by destroying the labyrinthine usages directly structuring women's lives under the old regime, by claiming a polity dictated by reason and justice rather than scribbled by tradition, welded a new consciousness of woman as both a politically determined and a consciously politically determining being.

The generation of philosophes preceding the Revolution, in particular Diderot and La Mettrie, had written of women with great sensitivity, though mainly within the same basically pessimistic biological context that colored their writings about the human condition in general. As Robert Niklaus points out, for Diderot the question of women's rights was subordinate to those of "mankind as a whole."[7] With the coming of the Revolution, some of the younger intellectuals seemed prepared to take a more radical stance. Certainly the most eloquent and prestigious French champion of female equality was Condorcet, who, in a series of publications from 1788 until the end

[5]"Feminism in the French Revolution," *American Historical Review,* 80 (1975), 46.

[6]"Women in the French Revolution," in Renate Bridenthal and Claudia Koonz, *Becoming Visible: Women in European History* (Boston: Houghton Mifflin, 1977), p. 239.

[7]"Diderot and Women," *Women and Society in Eighteenth-Century France.* ed. Eva Jacobs et al. (London: Athlone, 1979), p. 82. See John Falvey's "Women and Sexuality in the Thought of La Mettrie," in the same volume, pp. 55–68. In *Sex and Enlightenment: Women in Richardson and Diderot* (Cambridge: Cambridge University Press, 1984), Rita Goldberg compares the English novelist's religious preoccupations with the more physiological concerns expressed in *La Religieuse.*

of his life,[8] proclaimed not in passing but repeatedly and program-
matically that women should be "admitted to the rights of the city."
Constance Rowe summarizes Condorcet's prescription for improving
the status of women: "Neither a Puritan, nor a hedonist, Condorcet
believed that relations between the sexes would grow in beauty,
affection, and disinterestedness only when men and women could
stand together as equals in education, political expression, and full
participation in professional life."[9]

Condorcet, however, as an aristocratic intellectual, has been regarded
as speaking for an elite of propertied and privileged women rather
than for the more modest aspirations of the *lumpen-Frauenwelt*. Louis
Devance comments: "On the eve of the Revolution, it is Condorcet
who best represents, within the heart of the Enlightenment, the
current of feminism of aristocratic origin. In this area, Condorcet
appears the exact antithesis of Rousseau."[10] Pushing beyond the
biologically oriented theses of La Mettrie and Diderot, Condorcet
described both men and women as belonging to the category of the
human being, and in his philosophy all human beings were granted
the same essence and therefore the same political status. He went
further than his Encyclopedist friends by taking a rationalist rather
than an empirical position, to use Eva Jacobs's distinction: "It is
sobering to reflect that in the case of a leading *philosophe* [Diderot],
pragmatism and the empirical consideration of reality only served to
confirm the general belief in the otherness, and implied inferiority
of women. Empiricism, modern as it is as an approach to reality,
does indeed militate against the equality of women. There are too
many facts against it. Only rationalists, who, like those of the seven-
teenth and eighteenth centuries, are unencumbered by facts, can
hope to provide a radical case for women's emancipation."[11] As we
shall see at the end of this chapter, however, it was a group of
factually unencumbered rationalists who legislated women's subservience in October 1793.

[8]For a discussion of Condorcet's role, see David Williams, "Condorcet, Feminism,
and the Egalitarian Principle," *SECC*, 5 (1976), 150–63. Claire G. Moses placed
Condorcet's feminism within a current of individualism in "The Legacy of the
Eighteenth Century," *French Women and the Age of Enlightenment*, pp. 407–15.

[9]"The Present-Day Relevance of Condorcet," *Condorcet Studies I*, p. 25.

[10]"Le Féminisme pendant la Révolution française," *AHRF*, 49 (1977), 352.

[11]"Diderot and the Education of Girls," *Women and Society in Eighteenth-Century France*,

It is true that Condorcet took a position contrary to Rousseau's. When Rousseau envisaged the republic of virtue, he depicted women as a complementary category of being, whose existence was bound up with but supplemental to the central male figure.

The constitution and the Declaration of the Rights of Man and of the Citizen would seem to have been the appropriate places to clarify the legal status of women. In point of fact, however, these documents slipped around the question by means of what Leopold Lacour referred to as an "equivocation." "In the Declaration," he observed, "man means 'homo' and not 'vir.'"[12] The history of the next four years was marked by government efforts to apply the word "man" as "human" in some spheres, such as those of taxation and criminal justice, where women were equally liable, and "male" in others, namely, those concerned with political, educational, and social rights.

One woman who was intent upon clarifying the artful dodge that the word "man" represented was Olympe de Gouges, who believed that Jean-Jacques Rousseau was her "spiritual father." Ignoring Rousseau's insistence on natural female inferiority, she declared herself strongly identified with him as a being of persecuted virtue. She composed a "Declaration of the rights of women" in September 1790, which contained the following provisions: "All women are born free and remain equal to men in rights.... The aim of all political associations is the preservation of the natural and inalienable rights of men and women.... The nation is the union of women and men.... Law is the expression of the general will: all female and male citizens have the right to participate personally, or through their representatives, in its formation."[13]

While de Gouges's declaration had no success constitutionally, under the National and Legislative Assemblies women enjoyed the

---

p. 95. See also Blandine McLaughlin on "Diderot and Women," *French Women and the Age of Enlightenment*, pp. 296–308.

[12]Lacour analyzes the basic issue of defining a constitution for human beings as it was found out in 1789 and again in 1793. *Trois Femmes de la Révolution* (Paris: Plon, 1900).

[13]*Droits de la Femme* (Paris: n.p., 1790) [BN microfiche 14003]. Ruth Graham describes de Gouges's sad career as Rousseau's disciple in "Rousseau's Sexism Revolutionized," pp. 127–39.

beginnings of some direct influence in political affairs. According to Abray, "Once the Estates had met and representative government had begun, the feminists changed their tactics. They took to sending delegations to the government and to using clubs as platforms" (p. 47). A number of clubs admitted females to varying degrees of participation, including the Club des Indigents, Club des Halles, Club des Nomophiles, Club des Minimes, the Jacobins, and the Cordeliers.[14] Several publications, including the Abbé Fauchet's *Bouche de Fer*, pushed the cause of women's rights regularly and fairly aggressively.

Under the "Jacobin Republic" these steps toward defining "man" as "human being" rather than as "male" were halted in the name of virtue, according to Rousseau's arguments. Louis Prudhomme, editor of a publication called *Les Révolutions de Paris,* was the principle spokesman for the Jacobin-Rousseauvian male oligarchy until he criticized the expulsion of the twenty-two deputies of the Gironde in May 1793 and was himself arrested. On January 25 of that year, Prudhomme had launched the attack against feminine participation in political life with an address to a recently formed women's club at Lyons. He would not object to a little circle of "good mothers of families from the same neighborhood getting together at a certain hour, their children on their knees, sewing in their hands," to "sing the hymn to Liberty" or listen to "some citizen, the father of a family, telling them the news of the day and reading them a new law decreed by the National Assembly if it concerns them." This wholesome tableau, however, was a far cry from the behavior of the citizenesses of Lyons:

> What do they think they are doing, the club of Lyons women, teaching young girl citizens entire chapters of J.-J. Rousseau's *Contrat social?* In the name of the fatherland whose love they carry in their hearts, in the name of nature from which one must never stray, in the name of good domestic morality, of which women's clubs are the scourge... we implore the good citizenesses of Lyons to stay home, to look after their households... without claiming to understand the *Contrat social*.[15]

[14]See Marie Cerati, *Le Club des citoyennes républicaines révolutionnaires* (Paris: Editions Socials, 1966), and Olwen Hufton, "Women in Revolution, 1789–1796," *Past and Present*, 53 (1971).

[15]*Les Révolutions de Paris*, no. 185 [Jan. 1793], 19–26.

Here once again, as in the Girondin-Jacobin battle over moral supremacy, two scenarios of heroic Rousseauvian virtue clashed head on. The women of Lyons yearned to be part of the body politic, to contribute to their country as active citizens in the Plutarchian-Rousseauvian tradition. Prudhomme, on the other hand, explicated that tradition as a masculine fantasy of robust virility, presupposing a submissive domestic woman at home, as Rousseau had specified.

Prudhomme's denunciation was answered by a redoubtable antagonist, the strong-minded Blandin-Demoulin, president of the Société des Amies de la République à Dijon. She described the many activities of her organization on behalf of the Revolution. "We do not limit ourselves, Citizen Prudhomme, to singing the hymn to Liberty, as you advise, we wish to perform acts of patriotism." She objected to her critic's preference for ignorance in women. "Give up your system, Citizen Prudhomme, it is as despotic toward women as the aristocracy was toward the people," she exhorted. "It is time to operate a revolution in the mores of women; it is time to reestablish them in their natural dignity. Ah! What virtue could one expect from a slave?" Having neatly skewered Prudhomme with an argument from Rousseau, she finished him off with a quotation from Montesquieu: "In Asia from the earliest times we have seen domestic servitude marching in step with arbitrary government."

Prudhomme rose to the challenge and responded: "The sage who repeated endlessly that the most estimable woman is she of whom the least is said would have been pained to read the letter of President Blandin-Demoulin; Rousseau did not like so much wit and such fine reasoning in women." Furthermore, "we do not deny the good that these societies may have done the Republic but the citizenesses would serve it better still if they stayed home.... Let them not claim to be better than the women of Sparta and of Rome at its finest hour. If Cornelia had belonged to a club we would take back everything we have said according to nature, reason, and J.-J. Rousseau." Prudhomme returned to the attack from time to time, pointing out a few weeks later that "Julie Wolmar would not have taken her children to the citizenesses' club."[16]

---

[16]Quoted in Paule-Marie Duhet, *Les Femmes et la Révolution, 1789–1794* (Paris: Julliard, 1971), pp. 150–58. Elizabeth Fox-Genovese discusses the late eighteenth-century ideal of femininity for which Prudhomme spoke, one which dowered woman with authority in the home, as if in compensation for denying her autonomy in the

The Jacobins were not, however, opposed to women per se. They were enthusiastic to a remarkable degree about women who breastfed their babies. This activity had come to represent the capital virtue of the sex for the orthodox Jacobin, and devotion to the nursing mother was deeply felt. The Festival of August 10, 1793, arranged by the artist Jacques-Louis David, to celebrate the acceptance of the new constitution, began with a gathering at the Place de la Bastille. A great statue of a woman, representing Nature, was erected amid the debris of the fortress. Her arms were crossed and "from her fertile breasts, which she squeezed with her hands, sprang abundantly a pure and salutary water." The representatives of the nation solemnly drank from her waters and embraced one another as part of the dawn-to-dusk celebration which moved from place to place in Paris throughout the day. The new Jacobin constitution, however, was more explicit than the earlier one had been. It defined as citizens "every man born and raised in France, having reached the age of twenty-one," and added several other possible criteria, including "having married a French woman." Thus "man" was moved more decisively under the sign of masculinity.

Sébastien Mercier pointed out that for Rousseau, "modesty had to be the habitual source of women's virtue. He wants the law to show in its treatment of women the same sentiments that virtue inspires in those souls the most susceptible to delicacy."[17] But this vision of modest, breastfeeding mothers protected by masculine sensitivity had not much to do with the tough realities of French life in the fall of 1793, and the disparity between what the Jacobins thought women should be and what they actually were was becoming painful. Levy, Applewhite, and Johnson remark:

Initially the women of Paris were enthusiastic about the Jacobin government, and they responded with many acts symbolizing their loyalty. For

---

world. "Conjugal domesticity and motherhood were gradually seen to offer the perfect molds within which to reconfine female sexuality and female authority. They also had the advantages of offering women a new and flattering image of themselves, control of their own sphere—however marginalized—and a model with which women of different social and economic backgrounds could identify." Introduction, *French Women and the Age of Enlightenment*, p. 16.

[17]*De J.-J. Rousseau, considéré comme l'un des premiers auteurs de la Révolution*, 1: 37.

the first time, the women of the people were exalted as paragons who set the standards of morality in republican society.

The middle-class Jacobins preached the virtues of monogamous marriage and deplored libertine manners, drinking, gambling, and prostitution. By contrast, the *menu peuple* found enjoyment in cheap wineshops, and gambling filled their hours with a modicum of relief from their monotonous jobs. It was the Terror that finally undermined the unity between the Republic of Virtue and the women. [Pp. 62–63][18]

The fall of 1793 saw numerous episodes of street violence sparked by fights in the interminable lines before grocery and bakery shops, by slurs regarding lack of patriotism, and by charges of immorality slung back and forth between neighbors and even strangers.[19] Paris in general was edgy; the Terror excited some as it depressed others, and beneath the garish spectacle of trials and executions lay the numbing reality of shortages, hunger, and total uncertainty about the future. One such episode involved a brawl between a club of republican women and a group of women from the Halles who refused to wear the cocarde (a decoration made of red, white, and blue ribbons, symbolizing patriotism). This incident, as Levy, Applewhite, and Johnson demonstrate (chs. 2, 3), was the culmination of a long struggle between the Society of Revolutionary Republican Women, who were influenced by the radical faction "les enragés," and the Jacobins. Although the demotion of women's political status was decided by sectarian interests, it was used to deny women civil rights in France under the revolutionary government. The arguments for and against women's rights are worth considering in some detail, for they richly illustrate the quest for union with a representation of the virtuous people and for the exclusion of all real persons with whom "it was difficult to identify."

[18]Paule-Marie Duhet comments: "The Constitution of 1791 had established the distinction between active and passive citizens: women...were part of the second category." Under Jacobin hegemony, however, this antidemocratic discrimination was jettisoned in favor of a new distinction, that between the "general sense and the restricted sense of the word 'citizen.'" In this new way, "members of the sovereign such as children, the insane, minors, women, and condemned criminals would not be citizens.... But in actual usage this expression was applied to all who belonged to the social body." *Les Femmes et la Révolution, 1789–1794,* pp. 165–66.

[19]For an account of the tensions in Paris that winter and the role of the women's organization called the *Femmes Républicaines-révolutionnaires,* see Ruth Graham, "Women in the French Revolution," pp. 248–49.

On 8 brumaire a petitioner appeared before the Convention to demand "the abolition of all societies of women, because it is a woman who is responsible for the misfortunes of France" (*Moniteur,* 9 brumaire [October 30, 1793]). The reference was probably to Marie-Antoinette, whose trial was then taking place, although Olympe de Gouges was to be executed a week later also, Mme Roland the week after that, and Louis XV's old mistress, Mme du Barry, at the end of the month. A symbolic foursome, they stood for women's ambitions in their principal manifestations: two who had incarnated old-style success, by embodying royalty or seducing it, and two who had essayed republican paths, Mme Roland, who had exerted power through the ministry of her husband, and Olympe de Gouges, who had spoken in her own voice. All four were guillotined, and their execution lent weight to the condemnation of female claims that were taking place.

J. B. André Amar, who in April 1794 was to award Jean-Jacques Rousseau the honors of the Pantheon, spoke on 9 brumaire (the previous October), in the name of the Committee of General Security. He declared that no one could be forced to wear the cocarde, and then addressed himself to the three important questions: "(1) Must assemblages of women meeting in popular societies be permitted? (2) Can women exercise political rights and take an active part in government affairs? and (3) Can they deliberate in political or popular gatherings?" (*Moniteur,* 9 brumaire). The Committee of General Security decided in the negative to all these questions. First, "The citizen's political rights are to discuss and recommend resolutions relative to the interest in the state by deliberation, and to resist oppression. Do women have the moral and physical strength required by the exercise of these two rights? Universal opinion rejects this idea." "Universal opinion" was like the "general will" and the "public conscience." It was not ascertained by taking a poll or examining in some other way the real attitudes of other people, because real people were frequently wrong; it was to be found by searching within the heart of the virtuous patriot who was in touch with nature.

It was nature that answered the second question as well, for if women exercised political rights, according to the Committee:

> they would have to sacrifice the more important duties to which nature calls them. The private functions to which women are destined by

nature derive from the general order of society; this order results from the difference between men and women. Each sex is called to a kind of occupation which is appropriate to it; its action is inscribed in a circle it cannot break, because nature, which gave man these limits, commands imperiously, and obeys no law.

Now, said Amar, what were the natural characteristics of the two sexes? "Man is strong, robust, born with great energy, audacity, and courage; he braves the perils and the seasons by his constitution; he resists all the elements; he is good at crafts, at hard labor, [etc.] . . . and he alone is suited for the profound and serious meditations which demand great mental concentration and long study which women are not permitted to pursue." This paean to the origins of phallocracy was contrasted with an analysis of the true female nature: "What is the character of woman? Morals and nature have assigned her functions: to begin the education of men, to prepare the minds and hearts of children for public virtue. . . . These are their functions after taking care of the home: woman is naturally destined to make virtue loved." Thus, in a republic where men "made virtue reign," women were charged with "making it loved." In this way all people were the means to that supreme end that in turn was their fulfillment and reason for being: the republic of virtue.

Amar saw the issue as an essential one to the very foundation of the republic:

> This question is tied to morals, and without morals, no republic. Does the reputation of a woman allow her to show herself in public? In general, women are hardly capable of lofty conceptions and serious meditations; and if, among the ancient peoples, their natural timidity and modesty did not let them appear outside the family, do you wish, in the French Republic, to see them in court, at the podium, in political meetings like men, casting aside reserve, the source of the sex's virtues, and the care of the family?

Charles Charlier, although acknowledging himself impressed by Amar's exposition of "universal opinion," was nonetheless troubled by one problem: how could such an exclusion be logically justified? "Despite the inconveniences which have just been mentioned," he said, "I do not know what principle one can invoke to forbid women from assembling peaceably; *unless you deny that women are part of the*

human race, can you take away this right common to all thinking creatures?"
Charlier displayed his depravity in this response, for instead of
melting into the one true body politic of the republic of virtue, he
insisted on mouthing the individualistic notion of principles existing
apart from the hearts of patriots. Claude Bazire responded by
pointing out: "You have declared yourselves a revolutionary government, in that capacity you can take all measures necessitated by
public safety. For the moment you have thrown the veil over principles" (*Moniteur,* 9 brumaire). The decree read: "Clubs and popular
societies for women, under any name whatsoever, are forbidden."

Olympe de Gouges, who had been enraged that women could not
vote but could be executed, was guillotined on November 4 for
having published pamphlets critical of the Terror. She left a few
lines describing herself shortly before her execution: "Sick and
feeble and having no talent for public speaking, I resemble Jean-
Jacques in that regard as well as in his virtue" (Lacour, p. 422).

In the following weeks several groups of "republican women"
attempted to speak before the Convention, but were turned away.
After being warned on 29 brumaire that they were running the risk
of "following Marie-Antoinette, Olympe de Gouges, and Mme Roland"
(*Moniteur,* November 19, 1793), they were, for all practical purposes,
silenced. The Conseil général, however, did vote on 11 nivôse
(December 31) that at civic ceremonies patriotic women were to have
a special place, "where they will be present with their husbands and
children and where they will knit" (*Moniteur,* 11 nivôse).

CHAPTER TWELVE

Purging the Body Politic

In the fall of 1792 the Jacobins were largely expressing opposition to the war, a Girondin cause. By the following winter, however, the situation had changed and belligerence toward the European powers had become a predominant element in Jacobin speeches and writing. The war effort made it possible to redefine terms in ways that would have been unacceptable in times of peace. Those labeled émigrés who left France at any point in the Revolution could, because of the war, be called, first, suspects and, eventually, traitors.[1] The émigrés became the principle of evil to which the ills of the country could be attributed. As Prudhomme justified the elimination of women from the political corpus by quoting Rousseau, the deputy Isaac-René Le Chapelier invoked Rousseau's authority in pursuing and eliminating emigrants. In the *Révolutions de France et de Brabant*, he reminded his readers: "Have you forgotten that J.-J. Rousseau specified that *in moments of trouble emigrations may be forbidden?*" (2e série, October 1792, 1: 67).

---

[1]Marc Bouloiseau describes the concept of "suspect" as resulting from a fundamental distinction made by the government between citizens: "Those who collaborated in its policies deserved the protection of the laws; to the enemies of the Republic was owed only death." *La République jacobine* (Paris: Seuil, 1972), p. 109. In an *Almanach de la raison, an II,* Esope Desloges created a kind of catechism equating humanity with patriotism: "Are those who were born in France or naturalized and refuse to adopt the republican constitution to be considered French?—No, they are animals." Quoted by Gundula Gobel and Albert Soboul in "Les Almanachs de la Révolution (1788–1795)," *AHRF,* 50 (1978), 640.

The logic of the Jacobin position had always denied that there was inherent potential discord *within* the people; the belief in the body politic necessitated the corollary that all violence, corruption, and egotism invaded the people from outside. The people, represented as one undifferentiated pure body, had been persecuted by the rich and the powerful throughout history, but now, under the Republic, the metaphysical order had been reversed.

By 1793, however, the Republic had unquestionably seized power and, according to its own theories, justice, cooperation, and contentment should have been replacing the vices and miseries which characterized the *ancien régime*. Failure to achieve this state could not be explained by defects in the human constitution, for axiomatic to the Jacobin faith was the innate goodness of man. Evil was the attribute of those who differentiated themselves from the people of France. As Jacobin orthodoxy postulated an essentially pure fatherland, it exiled evil to beyond the frontiers. The enemies were Austria, Prussia, England, and the pope, described as infiltrating France with spies, assassins, and secret agents who caused plans to go awry, who corrupted innocent Frenchmen, and who conspired to restore the Bourbon monarchy. The xenophobia that increasingly marked radical discourse provided an ongoing rationale for the Terror. In this way the Terror made the war necessary as much as the war called forth the Terror.

Terror was made "the order to the day" on September 5, 1793. The Jacobins demanded that "all nobles be arrested and detained until there was peace." Jacques-Alexis Thuriot, the presiding officer, declared that "all the French will bless the Jacobins, and all the scoundrels will perish on the scaffold." Thuriot's comment reveals the prevailing emotionally polarized tone: all the French were in accord with the Jacobins, and all the wicked would die. This careful distinction between the French people in their Jacobin incarnation, on the one hand, and the evil ones destined to be destroyed on the other, was to be scrupulously maintained.

Jean Starobinski has analyzed the fatal causative link between the purity of the body politic and the evil of the other in these terms:

The autonomy of the self, excessively preoccupied with its own purity, flips over into submission, dependence, and idolatry. It becomes unjust and unreasonable in wishing to hold onto a permanent justification. I am thinking here of the Terror. Certainly not in order to see Rousseau as its theoretician (although Robespierre drew the essential part of his ideas from Rousseau), but because the Terror seems to me to be, on the political level, homologous with what unfolds on the mental level in the autobiographical writings of Rousseau. To safeguard the conviction of his own radical innocence, Jean-Jacques must reject the evil to the outside, to impute it to a universal plot formed by his enemies. It is absolutely necessary that evil come from others and from them alone.[2]

Terrorist language, the sign of purity by which virtuous patriots could recognize each other, was reduced to a constellation of simple referents to be expressed within a narrow network of permissible locutions. The virtuous, homogeneous fatherland was violent only toward its evil, menacing enemies. Jean-Baptiste Drouet, whose curious fate it had been to recognize Louis XVI as the king passed through Sainte-Menehoulde and to signal his attempted flight, reacted excitedly when Terror was made the order of the day. He rose to his feet and called upon his fellow delegates: "Since our virtue, our moderation, our philosophic ideas have done us no good, let us be brigands for the happiness of the people" (*Moniteur,* September 5, 1793). His suggestion, however, was not well received, because the proposal to jettison virtue and other terms of moral value was not at all in accord with the strict moral vocabulary upon which his colleagues insisted.

The terror is often depicted as grim. One gathers from reading the press and other documents of the period, however, that it must have been, in many ways, a time pulsing with excitement and surprises, frightening but exhilarating, infinitely more diverting than the bland existence of a peaceful, middle-class, parliamentary society. Three great theaters were operating in Paris during those years: the Conseil général of the Paris Commune, the Jacobin Society itself, and the floor of the National Convention. All three stages were crowded with throngs of delegates, spectators, and petitioners, and all three revolved around the written word as it was pronounced, as it was reported in the newspapers and journals and as it was interpreted. Resolutions arrived at by the Commune were put forth as requests at the Jacobin Club; the Jacobins petitioned the Convention with motions they had entertained the night before. The

[2]"La Mise en accusation de la Société," pp. 34–35.

Jacobins were in a permanent state of "purifying scrutiny," as various members were called on to speak of their own patriotism. According to the *Moniteur,* failing to pass the Jacobin test often mean arrest and execution, which effectively transformed the interrogations into hasty capital trials. The Conseil général appears to have been wilder than the other two; while slowly losing power, it entertained more irresponsible motions and offered more radical solutions to the matters under discussion at the club and the Convention.

Part of what makes accounts of the Convention so gripping was its function as a symbolic spectacle. Two new laws had led to great drama on the floor of the hall. The first, reflecting the movement against feudalism and the hegemony of the Catholic church, prohibited the use of "objects of superstition." The second was a decree permitting the finder of hidden assets belonging to a "suspect" to confiscate them, with one-twentieth of the proceeds going to the finder.

Every day people appeared at the Convention from all over France, dragging trunks filled with coins, bags of gold Louis, valises stuffed with silver, which they proudly "laid on the altar of the republic." This booty had been dug up from the places where it had been hidden by suspected persons, and its very existence demonstrated that those who owned such riches were guilty of selfishness and greed. Thus on 14 nivôse (January 4, 1794) the members of the Revolutionary Committee of the Fountain of Grenelle announced that they had found a great quantity of gold pieces, 37,628 livres, at the house of a certain Barbier. Their twentieth amounted to some 1881 livres. Delegates objected that in a free country, property was protected. According to the *Moniteur,* Fayau, representative from the Vendée, replied that "in a free country no one can or should disguise the interior of his home." The wish to hide oneself or one's belongings from one's fellow countrymen could be motivated only by a culpable desire for opacity, a separation so great from the goodness of the fatherland as to constitute a self-indictment.

Along with the sacks of coins on the Convention floor were daily piled heaps of religious objects. On 11 brumaire, 1793, citizens of Nevers appeared at the Convention. "They were carrying great gold crosses, crosiers, mitres, [statues of] saints, seventeen trunks filled with plate, a wash basin filled with the coins that used to be called 'double louis' and several sacks of *écus*" (*Moniteur,* 13 brumaire [November 3]). Loot from churches all over France was brought to help fight the war. Objects in bronze or lead could be melted down for fire arms and bullets, and precious metals could be used for coins. On 28 brumaire the shirt Saint Louis was said to have worn was burned.

One of the great moments of revolutionary iconoclasm must have surely been 20 vendémiaire, year II (October 16 1793), when Philippe-Jacques Rühl, representative of the Marne, went to Reims, holy center of Catholic-monarchical tradition where Joan of Arc had crowned Charles VII, and "had all the old men assembled in the public square to preach hatred of tyrants. He seized the 'Sainte Ampoule' in one hand and smashed it in the midst of the most lively applause" according to the *Moniteur.* The destruction of the "Sainte Ampoule," the physical link between the Holy Ghost and the French monarchy, was one of the most crucial symbolic acts of the Revolution, demonstrating how inextricably, for better or for worse, the Catholic church had bound its fortunes to those of the kings of France.[3] The Convention cheered wildly at the news, congratulating Reims. A few weeks later, the Jacobins at Tours informed the Convention that they too had "smashed the Sainte Ampoule." The passing from literal iconoclasm to its imitation is the sign of ritual beginning to form.

While the "Sainte Ampoule" was to be broken periodically, the destruction of objects of superstitition was taking forms which had not been prescribed in official Jacobin texts. There were constant improvisations, ever stretching the narrow confines of the acceptable. Throughout 1793–94, the *Moniteur* describes the Convention receiving groups of patriots bearing books, papers, paintings, flags, objects of all kinds which had been found in private homes, libraries, and collections, and burning them on the Convention floor while "dancing the Carmagnole in a circle around the flames." On October 23, Anne-Alexandre-Marie Thibault, former constitutional bishop of Cantal, had asked the Convention to clarify the situation. Were patriots really authorized to burn the belongings of their neighbors if they bore "signs of royalty or feudalism"? (*Moniteur*). Marie-Joseph Chénier replied cautiously that "there are some very republican

---

[3]Albert Soboul analyzed the complex strains of political, economic, and intellectual factors which combined in year II to render the movement toward dechristianization so powerful: Part 2, ch. 3 of *Mouvement populaire et gouvernement révolutionnaire*, pp. 204–17.

books which are dedicated to princes, for example those of Sydney [*sic*] and Jean-Jacques Rousseau." Chénier then passed to the order of the day, apparently unwilling to pronounce on which books and art objects might be destroyed. In the meanwhile the Abbé Grégoire, as spokesman for the Committee on Public Instruction, quietly made arrangements to have certain precious paintings and statues put under national protection. Nevertheless, every few days, the deputies were witness to the spectacle of cloth covered with fleurs-de-lys or paintings of Louis XIV or the king of Prussia ablaze on the Convention floor.

Everything had to be purified. "Everything," said François Deforgues, "even the language, must be regenerated according to the Republican system" (*Moniteur,* 30 frimaire [December 12, 1793]). On 10 brumaire "tu" had become the obligatory form of address, and decree after decree was passed against the persons and possessions of aristocrats. René Girardin, who had sheltered Rousseau in the last months of his life and conserved his remains on an island in a lake on his estate, the "Ile des Peupliers," refusing to surrender them for pantheonization in 1791, apparently alarmed at the rising tide of antiaristocratic sentiment, appeared at the Jacobins on 11 brumaire, 1793. He offered up the remains to the Republic, claimed to have been a close friend of Marat, and requested that "in recompense for the sacrifice he was making, he be cleansed of his original stain by a republican baptism, under the name of Emile" (*Moniteur,* 14 brumaire [November 4]).

Another personage from Rousseau's past, Charles Palissot de Montenoy, was, from newspaper accounts, also in trouble in the fall of 1793. He was unable to obtain a *certificat de civisme,* without which he was subject to arrest as a suspect, because he had insulted Jean-Jacques Rousseau in his play of 1760, *Les Philosophes.* He wrote repeated letters to the Conseil général denying "that he had ever put Jean-Jacques Rousseau on the stage, and declaring that the valet in *Les Philosophes* was no more Rousseau than a monkey is a man" (*Moniteur,* October 5, 1793). The same week the Convention decreed that a statue of Rousseau was finally to be erected (*Moniteur,* October 8).

As measures regulating ever more details of the lives of the citizenry were passed, the definition of who constituted the French people continued to narrow. After the trial of the Girondins, Jean-Baptiste Clauzel [Clausel] demanded the arrest of "the members of the Constituant Assembly who had protested the Constitution of 1791" (*Moniteur,* October 5). On October 10 Fabre d'Eglantine put forth a motion, amended by Robespierre, to arrest all English, Scotch, Irish, and Hanoverians residing in France and to confiscate their properties.

From time to time objections were voiced to the idea that France's destiny was to become "one virtuous body." Claude Bazire [Basire] spoke out against the Terror: "It is time," he said, "to free the patriots from this terror which destroys the magnanimous virtues" (*Moniteur,* 20 brumaire [November 10, 1793]). The very plurality of the moral substantives he invoked signaled his dangerous separation from the state of fusion that marked the true Jacobin. François Chabot, eccentric former monk distinguished by his deliberately dirty proletarian appearance at the Convention, protested the destruction of dissident voices in the Assembly and declared that an opposition was necessary. "If there is no longer a right wing," he announced brashly, "I'll form one all by myself, even if I lose my head." Ten days later he was arrested and was executed on April 5, 1794, along with Bazire.

Robespierre demanded that not only foreigners and nobles but priests and bankers be excluded from the Jacobins (26 frimaire; December 16, 1793). Thus Anacharsis Clootz, the "orator of the human race," despite his impassioned appeals for universal Jacobinism, was drummed out of the corps.

On Christmas day, 1793, the Committee of Public Safety sent out a message to the departments, drafted by Robespierre, Billaud-Varenne, and Carnot, explaining the "reform of the laws." All red tape and bureaucratic procedures had to be eliminated:

> Revolutionary intensity can only be exercised in a free space, which is why the legislator clears the road of . . . everything which is an obstacle. Thus you will perform a useful sacrifice to the public good and to yourselves in rejecting from your functions everything which may act to the detriment of the fatherland, and thus against yourselves. Up until now we have purified men, there remains the task of purifying things. . . . The genius of revolutionary laws is to soar without being hindered in flight: it would be less rapid if it multiplied circles around itself.[4]

[4]*French Revolution Documents, 1789–94,* ed. J. M. Thompson (Oxford: Blackwell, 1948), pp. 275–77.

Thus legal procedures of all kinds were to be stripped of cumbersome checks and balances; a kind of immediacy between the impulse and the result was the republican goal. The new order was the antithesis of the "moderate state" as Montesquieu had defined it in *L'Esprit des lois:* a government in which one power is limited by another, because "every man who possesses power is inclined to abuse it."[5] The republic of virtue was the one exception to that maxim because it had no leaders existing as independent personalities, only emanations of the unquestionable goodness of the people. The virtuous body politic, according to Robespierre, was energized by its total devotion to itself; where this absorption flagged, tonus deteriorated dangerously. "If it were necessary to choose between an excess of patriotic fervor and the nothingness of unpatriotism, or the morass of moderatism, one would not hesitate. A vigorous body, tormented by an excess of vitality, still has more resources than a cadaver" (10: 276). "There exists for all men but one morality, one single conscience," Robespierre said (November 21, 1793), and disagreement with that unique standard could signify only one thing: treason inspired by foreign gold. The revolts in the Vendée, Marseilles, Lyons, the Aveyron, and elsewhere presented conceptual problems to Jacobin orthodoxy along the same lines as the assassinations of Marat and Le Pelletier, for the insurgent peasants and workers, largely poor and uneducated, might be viewed as embodying the very people whom the Jacobins were sworn to incarnate, and their revolt against a distant government could display the exterior sign of an act of virtue. The explanation of this apparent anomaly was that the Vendée had been corrupted by foreign money and that the rebellious peasants were being bought by England. "Pitt's gold has fomented all the misunderstandings among patriots," Collot d'Herbois declared. On 11 nivôse a letter from Marie-Pierre Francastel was read at the Jacobins, announcing, prematurely, the destruction of the Vendée. "The Vendée will be depopulated," the letter read, "but the republic will be avenged and tranquil. Let terror never cease to be the order of the day and all will be well" (*Moniteur,* 16 nivôse [January 5, 1794]). Hérault de Séchelles, member of the Committee of Public Safety, was denounced as an aristocrat. He resigned from the Convention, reminding the deputies that the revered Le

[5]*De l'esprit des lois,* vol. 2 of *Oeuvres complètes* (Paris: Pléiade, 1966), p. 4.

Pelletier had also been a noble. "If having been thrown by the accident of birth into a caste which Le Pelletier and I did not cease to combat and scorn is a crime to be expiated, [I resign from the Convention]" (9 nivôse [December 29, 1793]).[6] He had never had any friendships with suspect persons, he declared, "I have had only one friend since I was six years old. Here he is [he displayed a portrait of Le Pelletier], Michel Le Pelletier! Oh thou! from whom I shall never be separated, whose virtue is my model, fortunate martyr! I envy your glory. Like you I would throw myself onto the liberticide daggers for my country; but must I be assassinated by a republican blade?"[7] Hérault was spared for the moment, but was arrested and executed on 16 germinal [April 5, 1794], at the same time as Bazire, Chabot, Danton, and Camille Desmoulins. Among his possessions were manuscript copies of *Emile* and *La Nouvelle Héloïse* in Rousseau's own hand, as well as a portrait of Mme de Warens (Michelet, 2: 1964).

Just as Louis XVI, in revolutionary discourse, had been found guilty of royalty rather than of any specific crime, so Hérault was culpable by metaphysical category. He was the first member of the Committee of Public Safety itself to be arrested. Michelet speculates on the panic of those who were unable to assure themselves of always harmonizing with Robespierre's vision of virtue. In his description: "The Jacobin of Jacobins, Montaut, said: 'of the seven hundred-fifty we are, it is possible two hundred will survive.' By April David himself feared his master: 'I believe that there will not be twenty of us members of the Mountain left'" (2: 753). Le Pelletier, of course, was protected by his martyrdom. On 28 nivôse the *Moniteur* noted: "The young students of the country announced that they had taken Pelletier for their patron in the place of Saint Nicolas." This did not, however, save his younger brother, Félix, from being expelled from the Jacobins for aristocracy.

The condensation in purity and the consequent surge in vital energy that the Jacobin leadership displayed in their texts was challenged in the winter of 1793–94 by British peace feelers. This

---

[6]For a discussion of the dilemma of such Jacobin former nobles, see Décembre-Allonier, 2: 124, and Michelet, 2: 1443–44. Colin Lucas discusses the revolutionary redefinition of elite status in "Nobles, Bourgeois and the French Revolution," *French Society and the Revolution,* ed. Douglas Johnson, pp. 88–131.

[7]Michelet, *Histoire de la Révolution française,* 2: 1964.

was the signal for a concerted Jacobin press campaign against the reputation of the English parliamentary system. Robespierre announced that it had become necessary "to pay attention to British crimes" (*Moniteur,* 21 nivôse [January 10, 1794]). Collot d'Herbois began by saying that there could be no common ground between the two governments. "He did not want to compare the English government with that of France; that would be putting the excess of all vices up next to the sum of all virtue" (*Moniteur,* 24 nivôse). Great Britain was epsecially to be castigated, not only because its naval assaults had made headway against the French, and because Pitt was attempting to raise counterrevolution, but because of its apparent readiness to discuss ending hostilities. Barère spoke up on 3 pluviôse (January 22) announcing that peace was an essentially corrupt impulse: "Monarchies need peace," he claimed, "the republic needs the energy of war. Slaves need peace, republicans need the fermentation of liberty" (*Moniteur*).

At the time that England's advances were being rejected, the quarrel between the radical elements of the Paris Commune, represented by Hébert and the Cordelier Club, and the Jacobins, who were now the government, produced ever more bitter pronouncements. Danton attempted to deflect the hostilities onto the aristocracy: "Let us subordinate our personal hatreds to the general welfare," he asked, "and accord the priority of the dagger to aristocrats alone" (*Moniteur,* 19 nivôse [January 8]).

The appropriate attitude toward women and sex continued to plague the Jacobin legislators. Was the union of "the man and woman who love each other to be considered marriage," as Saint-Just declared in his *Institutions?* Or was it the state's business to prescribe relations between the sexes at all? On March 23 "the *société populaire* of Condom demanded that celibacy be declared a capital offense and punished as such" (*Moniteur,* 4 germinal), whereas Merlin de Douai had a decree passed which permitted divorced men to remarry immediately but required women to wait six months, evidently to resolve any ambiguities over paternity. Pierre-Gaspard Chaumette denounced prostitutes before the convention, "inviting the police to prevent these dangerous women from corrupting morals" (*Moniteur,* 21 nivôse). On the other hand, the mistress of Marie-Joseph Chalier, who had been executed at Lyons and was considered a Jacobin martyr, was presented before the Convention to be awarded "the same pension as Thérèse." There were, nonetheless, rumblings from the more puritanical Jacobins against pensioning off former "concubines" on the same basis as "virtuous heroines of the Republic."

At the Jacobins proposals were put forth to disaffiliate all other societies which had been formed since May 31, 1793 (the expulsion of the Gironde), on the grounds that they were newcomers to revolutionary sentiment. *Sociétés populaires* were to be abolished as the women's groups had been. Garnier (delegate from l'Aube) insisted: "if we purge ourselves it is to have the right to purge France. We will leave no heterogenous bodies in the republic" (*Moniteur*, 16 germinal [April 5, 1794]). The military commission at Marseilles announced to the Convention that "the blade of the law strikes off the heads of the guilty every day; the more the guillotine works, the more firm the republic becomes" (*Moniteur*, 6 germinal).

On 25 ventôse Fouquier-Tinville, the prosecutor of the revolutionary tribunal, had Hébert (le Père Duchesne), arrested along with his co-conspirators Charles-Philippe Ronsin and Antoine-François Momoro, for plotting insurrection. They were executed on 4 germinal (March 24). Eight days later Danton was arrested also. Danton and his friends, who at this point were called *indulgents* and stood for conciliation, were executed 16 germinal. The people, who spoke through the Jacobins, had undergone still another reduction, in the quest for absolute purity.

The execution of Danton caused special consternation; to many people he had seemed a central representative of the republican movement. Robespierre and Saint-Just both pointed out that Hébert's and Danton's stated intentions of defending themselves were proof of their guilt, for since the virtuous people could wish only the good, he who feared the people must be separated from it and hence culpable. "Whoever trembles at this moment is guilty," said Robespierre, "for never does innocence fear public surveillance!" (*Moniteur*, 12 germinal [April 1]). Saint-Just claimed that Hébert had cried out: "They want to destroy me; defend me!" "Does an innocent person talk that way about defending himself?" he asked. "Does he have presentiments of terror before he is spoken about? The committees were prudently silent and public opinion and the people accused those whom I accuse before I did" (*Moniteur*, 10 germinal). Saint-Just claimed that Danton had retired to enjoy his new bride in Arcis-sur-Aube, "You isolated yourself from the Mountain," he said. "You attempted to corrupt public morals, you were the apologist for corrupt men. Wicked man, you compared public opinion to a whore . . . you said that glory and posterity were silly" (*O.c.*, 2: 323). "Danton," Saint-Just said, "that horrible man favored all the wicked people, he lived in pleasure" (*O.c.*, 2: 372). "Destroy all the factions," he exhorted the Convention, "So that there remains in the republic only the people and you."

A deputy from Cette, according to the *Moniteur,* became excited at the news of so many executions and cried out: "Make death the order of the day." He claimed that if another three hundred thousand heads were to roll, as Marat had wished, the Republic would, at last be purified. Tallien, presiding over the Convention, was offended, "Virtue, probity, and justice are the order of the day," he reprimanded him.

Thérèse appeared before the Convention, accompanied by a deputation of the Republican Society of the Commune of Franciade (formerly Saint Denis), demanding the honors of the Pantheon for Rousseau. The presiding officer, Amar, responded to the visitors by declaring that "the national representatives would not delay paying the debt they owed to the most intrepid defender of the rights of the people; to the one who consoled unfortunates while making them love that immortal Providence which watches over all men and forms the hope of unfortunate man in the brief voyage he has to make upon the earth."[8] The depressive undertone of Amar's response was increasingly typical of Jacobin oratory. A note of resignation, bitter or plaintive, was sounded more and more frequently in their addresses, as Jacobins seemed to turn away from the possibility of realizing their ambitions on earth and looked rather toward a divine reward. As Soboul pointed out, even the representatives of the two Committees in the provinces depicted the inhabitants as creatures far distant from the virtuous beings they were categorically declared to be: "The reality contradicted the Rousseauist myth at each instant . . . even the tone of their letters testified to this bitterness."[9] As the vision of

[8]For an account of motions brought before the Assembly regarding Rousseau's pantheonization and Thérèse's pension, see Blaudoin, *Honneurs publics rendus à la mémoire de Jean-Jacques, étude historique* (Geneva: Carey, 1878). Also *Jean-Jacques Rousseau,* catalogue of exhibition at the Bibliothèque nationale, ed. Julien Cain (Paris: BN, 1962).

[9]"Classes populaires et Rousseauisme sous la Révolution," *AHRF,* 34 (1962), 446.

the republic of virtue grew more somber and distant, the Convention decreed that Rousseau's remains be brought to the Pantheon—it was no longer a question of René Girardin's property—and that the Committee on Public Instruction prepare a report on the rationale for the pantheonization of Rousseau.

An uneasy truce had subsisted between the partisans of Rousseau's virtue and those of the Encyclopedists until the beginning of the Terror. Charles Villette, the dissipated old marquis who had been Voltaire's friend and host in the philosophe's last days, had managed to keep in step with public opinion through much of the Revolution, voting the incarceration of Louis XVI as deputy from l'Oise and avoiding the fate of the Girondins whose friend he had been. A letter he published in Camille Desmoulins's *Révolutions de France et de Brabant* is an attempt at autobiography intended to rewrite the past. Far from being enemies, he held, Voltaire and Rousseau were like brothers in arms, and Villette's association with the one in no way implied antagonism toward the other: "Brothers and friends, I have taken the liberty of effacing the inscription on the corner of my street which reads: 'Quai des théâtins' and I have replaced it with 'Quai Voltaire.' I invite the good patriots of the rue Plastrière to put the name of Jean-Jacques Rousseau on the four walls of their houses. It matters to sensitive hearts, to ardent souls, to think as they cross this street that Rousseau lived on the third floor." Villette recounted how he had run to the cafe Procope, Voltaire's old hangout, to announce his idea, and that the habitués had applauded it, suggesting that by the same token "the sewers of the city should be named Mallet-du-Pan, Abbé Royou, Rivarol, etc." Thus Villette attempted to pass himself off as the disciple of a single entity, Voltaire-Rousseau, champion of liberty.[10]

Voltaire's remains were brought to Paris on July 11, 1791, in the midst of considerable pomp. Rousseau's pantheonization, however,

[10]In "1878: Un Centenaire ou deux?" *AHRF,* 50 (1978), Michel Delon discusses the problem of forging a unified ideological picture of the Revolution from the violent discord of the participants themselves, with particular emphasis on Louis Blanc's efforts to squeeze Rousseau, Voltaire, and Diderot into some kind of ancestor portrait. Delon also points out a nineteenth-century tendency to see Robespierre as Rousseau's *fils spirituel* and Danton as the kindred soul of Diderot. Micheline Besnard-Coursodon analyzed the political significance of the Diderot-Danton rapprochement in the second half of the nineteenth century in "The Problem of a Filiation: Diderot and Danton as Seen by the Nineteenth Century," *DHS,* 10 (1978), 329–44.

did not take place until the fall of 1794, and it proved to be the more complicated, if ultimately more spectacular affair.

The Pantheon was thus in the process of gathering up the bones of those whom the Revolution called its ancestors, and for a time, attempted to reconcile Rousseau with the philosophes in the tomb. Camille Desmoulins described the Republic's need to gloss over its heroes' antagonisms and to weld them into a posthumous united front. At the same time that Mirabeau was placed in the Pantheon, "the remains of Voltaire and of Jean-Jacques will be transferred there as national property. Nations are divided between a thousand sects, and in the same nation what is the holy of holies for one sect is for another a place of blasphemy and abomination. But there will be no dispute between men over the holiness of this temple and its relics. This basilica will reunite all in its cult and its religion" (*Révolutions de France et de Brabant*, 72: 321).

It is not always enough to bury a quarrel, however; one must first be certain it is dead. Such was not the case, despite the shared apotheosis of Voltaire and Rousseau, not only because of the profound vibrations of their fundamental discord, but because certain philosophes inconveniently lived on. Frank A. Kafker, in an effort to determine whether the Encyclopedists who had survived into the Terror were active supporters of it, examined the revolutionary fortunes of thirty-eight men who had contributed to the great dictionary and concluded: "The collaborators of the *Enyclopédie* were not collaborators in the Terror."[11] The one exception to this aversion to the Jacobin republic among the former philosophes was Alexandre Deleyre, who had written ballads with Rousseau and had professed, in his letters, a passionate devotion to his collaborator which the latter, however, did not seem to reciprocate. Deleyre, deputy from the Gironde, moved to the side of the Mountain during the Terror.[12]

Although the majority of former Encyclopedists and other philosophes left letters and memoirs recounting efforts to make themselves inconspicuous during the Terror, three of the best known intellectuals of the *ancien régime*, Condorcet, the Abbé Raynal, and the Abbé Morellet, overtly refused to accept the revisionist interpre-

[11]"Les Encyclopédistes et la Terreur," *Revue d'Histoire Moderne et Contemporaine*, 14 (1967), 284–95.
[12]See Gagnebin and Raymond, *Oeuvres complètes*, p. 428, note 2, *Confessions*, for a description of Rousseau's relations with Deleyre.

tation of the Enlightenment which some Jacobins were attempting to propagate. According to his memoirs, the Baron Malouet, monarchist deputy who emigrated to England after August 10, 1792, arranged a dramatic stunt which embarrassed the Jacobins and revealed the schism which Desmoulins had been at such pains to disguise. He persuaded the Abbé Guillaume-Thomas Raynal, one of the fabled names of the philosophic group, to leave his retreat in Marseilles and come to Paris to address the National Assembly. The abbé, in August 1790, was still technically wanted under an arrest order from the parlement of Paris dating from May 25, 1781, for having written the *Histoire philosophique et politique des Deux-Indes*, a free-thinking work attributed in part to Diderot, profoundly offensive to both church and government and more honored by revolutionaries than read. The Assembly, moved at the thought of the old warrior's long struggles on behalf of freedom, declared the decree against him void and invited him to speak before the deputies. Malouet gleefully recounts setting up the situation, aware as the others were not that the unbelieving priest was as appalled by the Revolutionary government as he had been by the monarchy. Opposition incarnate in one human being, the elderly radical looked down on the adoring faces of the delegates and delivered a blast of venom against everything which had taken place since 1789. It was terrible, as if Saint Peter had appeared at a Catholic mass only to call the participants fools and knaves.

Robespierre handled the momentary ontological panic of the Assembly with great aplomb: "You see," Malouet quotes him as saying, "how the enemies [of liberty] dare not risk a frontal attack and are obliged to resort to subterfuge. The wretches drag forth a respectable old man from the edge of his tomb, and abusing his weakness, they make him abjure the doctrine and the principles which founded his reputation."[13]

Rather than parrying Raynal's attack, Robespierre's response simply dismissed him as a befuddled dotard and indeed the abbé's eighty years, sacrosanct name, and eccentric demeanor endowed him with an aura relatively impervious to more direct reprisals. Nonetheless, Robespierre subsequently expressed increasing rancor toward the entire group of philosophes, living and dead, and embarked upon a deliberate press campaign to destroy their reputation while enhanc-

---

[13]*Mémoires de Malouet* (Paris: Plon, 1874), 2: 135.

ing Rousseau's. To this end, in April 1792, he began publishing a journal, *Le Défenseur de la Constitution* (a misnomer since it had no bearing on the constitution), in which he expressed his opinion of "public affairs and the men who direct them."[14] The first targets of his pen were Mirabeau or rather Mirabeau's memory, and Condorcet, both former nobles imbued with intellectual prestige because of their connections with the philosophes and physiocrats of the old regime. In the first issue Robespierre took on Brissot, who had just made a speech in praise of Condorcet's long friendship with the Encyclopedist d'Alembert.

> M. Brissot, in the panegyric of his friend, while reminding us of Condorcet's liaisons with d'Alembert and his academic glory, has reproached us for the temerity with which we judge men whom he calls our masters in patriotism and liberty. For my part I would have thought that in those respects we had no other masters than nature. I could point out that the revolution has cut down many a great man of the old regime [here Robespierre used the sinister word 'rapetissé' which was a colloquial term for guillotining] and if the academicians and mathematicians whom M. Brissot proposes to us as models attacked and ridiculed priests, they nevertheless courted the great and adored the kings in whose service they prospered; and who is unaware of how implacably they persecuted virtue and the spirit of liberty in the person of this Jean-Jacques Rousseau whose sacred image I see before me, of this true philosopher who alone, in my opinion, among all the famous men of those times, deserved the public honors which have been prostituted since by intriguers upon political hacks and contemptible heroes. [4: 35–37]

The familiar signs of Rousseau's picture of virtue emerge from Robespierre's words; the unique man of nature martyred by a venal and malicious world. Yet circumstances had altered causes to an astonishing degree, for by the winter of 1792, according to newspaper accounts, it was beginning to be dangerous to have been an enemy of Rousseau's, and before the Terror ended, it had become very nearly a sentence of death. Michel-Edme Petit, in an *Eloge de J.-J. Rousseau* of October, 1792, sounded the increasingly distinctive tone with which allusions to Rousseau were being couched in some

---

[14]See Léonard Gallois in *Histoire des journaux et des journalistes de la Révolution française* (Paris: Schleicher, 1846), 2: 113–44.

Jacobin circles. "One must believe in God to love J.-J. Rousseau, and whoever loves him will become better." "God made use of a provincial academy to give Jean-Jacques to the earth!" Rousseau's work had, in effect, created a new nobility, and it was this that the Revolution was consecrating:

> The rich . . . lowering themselves from one excess to another in their enjoyment, imagined in their lowly arrogant ineptitude that they could make themselves something more than rich, more than even wise, and prostituting an appellation which belongs only to *virtue*, they constituted themselves a class apart, which they called nobility. I agree that the truths which Jean-Jacques came to teach us have at first glance a sort of terrible majesty, which one would like to mitigate by doubt; but if one freely abandons one's heart and mind to their impact, they take hold of one's entire soul, revivify it, raise it, and aggrandize it all at once . . . like the sun.[15]

This exaltation, expressed by a solar metaphor inversely symmetrical with Louis XIV's own, could be formulated in menace toward those who were indifferent to Jean-Jacques's virtue. The Abbé Morellet described in his memoirs the existence of the little group of doubters, those who might be termed liberal Encyclopedists and their friends, who had survived into the Revolution. Pierre Cabanis who had been Mirabeau's physician, Constantin de Volney, the Abbé Sieyès, André Chénier, Condorcet for a time and Mme Condorcet after her husband went into hiding, Mme d'Houdetot, who had so inflamed Rousseau, M. d'Houdetot, and a handful of others banded together in Auteuil at the home of Mme Helvétius, the widow of the well-known materialist philosopher. Sergio Moravia has characterised them as "adverseries of Rousseauvian democracy," commenting that they "firmly rejected the almost religious faith in the virtue of the people as Robespierre understood it."[16]

The purpose of this book is not the analysis of the political struggles between the factions themselves, it is the examination of the function which Rousseau as a figure of virtue served the revolutionaries. The increasing polarization of moral value along the line dividing those who were with Rousseau from those who were against him is illustrated by another anecdote from the Abbé Morellet. He

---

[15]Paris: Droits de l'homme, 1792, pp. 7, 13, 36.
[16]"La Société d'Auteuil," *DHS*, 6 (1974), 181–91.

recounts how one evening while dining near the Tuileries he over-heard one of Hébert's dinner companions telling the Père Duchesne that the sections were dispensing certificates of "civisme" too casual-ly. These certificates, awarded by neighborhood committees, were necessary for survival in revolutionary Paris, for without one a person was liable to arrest as a "suspect." "They gave one to a well-known aristocrat," Père Duchesne's friend announced indignantly, "the Abbé Morellet whom I had thrown out of the Tuileries section for having written against J.-J. Rousseau."[17] Morellet recounts scut-tling from the restaurant only to risk his neck on several other occasions, as in messidor of the year II, at the height of the Terror, when he rashly produced a bitter little satire suggesting that the Republic might well resort to eating the bodies of victims of the Terror in order to resolve its provisioning problems. The *Prejudice Overcome, or New Method of Sustenance Proposed to the Committee of Public Safety,* describing the "Jacobin eucharist" in terms reminiscent of Swift's *Modest Proposal,* did not lead the abbé to the guillotine as it might have done, and he escaped the fate which befell other mem-bers of the group in Auteuil, like the poet André Chénier, who was executed, and the luckless aphorist Sébastien-Roch Chamfort, who attempted suicide three different ways and yet managed to survive his last attempt for a few months.

The existence of this group with its lingering aura of political heroism, intellectual prestige, impeccable elegance and ironic *snobisme* drew fire from Robespierre much as it had from Rousseau, and on much the same grounds. The easy banter and unrepentantly elitist atheism of these old-time "liberals," to employ an anachronistic but not inaccurate expression, epitomized all the wicked individua-tion and coldly egotistical speculation which both master and disciple showed to be antithetical to true virtue.[18] In a speech at the Jacobin Club on December 5, 1792, Robespierre moved from verbal denun-ciation to symbolic act. He demanded that of the four busts decorat-

---

[17]Morellet, *Mémoires* (Paris: Ladvocat, 1821), 2: 97.

[18]Jan Biou applies this distinction to Rousseau himself, saying: "As he exalted man in opposition to humanism, Rousseau now exalts the liberty of the citizen in opposi-tion to liberalism." "La Théorie politique de Rousseau," *AHRF,* 50 (1978), 533. This is an accurate description of the antithesis between Jacobin political philosophy as interpreted by Robespierre and Saint-Just and the theoretical conceptions of the majority of former philosophes.

ing the hall, those of Mirabeau, Brutus, Rousseau, and Helvétius, two be struck down.

> I see here only two men worthy of our homage: Brutus and Jean-Jacques Rousseau. Mirabeau must fall. Helvétius must fall. Helvétius was a schemer, a miserable wit (*bel esprit*), an immoral creature, one of the cruelest persecutors of the good Jean-Jacques Rousseau, who is the only one worthy of our homage. If Helvétius were alive today, don't go believing he would have embraced the cause of liberty: he would have joined the crowd of conniving so-called wits who today are devastating the fatherland.

This speech touched off a wild display of approval at the club, according to the *Journal des Jacobins*. In the midst of shouting and applause, ladders were brought in, the busts of Mirabeau and Helvétius were thrown down and smashed, and the crowd, according to the account, "destroyed all those monuments to the profane cult which had been rendered up until then to men of letters, to scheming wits" (9: 143–44).

"Men of letters" and "wits" were, from this point on, in Jacobin texts, synonymous with traitors. In the months that followed, one theme was constantly reiterated: the Jacobins who embraced Rousseau's "virtue" *were* the people. They were individually and collectively the victims of the "philosophical conspiracy." Saint-Just declared that in his enemies he recognized the same people whose "envy and malice persecuted the good Jean-Jacques," and Anacharsis Clootz claimed, shortly before he himself was denounced by Robespierre as a foreigner and atheist, that "they want to punish me corporally as they did Jean-Jacques" (Jaurès, 8: 74).

When Condorcet replied to the accusations mounted against him and the philosophes his statements denounced the Jacobins for attempting to compensate for their lack of intellect and education by stirring up the gangs of *sans-culottes* who roamed the corridors and often the floor of the Convention. Of Robespierre he charged: "When a man has no thoughts in his head or feelings in his heart, when no learning makes up for his lack of wits, when he is incapable, despite his best efforts, of rising to the petty talent of combining words, and nevertheless he aspires to be a great man, what is there for him to do? By outrageous acts he must earn the protection of brigands."[19] Condorcet explicated Robespierre's texts and his sarcastic references to Robespierre's intellectual limitations, occasionally labored prose, and manipulation of the crowd cast ridicule upon the persona of the Incorruptible.

When the Terror moved into its most active phase with the fall of the Gironde in May of 1793, Condorcet went into hiding. A number of other intellectuals of the old regime were abroad, imprisoned, or dead. Grimm had fled to Gotha, Beaumarchais to England, Marmontel was hoping to escape notice in Normandy, while the critic La Harpe, the poet Ducis, the physiocrat Dupont de Nemours, and the fabulist Florian were in prison. Lavoisier, the chemist, and Bailly, the astronomer and former mayor of Paris were executed as was the novelist Jacques Cazotte.

A decree was passed on August 8, 1793, suppressing all literary organizations in France, including the Académie française. As Jacques-Louis David commented, "in general, those who are attached to academies are very poor patriots, and . . . if our revolution has experienced delays, it is to them chiefly that the cause must be attributed."[20] The Abbé Morellet wrote of hiding a group of portraits of academicians from bands of patriots determined to destroy them, as well as the document signed by Richelieu which had founded the institution.

At the meeting of the Jacobin Club on 18 floréal (1794), three months before Thermidor, Robespierre put the finishing touches on his indictment of the now defunct "coalition" formed by the philosophes in anticipation of the Revolution, which, according to him, they had foreseen. Among the philosophes before the Revolution, he said:

> The most powerful and the most famous coalition was the one known under the name of Encyclopedists. It included some estimable men and a great number of ambitious charlatans. This sect zealously propagated the belief in materialism which held sway among the great and the wits. Among those who were outstanding in the world of letters there was one man who, by the loftiness of his soul and the grandeur of his character, showed himself worthy of the ministry of preceptor of the human race. [10: 454–55]

---

[19]*La Chronique de Paris*, March 7, 1793.

[20]Quoted by Emile Campardon, *Le Tribunal révolutionnaire de Paris*, 2 vols. (Paris: Plon, 1866), 1: 6.

It is interesting to observe here that Robespierre no longer felt it even necessary to name Rousseau, so thoroughly accustomed had he and his followers become to the argument that the "preceptor of the human race" could refer only to Rousseau. "His upright male eloquence," Robespierre continued,

> depicted in strokes of flame the charms of virtue...The purity of his doctrine, imbibed from nature and from a profound hatred of vice, as well as his invincible contempt for the scheming intriguers who usurped the name of philosophes, called forth the hatred and persecution of his rivals and false friends. Ah! Had he been the witness of this revolution of which he was the precursor, who can doubt that his generous soul would have embraced the cause of justice and equality with transports of joy? But what did his cowardly adverseries do? They fought against the Revolution. [10: 455–56]

Echoes of Robespierre's impassioned discourse were heard in the speeches of other sincere believers in Rousseau's virtue. Typical was J. M. Guillaume's oration at Montpellier only two days later touching the same chords. "D'Alembert, Voltaire, above all Diderot had been enthusiastic friends of Rousseau. As long as he remained obscure and unknown, he put no obstacles in the path of their glory...but once they noticed that he was going farther than they, they joined together to crush him." The essential difference between Rousseau and his enemies, according to Guillaume, was the way in which his works involved identification with his virtue: "One may love *Brutus*, *Alzire*, *la Henriade* without loving Voltaire, but never will one read *Emile* and *Héloïse* without attaching oneself invincibly to the beautiful soul who did nothing but trace, in his immortal works, the virtuous feelings which inflamed him." "Mothers! Read *Emile*, let it be your gospel by the side of your children's crib. As soon as they began to speak, to lisp a few badly articulated sounds, teach them to mingle the name of *J.-J. Rousseau* to those dear and respected words of God, Fatherland, and Liberty." Guillaume had absorbed both sides of Rousseau's virtue, however, and he made the following pledge: "Oh Jean-Jacques! We swear to adore only virtue, and to exterminate all the wicked ones who have not been rendered better by our example and our advice."[21]

---

[21]*Eloge de J. J. Rousseau* (BN Lb40.1007), pp. 24, 28, 30.

Robespierre's denunciation of the "philosophic coalition" that June was accompanied by two other speech-acts which completed, in some sense his tribute to Jean-Jacques Rousseau: the institution of the Cult of the Supreme Being on 20 prairial (June 8), and two days later, the passage of the Law of 22 prairial.

CHAPTER THIRTEEN

The Supreme Being and
the Law of Prairial

Robespierre's report of 18 floréal was more than just a denunciation of his enemies; it was a complete declaration of faith in which
he spelled out his personal convictions regarding the meaning of
virtue in the Revolution. It has been called his "masterpiece,"[1] and it
is all the more astounding in having been produced by a man
wielding such immense political power at such a juncture in history.
A statement more than five thousand words long, it is perhaps the
most beautiful and forceful of Robespierre's discourses, for despite
Condorcet's snide comments, Robespierre had an expressive gift far
beyond "the petty talent of combining words"; he was endowed at
certain times with a great and tragic eloquence.

To appreciate the significance of this capital text, one must go
back two years, to the beginnings of the ardent "dechristianization"
of France, when Robespierre began to differentiate himself sharply
from both the crude anti-clerical *gauloiserie* of the Hébertistes and
the Epicurean indifference of the Dantonistes and to present evidence of a coherent vision of Rousseauvian virtue which he was
never to renounce. In 1792 the revolutionary government was seiz-

[1]In the opinion of his French biographer Gérard Walter: "If Robespierre's writings
are searched for the one which reflects his thought the most intimately and the most
profoundly, it is unquestionably this report of 18 floréal." *Robespierre*, 1: 429. For a
discussion of this document from a political perspective, see Georges Rudé, *Robespierre,
Portrait of the Revolutionary Democrat*, pp. 95–128.

[238]

ing church property to guarantee its paper currency, priests were swearing allegiance to the constitution, denouncing their former beliefs as superstitions, and marrying, while churches throughout France were being stripped of their sacred objects. Robespierre, however, the most influential of Jacobins, did not join the anti-Catholic bacchanal. His speech before the Société des Amis de la Constitution on March 26, 1792, set some of his fellow Jacobins' teeth on edge because of his reiterated references to "Providence." M.-E. Guadet, deputy from the Gironde who still sat with the Jacobins at that point, took offense at Robespierre's repeated gratitude for divine favors: "I keep hearing the word 'Providence' repeated in this speech; I even think I heard that Providence saved us despite ourselves. I confess I can make no sense of this idea. I would never have thought that a man who had worked with so much courage for three years to drag the people out of despotism's slavery could contribute to enslaving them with superstition."

Robespierre's reply was tinged with bitterness; he demanded that the Society of Jacobins vote that God, Providence, and the life to come were the bases of its politics. The printing of his speech, demanded and rejected in turn, was about to be put to the vote when a voice cried out: "No dumb sermons, Mr. President!" (*point de capucinades*). The witticism caused a scandal—it was the (constitutional) bishop Gobel who was presiding—, all was tumult, and the session ended without a vote.[2]

As out of step with his fellow Jacobins as Robespierre was on this issue in 1792, in a little more than two years he had Gobel executed on the charge of atheism (24 germinal, an II [April 14, 1794]), Guadet charged with treason, and the Festival of the Supreme Being celebrated on an unprecedentedly massive scale to introduce a new religion into France, replacing the frankly anti-Catholic Cult of Reason which the government had attempted to institutionalize in the winter of 1792–93.

Robespierre worked consistently for those two years to achieve the situation in which an essential part of Rousseau's concept of virtue could become real. Alphonse Aulard, the nineteenth-century historian, commented: "It quickly became apparent that the entire encyclo-

[2]F.-A. Aulard, *Le Culte de la raison et le culte de l'Etre Suprême (1793–1794)*, p. 260, quoting *Journal des Débats de la Société des Amis de la Constitution.*

pedist philosophy, the whole free lay spirit of the Revolution were menaced by this somber doctrinaire" (p. 260). This very "free lay spirit," however, this "encyclopedist philosophy" was what Robespierre saw as somber, as evil, as inextricably bound to the monarchy, as leading the Revolution down the road to moral decay.

Gérard Walter has described the situation five months before the floréal report:

> To understand its genesis, it is necessary to go back five months to that confused period of brumaire, an II when the revolt against sacerdotal ascendancy in reaction to the "priests' war" raging in the Vendée, was spreading through France. On 23 vendémiaire, after a vehement discourse by Chaumette, the Paris Commune had forbidden the public exercise of worship. Two days later, the same Chaumette read Fouché's celebrated decree and had it adopted. It announced: "Death is an eternal sleep." The provinces eagerly followed the capital and here and there even outdid it. The movement, called dechristianization, suddenly assumed an extreme importance. It reached its apogee in Paris between 17 and 20 brumaire: the abjuration of Bishop Gobel and the Festival of Reason. On 1 frimaire, at the Jacobins, Robespierre began his crusade against "atheism." From the beginning he meant to oppose atheism, which was "aristocratic," to the idea of a "great Being who watches over oppressed innocence," an idea that was "completely plebeian."[3]

In the report presented in the name of the Committee of Public Safety on 18 floréal, an II (May 7, 1794), as the Terror entered its most active phase, Robespierre elaborated his full vision of virtue, the republic, and the Supreme Being. The title, "On the connection between religious and moral ideas with republican principles and national festivals" (10: 442), announced what everyone already knew: that Robespierre's unwavering oratory differed profoundly both from that of cynical men of the world like Danton, and from that of rabid Catholic-baiters like Hébert, as well as from the statements of the by-now largely extirpated remnants of the philosophic free-thinkers.[4] The title also provided, at last, full and formal expression of the meaning of the Revolution as moral event.

[3] *Robespierre*, 1: 430.

[4] Cobban discusses Robespierre's tolerance of religious beliefs, commenting: "He was above all concerned with the influence over opinion that control of religion put into the hands of government. In opposition he had dreaded this power; in office he felt the need to employ it. His *culte de l'Etre Suprême* was patently sincere . . . and in fact

Rousseau's last writings were filled with expressions of pain at the "inexplicable moral chaos" he found in the world about him. In a letter to the Marquise de Mesmes he wrote: "I live in a generation which is inexplicable to me ... hatred has never entered my heart. They are nothing in my eyes; for me they are inhabitants of the moon, I have not the least notion of their moral being" (*C.c.*, 39: 98 [August 14, 1772]). Robespierre, who may not have even known the late works, began his report with a sentence that might have come directly from the *Rêveries du promeneur solitaire* or from Rousseau's correspondence: "The moral world, much more that the physical world, seems full of contrasts and enigmas." The contradictions Robespierre went on to describe were those Rousseau had denounced so movingly, the terrible gap between the goodness he found withing himself and attributed to other men, and the realities he observed. "Nature tells us that man is born for freedom," Robespierre continued, "and the experience of the ages shows us man enslaved." The sentence paraphrased Rousseau's famous "man is born free and everywhere he is in chains," and was followed by a significant elaboration: "His rights are written in his heart and his humiliation is written in history." This total antithesis between internal conviction and external event marked, more clearly than any other quality, the distance separating Robespierre's Rousseauvian mentality and the liberalism of the philosophes.

For Robespierre as for his mentor, what actually *was,* could not be accepted. "Time and the world are the spoils of crime and tyranny; liberty and virtue have scarcely touched an instant upon a few points of the globe. Sparta shines like a flash in the immense darkness. . . ." Ultimately, Sparta and Republican Rome, not Athens, held Robespierre's heart, not because Sparta and Rome represented cruelty or militarism but because they stood for communion in virtue, whereas Athens could offer only individualism, intellectual brilliance, and the opportunity for an urbane existence of no authentic moral value.

"Nevertheless, oh Brutus," Robespierre went on, "do not say that virtue is a phantom!" At this juncture he moved beyond the despair Rousseau had so movingly described, for even though human history

---

represented in his mind an alternative to Catholicism as a religion of the state. As such, it was not far removed from an attempt to put the last chapter of the *Contrat social* into practice." *Aspects of the French Revolution*, p. 179.

was vile, the past did not predict the future. If men could be forced to become as good as Robespierre knew they were capable of being by looking into his own heart and finding what his master had described, the world to come would be as shining as the old world was black. "What is there in common between what is and what was?" he asked, and the traditional answer to that question, human nature, was one he did not accept. France had shown the way to other nations by overthrowing the monarchy; all that was needed was a national commitment to virtue, and happiness would take the place of misery in the country. Just as Rousseau had planned to write a history of Sparta, showing "what man himself can do when he sincerely loves virtue," Robespierre wrote a predictive narrative: "This delicious land we inhabit, which nature favors in her caresses, is made to be the domain of liberty and happiness; this proud and sensitive people was truly born for glory and virtue."

By means of the Revolution the entire French people had reversed the order of pride and shame; the "transvaluation of values" Rousseau had preached and written of attempting to live had actually, according to Robespierre, come about. "In Europe," he said, "a worker, an artisan, is an animal raised for the pleasures of a noble; in France, nobles try to transform themselves into workers and artisans, and they cannot even obtain this honor."

At this point Robespierre addressed himself to the delegates of the National Convention, exhorting them to forget all other considerations and to dedicate themselves entirely to the task of making Frenchmen virtuous. "Vice and virtue decide the destiny of the earth: they are the two opposing spirits struggling over it. The source of both is in the passions of man. According to the direction given to his passions, a man raises himself to heaven or plunges into the filthy abyss. Thus the end of all social institutions is to direct men toward justice, which is at once public happiness and private happiness."

It is apparent that Robespierre was invoking a state that would create the citizens it desired, not one that would accommodate those it had. The very meaning of "Republic," in Robespierre's text, was the moral excellence of its citizenry. "Immorality is the basis of despotism," he continued, "as virtue is the essence of the Republic." Thus Montesquieu's theoretical distinction of 1748, that the principle of a monarchy was honor, while that of a "popular government" was virtue,[5] had edged toward the prescriptive in Rousseau's writings of the 1750s and 1760s and become, in 1794, programmatic.

Within this context Robespierre began to formulate the attack on the philosophes which was discussed in the previous chapter. The real crime of the philosophes was their atheism and their consequent indifference to eternal punishment, eternal reward, and the surrender of the self in virtue. To have denied the existence of God and the communion of believers in favor of some individualistic rational doctrines was to undermine the foundation of the republic of virtue. In Robespierre's model this was not an unintentional result of free-thinking speculation but a deliberate conspiracy to enchain the French through their senses and their frivolity. The Encyclopedists, in league with the aristocracy and the king, sought to weaken the moral fiber of the people through atheism. Far from calling religion "the opium of the masses," Robespierre depicted guiltless self-indulgence as the intoxicant to be feared. "They could not enslave the French people by force or by their own consent; they attempted to enchain it by subversion, by revolt, by the corruption of morals. They erected immorality not only into a system but into a religion."

Robespierre was accused of being a crypto-Catholic, working to restore the church's lost fortunes, but this is a misreading of his discourses. It was not the actual Catholic church for which he expressed admiration or respect, but rather the idea of a body of believers, held together in an ecstatic fusion of virtue. Robespierre did not even share Rousseau's equivocations: the "Supreme Being" whose cult he wished to inaugurate represented a theodicy that could never be reconciled with Christianity.

Robespierre, like Rousseau, did not deny the religious feelings he experienced on the grounds of rational doubt. The unlikelihood of the existence of gods of supreme beings was immaterial for both men; what mattered was the emotional state obtainable through one set of beliefs as opposed to another, not intellectual or scientific tests of those articles of faith:

> Consult nothing but the good of the fatherland and the interests of humanity. Every institution, every doctrine which consoles and elevates

---

[5]*De l'esprit des lois*, p. 215: "It does not demand much probity for a monarchical or despotic government to maintain or sustain itself. The force of the laws, in the one case, the clenched fist of the prince in the other, regulates or encompasses everything. In a popular state, however, it takes one additional motivation, which is VIRTUE."

the soul must be accepted; reject all those which tend to degrade the soul and corrupt it. Revivify, exalt all the generous feelings and all the great moral ideas which they wish to extinguish; through the charms of friendship and the bond of virtue link together the men whom they wished to divide. Who gave you the mission of announcing to the people that the Divinity does not exist, oh you who are thrilled by this arid doctrine and who are never thrilled by the fatherland? What advantage do you find in persuading man that a blind force presides over his destiny, and strikes crime and virtue by chance; that his soul is but a light breath extinguished by the tomb?

As Rousseau had written to Voltaire, "All the subtleties of metaphysics will not make me doubt for one moment the immortality of the soul or a benevolent Providence. I feel it, I believe it, I want it, I hope for it, I shall defend it until my last breath" (4: 1075).

The church was depraved not only because of the primacy of the doctrine of original sin, but because of the necessity of the priesthood for the administration of the sacraments. "What do priests have in common with God?" Robespierre asked. "Priests are to morality what charlatans are to medicine. How different the God of nature is from the God of priests! There is nothing which resembles atheism as much as the religions priests have made."

Robespierre wrote of his longing to melt into the infinite goodness, a desire so powerful and so compelling that he literally could not understand the mentality of those who rejected it, who preferred intellectual lucidity to emotional exaltation, ironic distance to rapturous communion, vulgar pleasure to the austere joy of renunciation, empty rituals to the plenitude of divine union. "The more a man is endowed with sensitivity and genius, the more he attaches himself to ideas that enlarge his being and elevate his heart; and the doctrine of this kind of man becomes the doctrine of the universe. Ah! How could such ideas not be true?" Here was stated with bald clarity the epistemology of virtue, a criterion for distinguishing truth from lie which would be incorporated the following month into the Law of 22 prairial. The truth, in Robespierre's lexicon, was that perception which made the good man feel "enlarged," and "elevated," and the validity of these enhancements of his potency completely superseded any merely mental reservations. Thus was the Terror morally justified: "National justice, in the storms excited by the factions, is able to distinguish error from conspiracy; it will seize with a steady hand all the perverse intriguers and will not strike one single good man."

The problem before the Convention, therefore once again, was not the establishment of carefully worded laws but rather how to forge from the chaotic disparity that France really was, the single virtuous body of which Robespierre so ecstatically spoke. "The masterpiece of society would be to create in [man] a rapid instinct for moral things, which, without the tardy assistance of reasoning, would impel him to do good and avoid evil." Thus, once again, Rousseau's project for a *morale sensitive* was put forth: a program not so much for leading men to virtue as for obviating the need for virtue by making men *instinctively* good.

At this point in his speech Robespierre referred to the antithesis between the depravity of the "philosophic coalition" and the "preceptor of the human race," Jean-Jacques Rousseau. He opposed the purity of his hero to the perfidy of the traitors who had actually led the Revolution and who were by "curious coincidence" all atheists. After denouncing Condorcet, "the traitor Guadet," Hébert, Vergniaud, and Gensonné, he came to Danton, with an accusation which defined the orator's corruption: "Danton, who smiled pityingly at the words virtue, glory, and posterity." That ironic curl to Danton's lip, symbolizing the refusal to become one with Robespierre, was the outer manifestation of an inner evil. "They knew that to destroy liberty they had to favor everything which tended to justify selfishness, to dessicate the heart and erase the idea of this beautiful morality that is the sole rule by which public reason distinguishes the defenders from the enemies of humanity."

Since the real purpose of the government was to make men come together into a virtuous mass, adoring the Supreme Being, its task was to find an "institution," in Rousseau's term, which would perform that function, and that institution Robespierre had found described by the master: "I want to speak of national festivals. Bring men together, you will make them better. Man is the greatest object existing in nature and the most magnificent spectacle is that of a great people assembled."[6]

[6]Paule-Monique Vernes presents an enlightening analysis of the polarity between loss of self in the group and isolation within the self against the group. "On the one hand, the goal of a community, which endows collective action with life and meaning, and the renunciation of personal interest in favor of the common interest, present themselves immediately to Rousseau simultaneously as unconditional necessities and

At the end of his discourse of 18 floréal, Robespierre issued the directives that would force reality to conform to the magnificent vision of fusion between the undifferentiated mass of humanity and the creator, all moved by the same pleasurable emotions of seamless self-adoration; one immense being, gathered, out of doors, to celebrate its own epiphany. Fifteen articles terminated his speech. The first one declared: "The French people recognize the existence of the Supreme Being and the immortality of the soul." Instead of employing the hortatory or causative forms to which Rousseau had resorted in his prescriptions for a patriotic theater, Robespierre uttered a simple declarative sentence, stating, as if it were a report from the real world, a reality of his inner life. This predictive narrative, in the articles that followed, delineated the new cult: "festivals will be instituted to recall man to the thought of the Divinity and the dignity of his being." The latter part of that sentence brings to mind the debt he claimed he owed Rousseau ("You taught me the value of my own being") and indicates the importance of a moral superiority he could experience sharing with the French people as a whole. The last article declared: "there will be celebrated next 20 prairial a national festival in honor of the Supreme Being."

Robespierre's ally Couthon demanded that the discourse not only be circulated throughout France but be "printed as posters and put up in all the streets... translated into all the languages and spread throughout the entire universe," pointing out that "Providence had been offended, and the Convention outraged by infamous men who, in order to bring despair to the hearts of the just, proclaimed materialism" (BR, 32: 381). An unnamed "orator of a deputation of the society of Jacobins" congratulated Robespierre on the decree, claiming that:

> They wanted to annihilate the Divinity, to annihilate virtue. Virtue was no longer anything but a phantom... certain men who had soiled the [Jacobins] perished on the scaffold; but they were not virtuous, they were never Jacobins. The real Jacobins are those who profess aloud the articles which must be seen not as religious dogmas, but as feelings of

as impossible realities." She shows how the overdetermined idea of a city-wide festival was invested with moral supremacy in his writings. *La Ville, la fête, la démocratie* (Paris Payot, 1978), p. 14.

unity, without which, Jean-Jacques said, it is impossible to be good citizens. The existence of the divinity, the life to come, the holiness of the social contract and the laws [*Du Contrat social*] are the immutable bases of the public morality which must seat our Republic, one indivisible and imperishable. [BR, 32: 384–85]

The following week, Jullien (a Paris delegate), who called himself an ardent admirer of Robespierre, proposed to the Jacobins that they congratulate the Convention for adopting the decrees of 18 floréal unanimously. He included, however, a provision by which "according to Rousseau, all those who do not believe in the Divinity must be banished from the Republic" (BR, 33: 68). After some acrimonious protest from the Jacobins, Robespierre spoke, stating that "this principle must not be adopted, it would inspire too much fear in a multitude of imbeciles and corrupt men. I believe we must leave this truth in the writings of Rousseau and not put it into practice" (BR, 33: 68–69).

Thus Robespierre, in the midst of the daily executions taking place in Paris, asserted the true identity of the French people and, at the same time, established the "institution" to create the very virtue it was to celebrate.

From the beginning of the Revolution, the writing of those devoted to Rousseau's concept of virtue had insisted that the sign of the good men was his persecution by evil. This fundamental tenet began to be referred to more and more urgently as the Terror gained intensity. Robespierre's references to his own imminent assassination seemed to multiply with the executions attributed to his aegis, as though to insist that the one true victim, in all circumstances, was Robespierre. Two incidents on May 23 and 24, 1794, reinforced this conviction. A man named Admiral (or L'Admirat) shot at Collot d'Herbois and announced that he had really been trying for Robespierre, and an adolescent girl, Cécile Renault, was arrested while attempting to see Robespierre. Two small knives were found upon her person. Robespierre's extreme and prolonged reaction to these two incidents in his speeches during the days that followed has given rise to a variety of interpretations among historians.[7] For the

---

[7]According to Gérard Walter, "The idea of dying before having finished his work, of leaving it to be destroyed by sacrilegious hands was to provoke in him the most violent reaction" (*Robespierre*, 1: 442). For Aulard, on the other hand, "he did not dare

spokesman of the Terror to voice his exaggerated emotions over two episodes that were not even very near misses—since Collot d'Herbois survived the attempt upon his life and Cécile Renaud and her "toy knives," as Michelet called them, hardly seemed to warrant more than a shrug—struck some observers as a sign of unusual cowardice or hypocrisy. Yet when we examine Robespierre's discourse, in light of his assumption of Rousseau's virtue, it becomes clear that assassination, which had made Marat and Le Pelletier into revolutionary saints, was represented as an object not of Robespierre's fear but of his aspirations.

Rousseau voiced a longing, near the end of his life, for the fate of the holy martyrs: "because if I have not the same faith as they, I feel my heart is worthy of the same prize" (*C.g.*, 19: 261). In Robespierre's speeches in the summer of 1794 he too portrayed himself as looking for assassination to avoid a far worse fate: being considered a wicked man. Just as the seal of virtue had been placed on Marat's ambiguous life by Charlotte Corday's knife, for the Jacobins, murder at the hands of overt anti-revolutionaries would have settled all questions of the significance of Robespierre's career forever. At the meeting of the Jacobins on 6 prairial (May 25), Robespierre evoked a vision of himself, chest bared before the tyrant's blade, awaiting the sacrificial stroke:

> I, who do not in the least believe in the necessity for living, but only in virtue and in Providence, I find myself placed in the state where the assassins wished to put me; I feel myself more detached than ever from human wickedness. Cowardly agents of tyranny, contemptible tools of the oppressors of the human race, come out of your dark hiding places, appear for what you are before the eyes of a people scandalized by your crimes! See us exposed before your homicidal daggers, chests bared, not wishing to be surrounded by guards. Strike, we await your blows.

Thus displayed for sacrifice, Robespierre placed his self-representation in the line of Marat and Le Pelletier: "We swear by the daggers red with the blood of the martyrs of the Revolution and since then sharpened against us, to exterminate utterly the scoundrels who

---

express the thought which swelled his heart, that the intervention of these daggers was a miracle in honor of the decree of 18 floréal." *Le Culte de la raison,* p. 299. See also Michelet, 2: 1146.

would attempt to take away our liberty and happiness" (10: 471). Vows to kill and calls for his own immolation had become opposite sides of the same moral imperative. The next day he returned to the charge, in prose that seemed energized by references to the attempts upon his life. "We have proclaimed the divinity and immorality of the soul; we have demanded virtue in the name of the Republic," he announced, "they are left with assassination. Let us rejoice and thank heaven that we have served our fatherland well enough to have been found worthy of tyranny's daggers" (10: 475).

For the Republic, according to Robespierre, was still in danger, despite the victories of the armies and the continuing executions of "conspirators." Again, as in the very beginning of the Revolution, there were:

> two peoples in France, the mass of citizens, pure, simple, athirst for justice; this is the virtuous people which sheds its blood to found the Republic; the other people is this mob of ambitious and intriguing people, this chattering, artificial, charalatan people who appear everywhere, who persecute patriotism; ... who abuse the education and the advantages the *ancien régime* gave them to lead public opinion astray; a people of scoundrels and foreigners who put themselves between the French people and their representatives to dupe the ones and slander the others. As long as this impure race exists, the Republic will be in pain and in danger. In saying these things, I sharpen the daggers against me, and that's the reason I say them.... I have lived long enough. [10: 477]

Two sets of "people" existed: one incorprating all that was good, an anonymous warmth within Robespierre's heart; the other an ubiquitous pseudopeople of cultivated tricksters for Robespierre to destroy, or with equivalent meaning, to destroy Robespierre. The latter, however, was increasingly the more compelling vision in the summer of 1794.

The famous Festival of the Supreme Being, it has often been noted, was the literal enactment of Rousseau's prescription for the celebration "appropriate to a free people." As Frederick Brown observed: "Insofar as the Terror may be said to have begotten a theater consonant with its doctrinal postulates, that theater resided in the *fêtes,* the great pageants of 1793 and 1794, which Louis David designed as *tableaux vivants* marshaling all citizens into Jacobinism's social cosmos."[8]

Carefully planned by David, the Festival of the Supreme Being involved every house in Paris in its decor and every citizen in its cast. The buildings of the city were garlanded with flowers and festooned with flags, and David had prepared a scenario of the appropriate attitudes to be struck by old men, mothers, twelve-year-old girls, and so on. From all reports, the various groups played their parts to perfection. The guillotine, to which twenty people had been sentenced the day before and twenty-three the day after, did not function on 20 prairial.[9] In the midst of the Tuileries a vast artificial mountain had been constructed, a multidetermined symbol of Robespierre's virtue. The "mountain" represented the Jacobin movement, and, as we have seen, it stood, according to Robespierre, for the "virtuous minority" of Athenians. Love of mountains had also become the mark of the superior soul, since Rousseau's descriptions of the Valais, his reiterated attribution of virtue to inhabitants of the Alps, and his *Lettres de la montagne*.[10] Robespierre too found moral elevation at the higher altitudes: "He who flees the tumult of the cities to raise himself to the summit of the mountains feels the calm

---

[8]*Theater and Revolution* (New York: Viking, 1980), p. 75. J. H. Thompson commented of the celebration that it was "based, perhaps on Rousseau's *Lettre sur les spectacles*, it was David's *chef-d'oeuvre*" (*Robespierre*, 2: 191). Harry Payne offers an interesting view of Rousseau's use of the festival to allay certain chronic anxieties: "His prescriptions on festivity seem to sense the power of rituals—both for cultivation of virtue and subversion of everyday social order." "The Philosophes and Popular Ritual: Turgot, Voltaire, Rousseau," *SECC*, 14 (1985), 312. See also Christie V. McDonald, *The Extravagant Shepherd*, *SVEC* (Oxford: Voltaire Foundation, 1973).

[9]Donald Greer, in *The Incidence of the Terror during the French Revolution: A Statistical Interpretation* (Cambridge: Harvard University Press, 1935), discusses the anomaly of increased executions coinciding with military victories and the almost total suppression of overt counterrevolution in the two months preceding Thermidor. He concluded that the Terror "was operated by a small group of men who, for a few months at least, lived in that dangerous world where ideas, principles or dreams count for more than anything else" (pp. 127–28). The "few months" implies that before the summer of 1794, Robespierre, Saint-Just, Couthon, and their colleagues had lived in the same ordinary world as their compatriots. This, as we have seen, was not the case; their devotion to virtue did not suddenly flourish in May 1794, it was the constant subject of both their political and their private discourse.

[10]J. L. Carr also draws attention to the "philosopher's mountain," a central Rosicrucian symbol of regeneration, as a source of inspiration for Robespierre, who had belonged to the Rosati society in Arras, a club Carr refers to as a possible "cross-fertilization" between the Masonic and Illuminati movements (p. 84).

VUE DE LA MONTAGNE ELEVÉE AU CHAMP DE LA REUNION
pour la fête qui y a été célébrée en l'honneur de l'Être Suprême le Décadi 20 Prairial de l'an 2.me de la République Française.

A Paris chez Chéreau Rue Jacques, aux deux Colonnes ; près la Fontaine Severin, n° 257.

Festival of the Supreme Being, 20 prairial, year II. (Courtesy of the Bibliothèque nationale, Paris) of nature penetrate his soul, and his ideas are enlarged with the horizon," he remarked in the Prospectus of the *Défenseur de la Constitution* (5: 3), referring to his new position as "having descended from the rostrum of the French senate" to "climb to the rostrum of the universe."

On the day of the celebration more than half a million people assembled as the members of the Convention solemnly made their way in the sunshine from the Tuileries to the Mountain, led by Robespierre. Commentators have put various interpretations on the fact that Robespierre appeared conspicuously separated from the rest of the representatives. Elected unanimously to the presidency of the Convention a few days before, he walked alone, the others falling behind, whether, in Aulard's words, "because he wanted it that way or whether his colleagues maliciously did it on purpose" (p. 318).

Michelet described the scene: "Robespierre usually walked fast, with an agitated air. The Convention did not in the least keep up with him. Those in front, perhaps maliciously and with perfidious respect, stayed clearly behind him, thus leaving him isolated" (2: 870). Barère, on the other hand, commented after Thermidor that "this proud affectation of being the first among the deputies, who were all equal, was offensive" (*Mémoires*, 2: 130). The phenomenon of distance from his colleagues on that day of spectacle was generally attested, even if readings of its significance were in conflict. It was also documented that in some way Robespierre's costume differed from that of all the other deputies. Some, for instance, Carr (p. 210), say they were wearing black, while Thompson (2: 191) describes them as wearing blue, but it is agreed that Robespierre himself was attired in yellow pants and a blue jacket in some way distinguishable from the garb of all the other deputies. According to Michelet, his costume "was a little bit different because of a slightly paler or more celestial shade of blue" (2: 869).

What has not been pointed out, to my knowledge, however, is that this combination carried a very specific significance in Europe in 1794, for it was the "Werther costume." Young Werther, the hero of Goethe's 1774 novel which owed so much to Rousseau's *Nouvelle Héloïse*, wore "robins-egg blue and yellow" when he shot himself.[11] Irving Marder writes that the novel "had an immediate influence on

[11]*The Sorrows of Young Werther,* trans. V. Lange, *Great German Short Novels and Stories* (New York: Modern Library, 1952), p. 99.

thousands of young people throughout Europe.... Many of them identified with the hero to the extent of adopting his costume: blue frockcoat and canary yellow waistcoat. Others, following his tortured logic to the end, killed themselves."[12] Thus the combination carried the connotations of the "suicide costume," and Robespierre's presentation of his public person attired in this widely understood sign of impending sacrifice carried the message that the Terrorist was to be known as his own victim.

He was not alone in calling for his own immolation as a martyr to virtue. Saint-Just had demanded Danton's death and only a few days after that execution he wrote:

> The *man obliged to isolate himself from the world and from himself, casts his anchor into the future, and presses against his heart posterity, innocent of present evil....Circumstances are difficult only for those who recoil before the tomb* [emphasis Saint-Just's]. I beg for it, the tomb, as a favor from Providence, no longer to witness crimes committed against my fatherland and humanity.... I despise the dust which composes me and which speaks to you, they can persecute that dust and kill it; but I defy them to deprive me of that independent life I have made for myself in the future centuries and in heaven. [2: 294]

Jaurès comments: "These men seemed to be as if hypnotized by the door to death they had opened for so many others. And at the very moment when they should have given the Revolution confidence in the goodness of life and reassured hearts obsessed with bloody memories, they themselves kept attempting, in their minds, to lie down in the tomb" (8: 396–97). Jaurès, however, failed to see that the "goodness of life" was remote from the identification with virtue. Only the infinite value of virtue was to be coveted, and that value could not be definitively acquired this side of the grave. Rousseau had known about moments of love, the sweetness of seasons, the joys of the senses, and the seductive plunge into *dolce far niente*. These, however, were not the aspects of Rousseau that formed models for the leaders of the republic of virtue. Their identification with his virtue was all the more powerful for not being muddled with the sensual tug of life's easy happiness. It was not the gathering of neighbors on the grass, the flow of wine, the glow of flesh, and the

[12]*International Herald Tribune*, Dec. 24, 1974, p. 6.

surprises of human conviviality which tempted them, but rather a different joy. The great party of Robespierre's life was the Festival of the Supreme Being.

On that occasion Robespierre addressed the crowd as president of the Convention. He proclaimed that "it has finally arrived, this day forever blessed which the French people consecrate to the Supreme Being; never has the world, which he created, offered him a spectacle as worthy of his regard." "French Republicans," he exhorted, "it is up to you to purify the earth [the tyrants] have sullied.... Liberty and virtue were born together from the bosom of the divinity, one cannot exist without the other in the human race" (10: 482). Robespierre then used the torch he was carrying to set fire to an immense paper statue of "Atheism," from whose charred ashes emerged "Wisdom." "At the sight of it," David's scenario read, "tears of gratitude flowed from all eyes."[13]

Robespierre announced: "It has gone back to nothingness, this monster which the spirit of kings had vomited upon France; with it let all the crimes and misfortunes of the world disappear!" Once again, Robespierre had linked two objects of Rousseau's rancor in the same condemnation, even though atheism and the monarchy were traditionally and, indeed, fundamentally antithetical before the Revolution. The real significance of this rapprochement, however, was revealed a few sentences later: "Man, whoever you are, you can conceive lofty thoughts of yourself once again, you may link your brief life to God himself and to immortality."

Materialism, which deprived man of his central role in the creation and his privileged place in the universe, was as humiliating in its way as the doctrine of original sin. Robespierre demonstrated how to reestablish self-esteem based upon virtue for all men willing to merge with him into the fatherland. "Let us rely only upon our constancy and our virtue, single but infallible guarantees of our independence; let us crush the impious league of kings by the greatness of our character even more than by the force of our arms" (10: 483).

It was the finest hour of his word, not because he believed he was manipulating the Convention into accepting his dictatorship, an

---

[13]Quoted in Albert Duruy, "Les Fêtes nationales pendant la Révolution," *Revue de France,* July 15, 1878, p. 310.

ambition which is ultimately unknowable and undemonstrable, but because he verbally delineated "celestial voluptuousness" (10: 554), the surrender of separate consciousness to the mass of virtuous people physically before him. A few weeks later, in his last speech before the Convention (8 thermidor), he returned to his happiness that day. "Seeing that sublime meeting of the first people of the world, who would have believed that crime still existed upon the earth? But when the people, in whose presence all private vice vanishes, returns to its domestic hearth, then the role of the charlatans begins once more" (10: 561). As a single undifferentiated body of primal goodness, the French people were the object of Robespierre's total devotion, because they were himself writ large. Falling back into their individual selves, however, they became once more riddled with the poisons of egoism and lowly impulses, vices of which his self-representation was free.

Two days after this glowing apotheosis of the people and its intrinsic collective worth, Robespierre and his friend Couthon were responsible for the passage of the famous law of 22 prairial, the legal embodiment of the Terror.[14] This law was intended to expedite trial procedures, for Robespierre explained that new traitors were being spawned faster than the revolutionary tribunal could strike them down. It was to sweep through the courtroom like a tornado, blowing away the artificial regulations that stood between the pure patriot's conviction of an individual's guilt and his execution. Traditional courtroom procedures, cumbersome rules of evidence, rights to counsel and to defense were all obstacles to the swift purification of the body politic, and were removed by the new law.

The law of 22 prairial contained the following provisions:

The Revolutionary Tribunal is instituted to punish the enemies of the people.
Enemies of the people are those who seek to annihilate public liberty,

---

[14]According to Walter, "Presented to the Convention in the name of the Committee of Public Safety by Couthon, this law is generally considered to be the personal work of Robespierre." *Robespierre*, 1: 443. Georges Lefebvre examined the problems of the law's authorship and purpose in an article: "Sur la loi du 22 prairial, an II." It was his opinion that the immediate cause of the law was the reaction of Robespierre and Collot d'Herbois to the attempts on their lives. Lefebvre says that "the law was prepared by Couthon, which could only have been done in collaboration with Robespierre, who also made sure it was passed." *AHRF*, 23 (1951), 244.

either by force or by ruse,...those who support the projects of France's enemies...by abusing the principles of Revolution, the laws and the government's measures, by false and perfidious applications. The punishment applied to all offenses of which the Revolutionary Tribunal is aware is death. The proof necessary to condemn the enemies of the people is any kind of document, whether material, moral, verbal, or written, which is able naturally to obtain the assent of all just and reasonable minds. The rule of judgment is the conscience of jurors enlightened by love of the fatherland. If proofs, material or moral, exist independently of witness's evidence, no witnesses will be heard. The law gives slandered patriots patriotic jurors as a defense; it gives no defense at all to conspirators.[15]

The Law of 22 prairial did not represent a departure from legal procedures under the Terror, but merely the codification of the epistemology of sentiment which had come to dominate judicial proceedings since the trial of Louis XVI. Louis, the first Frenchman to be condemned and executed as an "enemy of the people" rather than as a criminal, led the long procession to the guillotine of those who had been found guilty not on the basis of evidence but by reference to the promptings of the "public conscience."[16] The law explicitly formulated the suppositions that had led to the verdict of Louis's guilt, and now made these premises the juridical foundations of the revolutionary tribunal.

The first provision of the law (after the naming of personnel) announced that the purpose of the revolutionary tribunal was to "punish the enemies of the people." Thus *punishment* was substituted for *judgment* as the proper function of the court, and instead of referring to the "accused," the law stipulated its relation to "enemies of the people." Purgation, not equity, was the law's explicit objective. In Couthon's presentation of the law before the Convention, even

---

[15]Campardon, *Le Tribunal révolutionnaire de Paris*, 1: 336–38.

[16]As early as 1791, the underlying premises of the new system were in the air. Pierre Gin commented: "Have we not heard it advanced, as the basis of our so-called liberty, that the interior conviction of jurors, without legal proof, ought to suffice to declare the accused guilty and necessitate the application of the punishment! Great God! What centuries of horrors would be reserved to us if such a maxim gained credit among us!" *Des Causes de nos maux, de leur progrès et des moyens d'y remédier* (Paris: Barois, 1791); Barny 6033, p. 67. Gin went on to compare this new notion with the ordonnance of 1670, demanding legal safeguards and the establishment of uniform rules of evidence in French courts of law.

the word "punishment" seemed to him too anodine: "The delay before punishing the enemies of the people must be only the time to recognize them; it's less a question of punishing them than of annihilating them" (Campardon, 1: 331).

"Enemies of the people" were defined first as "those who seek to annihilate public liberty," and those who "support the projects of France's enemies." The law did not, therefore, address itself to middling offenses or moderate punishments. The crimes were nothing less than metaphysical murders, all the more awesome as they were intangible: liberticide and patricide. The punishment, as absolute as the crime, was the death penalty for those guilty of offenses "of which the Revolutionary Tribunal is aware." According to this wording, knowledge of crime was anterior to and independent of evidence. The law went on to provide that the prosecution bring forth evidence of the crime "which is able naturally to obtain the assent of all just and reasonable minds." This evidence, however, could in effect be anything; the law admitted no limit to the prosecution's resources. Hearsay, anonymous allegations, and circumstances were acceptable as evidence providing they conveyed the immediate sensation of certitude to the juror.

Couthon emphasized the antirational rationale of the Law of 22 prairial by contrasting its spirit with that of criminal justice under the old regime: "The reign of despotism had created a judicial truth which was not moral and natural truth ... evidence was not permitted to convict without witnesses or written proofs" (Campardon, 1: 329). The word "evidence" in French means "that which is perfectly obvious," and Couthon was condemning the system of justice which required independent testimony to corroborate a "patriot's" intuitive impression. In this way, the logical aspects of justice were eliminated in line with an adherence to Rousseau's principle of the moral primacy of conscience over reason.

Rousseau had expressed his revulsion and indignation toward the cold, formalized, proof-oriented criminal proceedings of his day in a letter to David Hume in which he pointed out that "the first concern of those who plot iniquities is to protect themselves from juridical proofs; it does not do any good to bring them to court. Interior conviction recognizes another type of proof which is governed by the feelings of an honest man" (*C.c.*, 30: 29). Rousseau despaired of prosecuting his tormentors in the courts because the law of his day demanded certain types of evidence rather than relying upon "interior convictions." The Law of 22 prairial, the appropriate instrument of justice in a "republic of virtue," relied exclusively upon the "conscience of jurors enlightened by love of the fatherland." The patriotic juror would immediately distinguish the "enemy of the people" from the "slandered patriot"; he would protect the latter, at any price, while the former was afforded no defense. Thus the entire elaborate edifice of criminal justice as it had been practiced toward the end of the *ancien régime* was radically simplified at a stroke. The awkward rules of evidence and the burdensome rights of defense, so laboriously established in the Enlightenment's battle with arbitrary feudal law, were replaced by one single criterion: the jury's immediate impression of the accused's morals. The equity of this appraisal was assured, according to Couthon, "by putting the exercise of justice into pure and republican hands" (Campardon, 1: 333).

The abolition of the right of defense was critical in Couthon's text. He pronounced contempt at the idea of anyone willingly speaking on behalf of the wicked. The professional defense lawyer was an abominable relic of monarchical times, when *contending* interests were pitted against one another in the courtroom. In a "republic of virtue," however, where all the good people's wills fused together to form one general will, there was no place for defense because no good person could wish to defend himself against his own wishes. Indeed, the very desire to defend oneself against the state was the definition of guilt. As Couthon expressed it, "defending the cause of tyrants is conspiring against liberty" (Campardon, 1: 332). In other words, the Law of 22 prairial made defense before the law a capital offense.

The juxtaposition of the two documents, the prescriptive scenario of the Festival of the Supreme Being and the Law of 22 prairial, has offered difficulties for interpreters, who, finding a fundamental disparity between them, concluded that the author must have undergone a radical metamorphosis. "It is Robespierre who drew that up,—the virtuous, the incorruptible Maximilien! Obviously it is not the same man," wrote Albert Meynier.[17] Mathiez, faced with the dilemma, attempted to deny Robespierre's connection with the law. "His efforts to make virtue the order of the day, his tender solicitude

---

[17]*Jean-Jacques Rousseau, révolutionnaire*, p. 173.

for the religious prejudices of the people, his Festival of the Supreme Being, everything proves that Robespierre was gradually preparing to suppress the exceptional measures and to return, through appeasement, to a normal regime."[18]

It was, however, the same author who narrated the Festival of the Supreme Being and who drew up the Law of 22 prairial; they were but two facets of the same phenomenon, the republic of virtue. As Robespierre had clearly stated on 17 pluviôse, "the strength of popular government in revolution is at once *virtue* and its emanation *terror:* terror without virtue is malignant; virtue without terror is impotent" (10: 357).

To be both good and potent; not the one or the other, but both simultaneously, this was the essence of "making virtue reign." The Law of 22 prairial was not the antithesis of the Festival of the Supreme Being; it was its necessary and inevitable complement, two aspects of the world Robespierre dreamed of, one which was not in the least Mathiez's notion of a "normal regime," that stagnant realm of moral ambiguity and individualistic antagonisms.

[18]*Autour de Robespierre* (Paris: Payot, 1926), p. 223.

CHAPTER FOURTEEN

Death of the Republic of Virtue

Two great documentary prescriptive acts had been promulgated—the scenario for the Festival of the Supreme Being and the Law of 22 prairial, one demanding the celebration of virtuous exaltation, the other codifying the annihilation of the wicked. Yet, in the discourses of the weeks that followed, the body of France was still perceived as menaced from without, betrayed from within.

Even these two master texts did not seem to create the alchemy to distill France into one undefiled being with which virtuous Frenchmen could merge. On the contrary, in the speeches and writings of Robespierre, Saint-Just, and Couthon are to be found more and more allusions to anguished feelings of separation from their fellow citizens. Although Robespierre's speeches of messidor and early thermidor continued to be applauded at the Jacobins, according to the *Moniteur* he repeatedly referred to a distancing of his colleagues, to a certain restraint in the air, to carefully impassive faces, to an ironic tinge to his colleagues' compliments, to muttered confidences which concerned him but from which he was excluded. He alluded to rumors: a number of deputies to the Convention no longer slept in their beds, fearing arrest in the middle of the night. Some of the Jacobins who clapped enthusiastically at his discourses were said in private to be terrified, others deliberately spread reports of imminent arrest to manipulate the fears of their colleagues.

On 24 prairial, Bourdon (delegate from l'Oise) and Merlin (from Douai) demanded an amendment to the law of 22 prairial which would exclude the members of the Convention themselves from arrest, trial, and execution under its provisions. Robespierre rose and put forth a definition of the revolutionary persona that would structure the situation within the model of virtue. He stated that Bourdon was attempting to

> separate the Committee [of Public Safety] from the Mountain. The Convention, the Mountain, the Committee," he explained, "that's all the same thing. All representatives of the people ready to die for the Fatherland are of the Mountain." (The members of the Convention stood up and applauded.) "The Mountain is nothing other than the heights of patriotism; a Montagnard is nothing but a pure, reasonable, and sublime patriot: it would be an outrage," Robespierre continued, "it would be assassinating the people to permit some schemers to drag off a portion of this Mountain and make themselves party leaders."
>
> Bourdon's reply was to deny the role Robespierre assigned him. "I never intended to make myself a party leader," he protested. "I demand that what was just claimed be proven; I have just been called a scoundrel...."
>
> "I did not name Bourdon," Robespierre replied. "Woe unto him who names himself. If he wishes to recognize himself in the general portrait that duty forces me to trace, I cannot stop him. Yes, the Mountain is untainted, it is sublime, and schemers are not part of the Mountain."
>
> A voice called out: "Name them."
>
> "I will name them when the time comes," Robespierre replied. [10: 492–94]

Thus the original dichotomy between the good innocent ones and the wicked who deserved to die continued unchanged, although the identities of the latter changed with each round of executions. The king, the monarchists, the aristocrats, the Girondins, the Cordeliers, the Dantonists, the Hébertists, the "enragés," had been followed by the tyrants, the hoarders, the conspirators, and now the scoundrels. Robespierre's text, at this juncture, described the enemy but refused to give him a face. His listeners were to compare their visions of themselves with his depiction of the guilty, and if his speech held up a mirror reflecting their depravity, they would know that they too were outside the city. Robespierre announced that "it has been proven that there are still some who want to degrade the National Convention. Strange discourses have been pronounced by some members, publicly stating the fear inspired in them by the idea of national justice."

"Who told those people the Committee of Public Safety intended to attack them?" he asked. "Did the Committee even threaten them? If you knew everything, Citizens, you would have the right to accuse us of weakness. When morals are purer and love of the Fatherland more ardent, generous accusers will come forth and reproach us for not having shown enough firmness against the enemies of the Fatherland" (10: 495). In Robespierre's depiction of himself a weakness appeared; it was not cruelty, however, but lenience, the inability to act as implacably as virtue demanded.

Tallien wrote to Robespierre on 25 prairial, presenting his own self-image to be judged against the discourse of others: "I know that they depict me as an immoral man in the eyes of the committees," he told him. "Very well! Let them come to my house, and they will find me, with my old and respectable mother, in the retreat we have occupied since before the Revolution. Luxury is banished from it and aside from a few books, what I possess has not increased by one sou. I have probably committed some errors but they were involuntary" (BR, 33: 225). Tallien, the cynical politician, offered a self-portrait inscribed in the vocabulary of virtue: he had no interest in luxury and he committed only "involuntary errors." Such were the attributes of virtuous Republicans.

While the writings of Robespierre's colleagues radiate panic-stricken hypocrisy, in his own discourse he complained of a great ache of loneliness, as though he were locked out of a warm house on a cold night and could only long for the comfort within. His rhetorical self, shyly and a bit stiffly at first and then pleadingly, implored the Convention to remerge with him in a union of goodness. "Notice that we need encouragement," he said, speaking for the Committee of Public Safety.

> Notice that they have done everything to make our career painful. It is bad enough to have to struggle against the conspiring kings and against all the monsters of the earth, without finding enemies at our sides. Come to our aid; do not let us be separated from you, since we are only a part of you, and we are nothing without you. Give us the strength to carry the immense burden, almost beyond human capacity, which you

have imposed upon us. Let us be always just and united despite our common enemies." [10: 496]

A few weeks before passage of the Law of 22 prairial, a decree was drafted and passed under Robespierre's aegis declaring that no English or Hanoverian prisoners would be taken. This document served to destroy the conventions protecting prisoners of war just as the Law of 22 prairial dismantled the safeguards erected for those accused of crimes. Shortly thereafter, the English decreed denial of mercy, quarter, or acceptance of surrender of troops. Thus the old monarchical tradition, which had held that war was a bit of a game, one the soldier could sometimes quit before he lost too heavily, was abolished. The warrior became consubstantial with the man, his fate was to win or die, and a new era of international relations had begun, in which the cynicism and contractual obligations of the old regime were replaced by total moral identification with the fatherland.

Robespierre's response contemptuously dismissed the Duke of York's pleas for French clemency toward captured soldiers: "What does liberty have in common with despotism?" he asked, "virtue with vice?" This was the same argument which Saint-Just had used to send Louis XVI to the guillotine. Louis was a king, kings were the enemies of the people, the people and its enemies had nothing in common but the blade. Here Robespierre was applying the concept "enemies of the people" to British soldiers and hence they too were excluded from the goodness of humanity and were to be killed: "That soldiers fighting for despots might give a hand to defeated soldiers to return to the hospital together, that is understandable; that a slave might deal with a slave, a tyrant with a tyrant, that also is conceivable, but a free man compromising with a tyrant or his satellite, courage with cowardice, virtue with crime, that is inconceivable, that is what's impossible" (10: 499).

Thus in international affairs the world was divided into two moral camps; the French, and theoretically a few other republics[1] personified virtue, while all other countries incarnated vice. Virtuous France's duty was to kill the wicked nations. But within France the homogeneity

---

[1]For a study of revolutionary France's attitudes toward other nations, particularly the United States and the Swiss republics, see R. R. Palmer, *The Age of the Democratic Revolution* (Princeton: Princeton University Press, 1959), 1, chs. 9 and 11.

of virtue disappeared, and the country itself was split between the good and the bad. That the same person could be regarded as *virtuous*, since he was part of France in relation to a foreign power, and *vicious*, since he opposed the Committee of Public Safety, did not offer Jacobin leadership a conceptual difficulty. As Robespierre had commented after the Festival of the Supreme Being, the *mass* of people was always pristine; to the extent that a person distinguished himself from that mass, either as an individual or as part of a group, he was corrupt. "France," Anacharsis Cloots had written in the fall of 1793, "you will be happy when you are finally cured of individuals."[2]

The press, which had enjoyed a period of unprecedented liberty starting several years before the Revolution and lasting until the censorship decrees of August 1793, had become by the summer of 1794 a totally Jacobin organ.[3] By the beginning of messidor, however, Robespierre and Couthon began to react suspiciously to the *Journal de la Montagne* itself, to the *Moniteur*, which merely reprinted what was written in the Jacobin journal, and to the *Mercure universel*. It was not that these newspapers criticized the Committee of Public Safety, the Mountain, or the Jacobins. On the contrary, articles concerning those bodies were larded with flattery bordering on servility. Statements in these publications revealed a profound devotion to, and understanding of, the republic of virtue. In the *Mercure universel*, for example, fidelity to the republican repudiation of original sin was demonstrated in the statement: "Men are only what the government makes of them. In a democracy (under a sky so pure, under such a beautiful government) the mother gives birth without labor pains...she blesses her fertility and counts her true riches in the number of her children."[4]

Robespierre registered annoyance at the obsequious compliments paid him in the journals, and at certain inexactitudes he had perceived. He protested that an ironic inflection he had put into a

---

[2] *Appel au genre humain* (Paris: N. p. frimaire an II; BN Lb41. 946), p. 11.

[3] J. Gilchrist and W. J. Murray describe the suspension of freedom of the press in the period of Jacobin ascendancy: "Following 10 August [1793], the arrest of all counter-revolutionary authors was ordered and their presses distributed among the patriots. Marat, Gorsas, Hébert, Carra and some others were the main beneficiaries in the share of these spoils. Durosoi of the *Gazette de Paris* was executed on 25 August—the first journalist to be condemned to death by the new Revolutionary Tribunal." *The Press in the French Revolution* (London: Ginn, 1971), p. 12.

[4] 1 messidor, an II (41: 122).

particular sentence was not reported. The enemies of the Revolution had many ways of undermining it, he pointed out on 6 messidor, "and one of the simplest and most powerful is to lead public opinion astray in regard to principles and men: this is why newspapers always play a role in Revolutions. The enemy has always hired writers; hence this competition organized by the factions for moral means which journalists furnish the enemy outside and the enemy inside" (10: 503).

After this rebuff the *Journal de la Montagne* and the *Moniteur* did not publish his next speech before the Jacobins, claiming that they feared that "the notes we have been given may not have all the exactitude we desire" (10: 504). That speech was in response to the trial of Catherine Théot but the real accused was understood to be Robespierre himself, and the accusation was that of aspiring not to dictatorship but to divinity. The records of the trial of Théot suggest an atmosphere of farce, as if the contextual message of sarcasm undermined the serious manifest nature of the proceedings. The content of the affair, nevertheless, demonstrates to what extent the role of holy martyr must have accorded with Robespierre's public self-representation, and how plausible the notion must have seemed to many people that he might display himself as a new savior.

Catherine Théot (or Théos), servant in a Paris convent, had declared herself the "new Eve" in 1779 and had been shut up for her visions, first in the Bastille and then in a lunatic asylum. During the Terror she was said to preside over a little circle of like-minded mystics, and in her incarnation as the "Mother of God," revealed the mysteries linking Christianity to the Revolution. Vadier and Barère presented a report in the name of the committees of Public Safety and General Security, claiming that "the Mother of God" was addressing Robespierre as her "first prophet, the son of the Supreme Being, the Redeemer, the Messiah."[5]

Robespierre's reaction demonstrated the parameters of self-generated virtue in the same way that *Rousseau juge de Jean-Jacques* had done. The initial impulse to examine the self, find it good, and project that value outward was followed by an unchecked expression of hatred against others who refused to accept the attribution. Both Robespierre and Rousseau, after long, persistent, and successful

[5]Michelet, 2: 896–98; *Moniteur,* 27 prairial (June 17, 1794).

efforts to center attention upon their revealed selves as incarnations of virtue, struggling with the evil of the world, uttered reactions of surprise and hurt when they suddenly experienced that attention as unfriendly. Robespierre, in the report which the journals did not print, spoke of supper parties where "pure" men were invited and heard slander against the "true patriots."[6] "Why is it," he asked, "that we always have to mention ourselves?"

> Why can we not defend the public good without defending ourselves? Why have they so bound us to the public interest, that we cannot speak in favor of the government, of the principles of the National Convention, without seeming to speak of ourselves? When Brissot attacked us, he was following the same system; and when we rejected his slander he used to say we were always apologizing; he wanted to make us look ridiculous in order to ruin us. But I despise all these insects and I go to the point: truth, liberty. [10: 507]

Robespierre, like Rousseau, was claiming the right to experience in a passive way as external evil the situation he had actively created, as internal good, in his oratory and writing. When Robespierre asked "Why have they bound us to the public interest? (pourquoi nous a-t-on liés à l'intérêt général?)," the identity between himself and the people, upon which he had so intensely insisted, he now described as an alien and suspicious connection, one designed to make him seem contemptible. It was as if the heroic figure that he called himself were suddenly exposed in a different light, in which it took on a comic aspect. And indeed, the report on Catherine Théot made the Convention laugh. Joachim Vilate, an agent of the Committee of Public Safety who later claimed that the documents identifying Robespierre as Catherine Théot's "savior" were forged by the Committee of General Security to embarrass Robespierre, commented: "this affair was of a type to amuse and captivate public attention...they expected the greatest success from the ridiculous contrast between

---

[6]According to newspaper accounts, Robespierre had been accused of participating in a supper party given by the suspect Mme Sainte-Amaranthe, at which gambling and other unpatriotic activities were alleged to take place, in a salon decorated with portraits of Louis XVI. In reality, it was his brother Augustin who had enjoyed the indiscreet evening, and Mme Saint-Amaranthe was executed along with Cécile Renault, Amiral, and fifty-two others (BR, 33: 234–35). See Michelet's detailed account of how this affair was used to discredit Robespierre, 2: 887–89.

this travesty and his proud role at the Festival of the Supreme Being?"[7]

The following day, 17 prairial (June 2) another theatrical political event took place. Fifty-four persons labeled "Robespierre's assassins," all dressed in the red costume of the "parricide" which only Charlotte Corday had worn until that moment, were guillotined. The procession and the executions took four hours, during which public attention was focused sharply on the question of the locus of moral value. Who was the victim, and who was the assassin?

Robespierre's discourse claimed that the fifty-four were the aggressors and that he and the rest of the Committee of Public Safety were helpless victims. "You see the deplorable situation of the Committee of Public Safety," he told the Jacobins on 9 messidor. "Its enemies watch it incessantly and there is no infamous means which they do not employ every day to second the projects of assassination which we despise, but which surround us" (10: 508).

Robespierre insisted that his persona be universally recognized as virtuous. He stated that the fear which haunted him was not of being killed but of being labeled ridiculous or, worse, wicked. "They suppose we have a vile soul, if they believe that we are capable of forgetting our duties in the hope of conserving our life....No, let them assassinate us, but the next day may they not lump us with the scoundrels who will have plunged the dagger into our heart" (10: 508). In the pursuit of ultimate virtue, Robespierre, like Rousseau, reached the point of sacrificing every other value, including life

[7]H. d'Alméras, *Les Dévotes de Robespierre: Catherine Théot, et les mystères de la Mère de Dieu dévoilés* (Paris: Soc. fr. d'imp. et de lib., 1905), p. 91. For relevant texts see BR, 33: 244. The report was, in effect, a piece of neo-Voltairian satire of religious ceremonies. "One must be in a state of grace," it read, "and abnegate the temporal pleasures to approach the holy mother; one prostrates oneself before her, and her disciples become immortal when they have kissed the venerable face of the *Word's* mother seven times [laughter]. These mysterious kisses are distributed in circular form: two on the forehead, two on the temples, two on the cheeks, but the seventh, which is the complement of the seven gifts of the Holy Ghost, is applied respectfully to the prophetess's chin [laughter] which the novices suck with a kind of sensual thrill" (BR, 33: 246–47). The parody of religious ceremony and the mockery of Robespierre's ascetic posture produced a kind of anti-text to his report of 18 floréal.

G. Lenotre, in *Le Mysticisme révolutionnaire, Robespierre, et la "Mère de Dieu"* (Paris: Perrin, 1926), attributes Robespierre's doctrines to the "irreligious piety of the author of *Emile*." See also A. Mathiez, "Robespierre et le procès de Catherine Théot," *AHRF,* 6 (1929), 392–97.

itself, to an exemplary reputation. As Rousseau wrote to François Coindet in August 1767, "I can stand everything except blame; as long as it pursues me I will always flee, even if to the bottom of a precipice . . . or the midst of a bonfire" (*C.c.,* 34: 53).

Robespierre's speeches, declarations, and editorial work had been centered around the Convention, the Committee of Public Safety, the Jacobins, and the Commune. At the height of his authorial confidence, he had declared all of these bodies identical extensions of his own virtue, "all the same thing." Yet his speeches at the Convention ceased after the vote on the Law of 22 prairial. Now, on 11 messidor, the committees of Public Safety and General Security met together, a fight erupted, accusations that he wanted to become a dictator were hurled at Robespierre, and he stopped attending the meetings of the Committee of Public Safety.[8]

For the two weeks that followed, Robespierre addressed only the Jacobins. As Gérard Walter has pointed out, it was a strange situation: "Having broken off all personal relations with the members of the Committee of Public Safety and ceased all contact with the Convention, where he had not appeared since the vote on the Law of 22 prairial, Robespierre withdrew to the Jacobins and used their forum to deal with the committees and the national representatives."[9] His speeches at the Jacobins consisted of a series of denunciations and accusations of the wicked, combined with protestations of his own virtue and impending martyrdom. It was absolutely essential, according to him, that the Terror be seen as a regime of goodness and not of wickedness. "The enemies of the Fatherland have always wanted to assassinate the patriots, both physically and morally. Today, as always, they were trying to cast a mantle of injustice and cruelty over the defenders of the Republic; they denounce the

---

[8]"An examination of the registers and the papers of the Committee shows that Robespierre stopped coming only after 15 messidor," according to Mathiez, *Etudes sur Robespierre* (Paris: Editions Sociales, 1958), p. 83. Bouloiseau and Soboul claim, however, in their introduction to Robespierre's speech of 13 messidor, "it is immediately after this scene of 11 messidor that he ceased taking part in the deliberations of the Committee of Public Safety, leaving the field open to his adversaries" (10: 511). Thus attempts at reconstructing a model of Robespierre's mental acts depend on interpretations of ambiguous documents. Although the chronology of events is obscure during this period, it is agreed that Robespierre, for whatever reasons, was engaged in withdrawing himself from one after another of the groups to which he had formerly attributed a goodness indistinguishable from his own.

[9]*La Conjuration du neuf thermidor,* p. 99.

severity used against conspirators as assaults upon humanity." Thus the problem for Robespierre was that the organizers of the Terror were being regarded with fear, rather than with admiration and love. This could only be the result of an alien influence upon the people, because unsullied humanity and Robespierre were one.

> The humane man is the one who devotes himself to humanity's cause and who pursues humanity's enemy rigorously and justly; he will always be seen holding out a helping hand to outraged virtue and oppressed innocence. The barbarian is the one who is sympathetic to conspirators and unmoved by virtuous patriots. This system should have no other name than *counterrevolution* because it tends to kill the defenders of the Fatherland and cast a dreadful mantle of cruelty upon them. [BR, 33: 321]

Those calling for an end of the Terror and a return to normal life, Robespierre claimed, were really the same as the aristocrats, the Dantonists, and all the previous enemies of the fatherland: "The faction of the indulgents is mixed up with the others; it is their support. The first duty of a good citizen is to denounce it in public."

Up to this point Robespierre had most often spoken in the first person plural, even when this usage sounded rather awkward. Now, more frequently, he began to refer to himself alone, as if withdrawing his projected image even from the committee. "Undoubtedly it has been noticed," he told the Jacobins, "that a certain patriot who wants to avenge and affirm liberty is ceaselessly hampered in his operations by slander, which shows him to the eyes of the people as a frightening and dangerous man. It gives virtue the appearance of crime and the baseness of crime the glory due to virtue" (BR, 33: 322). "If Providence was willing to wrench me from the assassins' hands," he went on, "it was to engage me in using my remaining time usefully."

Robespierre had become, in his own texts, the entire Revolution. The worth of his self-representation was the worth of the Revolution, and the world conspiracy to kill him was the seal which the divinity had placed upon the metaphysical value of the Revolution. The rest of his speech was an emotional enumeration of insults and slanders of which he was the object in London and in Paris. "This is how they absolve tyrants," he declared, "in attacking an isolated patriot, who has on his side only his courage and virtue." "Robespierre," a citizen in the grandstand shouted, "you have all the French on your side." But Robespierre declined the offer to reestablish solidarity with him. "Truth is my only refuge against crime," he protested, "I don't want supporters or praise: my defense is in my conscience."

During the following week it became more and more apparent that a power struggle of major proportions was taking place. Soboul and Bouloiseau comment: "Since the middle of messidor, the crisis has been obvious. It affects not only the relations between the Revolutionary government and the popular movement, but those between the government and the Convention and those of the two Committees" (10: 518). Robespierre's spoken and written utterances did not seem appropriate to most commentators. Georges Rudé summarizes the peculiarity of Robespierre's behavior as it has been described during this period:

> Why, for example, did he choose to stay away from the Committee of Public Safety and the Convention during those critical weeks in June and July 1794 and stubbornly refuse to listen to Saint-Just's advice to be a little more accommodating toward his critics on the Committees? This cannot be explained, even in its broadest essentials, in terms of the "force of circumstance" or of basic political or philosophical beliefs. So, inevitably, some element of purely personal choice (or a physical factor like sickness, fatigue or a breakdown in normal responses) must be brought into play to determine why, at that moment, he made that choice and no other. The historian...can hardly avoid the conclusion that Robespierre's behavior in the weeks preceding Thermidor was almost unbelievably foolish and by lending credence to the suspicion that he was engaged in behind the scenes intrigues with a cabal of his intimates, played right into the hands of his opponents. [P. 213]

Rudé's criticism of Robespierre's behavior as unbelievably foolish depends on a Robespierre envisaged from the outside as seeking political power, a stable government, or the enactment of the republican constitution. However, as we have seen, Robespierre's own discourse explicitly repeats that his objective is *not* those ordinary aims but an entirely different goal, the achievement of a rapturous union in virtue with all of France. Robespierre has been both blamed for failing to accomplish what he did not set out to do, on the one hand, and praised for "saving the Revolution and France" by reaching for "exceptional means."[10] Yet neither evaluation of his career pays attention to what was central to his expressed thought, and the artifacts of his political and personal existence. On 21 messidor, in the midst of the desperate crisis, the most important message he had for the Jacobins was the following:

> Of all the decrees which have saved the Republic, the most sublime, the only one that wrenched it from corruption's grasp and freed all the people from tyranny, is the one which made virtue and probity the order of the day [18 floréal]. If this decree had been executed, liberty would have been perfectly established and we would not need to make the grandstands ring with our voice; but the men who wear only the mask of virtue put the greatest obstacles into the execution of virtue's own laws. [10: 519]

The following week he returned to the charge:

> When virtue was solemnly made the order of the day, the enemies of the Republic did not associate the idea of every man and every citizen's sacred and sublime duties toward the Fatherland and humanity with the word virtue, but rather they linked virtue to a certain exterior decency and at best an equivocal probity which consists of not breaking into somebody else's safe, but which does not prevent conspiring against liberty. At most they understand by the word virtue a faithfulness to certain domestic and private obligations, but never the public virtues, never the generous devotion to the cause of the people which is the heroism of virtue and the only support of the Republic, the only pledge of the happiness of the human race. [10: 531]

Accounts of the last few days before the great crisis of thermidor are marked by a succession of bizarre anecdotes, a kind of interfering static of peculiar subtext which suggests a repressed narration forcing itself up into the official reports of the government.[11] At the Jacobins a letter was read concerning a young soldier who had lost his forearm in battle and who wished to "make a sheath for his knife

---

[10]Rudé provides an equitable summation of the conflicting evaluations of Robespierre's effectiveness in ch. 3 of his *Robespierre*, "The Revolutionary Leader."

[11]See Mathiez, "Robespierre et la Commune le 9 thermidor," *AHRF* 1 (1924), 289–314.

from his bone." Robespierre answered that he personally felt he was being mocked by "exaggerated expressions of patriotism." He rose in anger, denouncing the letter as a fraud, and claiming that the words which had just been read "never came from the mouth of a republican hero" (10: 538). He went on to demand that "the Jacobins and all the good citizens seize and arrest upon the spot anybody who dares to insult the National Convention" (10: 540).

Those who criticized the Convention were to be arrested, as well as those who seemed to mock the figure of the Incorruptible by exaggerating his principles, and those expressing opposition to the Supreme Being. It is difficult to ascertain whether the petition of Magenthies (Majenki) was an authentic representation of its author's wishes or whether it too was meant as an "anti-text," a parody intended to humiliate the apostle of the Supreme Being. Published as a pamphlet entitled "Petition to the National Convention," it demanded the death penalty against anyone daring to say: " 'Sacred name of God.' He trembles, he says, from having written those four words." Robespierre demanded that Magenthies be arrested.[12]

Robespierre's last speech, on 8 thermidor, took place before the Convention, where he had not appeared since 24 prairial. He spoke for more than two hours, and this vast discourse in some sense resumes the visionary history of the republic of virtue and Robespierre's place in it. He began by assuring the deputies that he had come to "defend before you your authority which has been insulted; liberty which has been violated. *If I speak to you about the persecutions of which I am the object, you will not make a crime out of it; you have nothing in common with the tyrants whom you combat.* The cries of outraged innocence do not offend your ears."

Robespierre attempted, one last time, a speech to convince the Convention that its members were bonded to his vision, and his political self was above all a moral being, frightening not to good people, only to the evil ones.

> Whom do we terrify, the enemies or the friends of the Revolution? Who should fear us, the tyrants and the scoundrels or the good people and the patriots? We, frightening to patriots! We, frightening to the National Convention! And what are we without the Convention? We are the ones they are assassinating and we are the ones they depict as frightening!

[12]Walter, *La Conjuration du neuf thermidor,* p. 447.

And what are these great acts of severity with which they reproach us? Who were the victims? Hébert, Ronsin, Chabot, Danton, Delacroix, Fabre D'Eglantine, and a few other accomplices. Is it their punishment we are reproached with? No one would dare to defend them.... Who can accuse us in advance of injustice and tyranny except those who resemble them? No, we have not been too severe, I swear by the Republic which breathes! They speak of our rigor and the fatherland blames us for our weakness. What facts justify the horrible idea that they wanted to give of us? Since when does the punishment for crime terrify virtue? To appear an object of terror in the eyes of those one respects and loves, that is for the sensitive upright man the most atrocious of tortures, to make him suffer it, the greatest of crimes.

Robespierre's utterances had never been intended to frighten the good people; only the corrupt ones. Now, at the sight of the deputies he said he loved as an abstract entity, he labeled what he saw in their individual faces fear rather than the admiration that he knew Robespierre deserved. How could such an anomaly exist? Only those given to evil had reason to fear him; if the rest were frightened as well it must be the result of a conspiracy, a campaign to distort and slander his intentions. What worse blow could his enemies deal him than to disfigure his image so that he appeared a homicidal menace rather than the spokesman of the people's will he acknowledged himself to be?

"I know of only two parties," he continued, reverting to the Manicheanism which had consistently marked his revolutionary discourse, "that of the good citizens and that of the bad citizens; patriotism is not a question of party but of the heart. There are certain signs by which one can distinguish the dupes from the accomplices, the error from the crime. Who will make this distinction? Good sense and justice."

He described how he had been accused of wanting to become a dictator. This charge demonstrated how his accusers failed to comprehend the meaning of virtue.

What am I saying, *Virtue!* It is undoubtedly a natural passion but how could they know it, those venal souls who open themselves only to cowardly and ferocious passions? But it exists, I swear it to you, pure and sensitive souls, it exists, this tender, imperious, and irresistible passion, the torment and delight of magnanimous hearts; this profound

[273]

horror of tyranny, this compassionate zeal for the oppressed, this sacred love of the fatherland, this most sublime and most holy love of humanity without which a great revolution is but a dazzling crime which destroys another crime; it exists, this generous ambition to found upon the earth the first Republic in the world. This egotism of uncorrupted men, who find their celestial voluptuousness in the calm of a pure conscience and in the ravishing spectacle of public happiness; you feel it burning in your souls at this moment, I feel it in mine. But how would our vile slanderers guess it? How would someone born blind have an idea of light? Nature refused them a soul; they have some right to doubt, not only the immortaility of the soul, but its existence. What am I, me whom they accuse? A slave of liberty, a living martyr of the Republic, as much the victim as the enemy of crime. Take away my conscience and I am the most miserable of men. [10: 554–56]

This impassioned discourse described, for the last time, Robespierre's dynamic model of the French Revolution as a fusion in virtue. It was not the destruction of the monarchy and its replacement by a representative system of government. These were merely external forms, shadowy legal fictions that were never, in Robespierre's discourse, worth the shedding of human blood. To overturn the monarchy in favor of a different polity was "but a dazzling crime which destroys another crime," for *any* form of government distinct from the governed was inherently criminal.[13] The legitimate fatherland had no government apart from the burning sensations of "celestial voluptuousness" which melted all Frenchmen into one virtuous individual. Just as Rousseau, at the end of his life, had become convinced that the creatures around him were not really human, but "automatons without souls," so now Robespierre saw that his enemies too existed without souls and this original deficit made them constitutionally incapable of comprehending the ecstatic surrender to virtue which gave meaning to his life.

Like Rousseau, who spoke of himself as "buried alive among the living," Robespierre described himself as a "living martyr"; already immolated by the forces of evil, still somehow continuing to exist. He

[13]Camille Desmoulins had defied that postulate in one of the last issues of the *Vieux Cordelier:* "If virtue were the only motivation of the government, if you suppose all men to be virtuous, the form of the government is unimportant and they are all equally good. Why is it then that there are detestable governments and others which are good?" (7, quintidi, pluviose, 2e décade).

spoke of the fundamental truth of his being: "Take away my conscience and I am the most miserable of men." The only justification
for his career was his dedication to virtue; without that raison d'être
he was just another politician, one who far from having "saved the
Revolution" had brought it to such an impasse that its legislators
could debate only one topic: the moral value of Robespierre.

Those who wished to see the Terror end, who spoke of reconcilia-
tion and compromise among the various parties and factions, of
"amnesty in favor of lying deputies," these proponents of appeasement were the real enemy. To call a halt to the Terror before all the
wicked ones were annihilated "is more than protecting crime, it is
sacrificing virtue to it!" (10: 574).

The incorrigible vice of Robespierre's enemies was a subject for his
gratitude; it made the distinction between him and them firm:

> Seeing the multitude of vices which the torrent of the Revolution has
> spewed forth pell-mell with the civic virtues, I have sometimes trembled
> for fear of being soiled in posterity's eyes by the impure proximity of
> these perverse men who mixed into the ranks of the sincere defenders
> of humanity; but the destruction of the rival factions [the *enragés* and
> the *modérantistes*] has emancipated all the vices...and traced the line of
> demarcation between them and the good men.

The end was in sight, yet although both the virtuous and the
wicked were about to perish, Robespierre claimed that the ultimate
fate of the two was antithetical: "the good and the bad, the tyrants
and the friends of liberty disappear from the earth, but on different
conditions. No,...death is not an eternal sleep! *Death is the beginning
of Immortality.*"

Robespierre concluded his discourse by calling for the only measures that could save the Republic: "Punish the traitors, restaff the
Committee of General Security, purify this Committee, and subordinate it to the Committee of Public Safety, purify the Committee of
Public Safety itself, constitute the unity of the government under the
supreme authority of the National Convention" (10: 576). Thus,
once more, he demanded purification and punishment of the wicked, but this time the accused were within the two committees which,
in effect, were the government. According to the *Moniteur,* his speech
set off alarmed reactions among the deputies. "They don't want to

kill you," André Dumont protested, "It's you who are killing public opinion."

"The men I denounce are in the two Committees," Robespierre replied, "Must they themselves be my judges?" He nonetheless persisted in refusing to specify the persons whom he was charging with treason. The blank space in the accusatory narrative was to be filled by names of traitors, in his reading, or of victims, as many of his listeners feared. The session ended without a clear victory for either side, the definition of the traitors was not yet complete. That evening at the Jacobins a dispute broke out over whether Robespierre was to be given the floor, to reread the discourse he had addressed to the deputies that morning, or whether Collot d'Herbois or Billaud-Varenne would be able to seize the podium. To seize command of the word was to achieve dominance over the Jacobins. Robespierre won; those who had voted against the printing of his discourse that morning were thrown out of the meeting, and Robespierre announced that he was grateful to his opponents: "I thank them for calling attention to themselves in such a pronounced way, and letting me recognize my enemies and those of the fatherland better" (10: 587). Thus the author now announced his recognition of his antagonists; he had yet to insert their names into his requisition.

The events of the following day, recounted, debated, and subjected to intense scrutiny by generations of commentators, still remain ambiguous, both because Robespierre and his friends seem to historians to have behaved with inexplicable passivity, and because, in the wake of Robespierre's fall, so many people were interested in exculpating themselves by means of post-facto narrations.[14] The examination of the documents collected by Buchez and Roux, however, makes at least one point indisputable. The majority of deputies were reserving their word until they were assured of speaking as a chorus. When they sensed that opposition had reached a securely critical mass, they hurled accusations at Robespierre in an assault

[14]J. M. Thompson (1: xx) traces the post-Thermidorean efforts to scapegoat Robespierre for all excesses committed during the Terror as beginning with the deputy E.-B. Courtois's *Rapport fait au nom de la commission chargée de l'examen des papiers trouvés chez Robespierre et ses complices,* which was presented to the Convention on January 5, 1795 and printed by its order. According to Décembre-Allonier (1: 536), Courtois became a fervent Bonapartist and then one of the richest property-holders in Paris before being exiled as a regicide.

bordering on pandemonium, including such disparate charges as having "always hidden during the great dangers to the fatherland" ([Tallien], 10: 592), and having "six spies who followed members of the Convention each day" ([Vadier], 10: 592). Rather than representing authentic charges, these verbal assaults seemed to be aimed .at stifling Robespierre's discourse.

In the midst of the tumult he raised his voice to exclaim: "I demand to be put to death" (10: 593). The Convention voted to arrest him and, a few minutes later, his brother Augustin, Couthon, Saint-Just, and Le Bas.

By the next day they were all dead. Robespierre's end, in a way, had been the worst, because, shot in the jaw either by his own hand or that of a soldier, Merda (Méda), he was carried to the guillotine on a plank, his head held together by a bloody rag.

On the day Robespierre was executed, Collot-d'Herbois delivered a summation of what he now termed a conspiracy. "He protested," according to the *Moniteur* of 9 thermidor (July 27, 1794), "that the conspirators' system was not to make justice and virtue triumph, by always speaking of their advantages, but to crush all those who did not wish to obey them." This summation of the crusade for virtue typified the Thermidorians' public attitude toward Robespierre, Saint-Just, Couthon, and their lesser allies, once they had been forever silenced. And yet it posed a contradiction where none existed, for the wish to make virtue triumph was not antithetical to the impulse to "crush all those who did not...obey." Twin faces of the same coherent policy, "virtue and its emanation, terror," were the faithful realization of a reading of Rousseau; a narrow, rigid, unnuanced interpretation to be sure, but nonetheless authentically faithful to a central core of the master's teachings.

While in the immediate instance Robespierre's identification with Rousseau's virtue had been crushingly repudiated, the powerful emotional fusion was not forever lost. In 1831, a young militant republican, Albert Laponneraye, set himself to editing the discourses of Robespierre. Laponneraye, who spent most of his brief life in prison for his violent revolutionary activities, expressed the transcendental significance of his master's career:

Here is one of the most powerful individuals of the French Revolution, the militant leader of the Jacobin party, of which Rousseau had been the theoretician and Jesus the initiator. Jesus, Rousseau, Robespierre, three names which march inseparably together and which are deduced logically one from another, like three terms in the same theorem; a holy and sublime trinity which contains the principle of equality and fraternity. Of these three men, the first and the last suffered the agony of an infamous death. The second, without having been dragged to the gibbet, expiated no less cruelly than the Galilean and the martyr of Thermidor, the immense services he had rendered humanity.[15]

Laponneraye explained that the divine succession of Christ, Rousseau, and Robespierre had been given to men in order to lead them beyond themselves, and that while it was selfishness and egoism that had martyred them, their sacrifice to virtue had been ordained by God.

In the immediate post-Thermidorian period, however, Rousseau's virtue was wrenched away from associations with Robespierre and Saint-Just. The strong emotional attraction did not die overnight, but instead split into two separate movements which had their day before submerging into the general currents of political and personal life. The survivors of Thermidor took over the still existing cult of Rousseauvian virtue, but altered its character in such a way that it could be integrated into the new regime. At the end of the following month, the Committee on Public Instruction finally presented its long-awaited report of Rousseau's qualifications for pantheonization. Prepared and delivered by Joseph Lakanal, the report marks the end of the Terrorist Rousseau, at least for the moment, and the emergence of a different folk-hero: Jean-Jacques as sentimental champion of the disinherited and reformer of female morals. A softening of Rousseau's Spartan rigor was distinguishable in this discourse; for Lakanal, the battle against vice was finished and the time had come for "last rites," a "solemn act of national justice,"

[15]Introduction to *Oeuvres de M. Robespierre* (Paris: published by the editor, 1840), 1: 5. In Walter's words, Laponneraye, who befriended Charlotte Robespierre in her last years, "played a capital role in the diffusion of Robespierre's work. His frenzied apostleship is a unique case in the story of Robespierrism" (*Robespierre*, 2: 176). Laponneraye may have been the ultimate disciple, but he was not alone in finding Christ in Robespierre. Michelet remarked sarcastically that Ernest Hamel's biography elevated Robespierre above humanity. "From childhood on, [Hamel portrays Robespierre] as a saint, he makes little chapels. He has only one love, his doves. M. Hamel twice compares him to Jesus." *Histoire de la Révolution française,* 2: 1017 (Preface to ed. of 1869).

when the doors of the Pantheon were opened to "the author of the *Contrat social* and the *Emile*. The voice of a whole generation nourished on his principles, and, so to speak, raised by him, the voice of the entire Republic calls him hence."[16]

Lakanal carefully avoided all references to the divisive identification with Rousseau that Robespierre had so often employed; instead he insisted upon the great reversal in moral values that Rousseau had taught the French people. With marked astuteness Lakanal pointed out that all the revolutionary publicists had extolled the influence of the *Contrat social* as well as Rousseau's other political writings. But, he continued, the great maxims developed in the *Contrat social*, as obvious, as simple as they appear to us today, produced little effect at the time. In fact, nobody had understood them, for they were beyond the comprehension of ordinary minds. To this Lakanal added: "In one way or another it was the Revolution which explained the *Contrat social* to us. It took a different book to lead us to the Revolution, to raise us up, to instruct us, to prepare us for it; and that work is *Emile*." In *Emile*, Lakanal went on to say, "the road to virtue was leveled like the road to knowledge; mothers who had been led astray until then by worldly dissipation, finally called before the tribunal of Nature, were brought back to the sweetest and to the most sacred of their duties by irresistible eloquence and the appeal of enjoyment" (Paris, 62–64). And what was Rousseau's greatest contribution to revolutionary thought, according to Lakanal? He chose a number of remarks in which Rousseau compared the rich unfavorably to the poor, asking bluntly: "Are these not, citizens, revolutionary maxims, . . . from this revolution which is your own and which you want to turn entirely to the profit of the people and of virtue?"

He then cited Rousseau's predictions that the monarchy had not long to endure, and concluded by observing that Rousseau could also make mistakes, as when he criticized the arts and sciences. He called for a great procession to accompany the transference of the remains. The procession should consist of (1) musicians playing tunes from *Le Devin du village;* (2) botanists carrying plants; (3) artisans; (4) deputies from the Paris sections bearing the Declaration

[16]J.-M. Paris, *Honneurs publics rendus à la mémoire de Jean-Jacques Rousseau, étude historique* (Geneva: Carey, 1878), p. 59.

of the Rights of Man; (5) mothers dressed in classical style with babes in arms; (6) and (7) inhabitants of Montmorency, Ermenonville, and other places associated with Rousseau's life; (8) Genevans; and (9) the National Convention totally encircled by a "tricolore" ribbon, preceded by the *Contrat social*.

On 18 vendémiaire, an III (October 15, 1794), the grand procession began. Rousseau's funeral urn was carried from the Ile des Peupliers where he had been buried to the commune of Emile, formerly the town of Montmorency. The following day a deputation from the Convention went to receive the remains, which were placed on a cart decorated with willow branches, to the accompaniment of songs from *Le Devin du village*. In the middle of one of the pools of the Jardin national, formerly the Tuileries, an island surrounded by weeping willows had been constructed, surmounted by a little building "of antique form" in which the urn was placed. Throughout the night visitors streamed past the site, and the next day Rousseau was at last laid to rest in the Pantheon. Jean-Jacques Cambacérès, the president of the Convention, who, under Napoleon was to become the Duc de Parme and effectively arch-chancellor of the Empire, read the decrees:

> It is to Rousseau that we owe this salutary regeneration which has caused such fortunate changes in our morals, in our customs, in our laws, in our minds, and in our habits.... He has led Nature back from where she had gone astray, and at the sound of Rousseau's voice, mother's milk poured onto the lips of babes. Citizens, the hero of so much virtue was destined to be its martyr! His life will mark an era in the glories of virtue and this day, these honors, this apotheosis, this accord of an entire people, this triumphal celebration is an effort to repay the philosopher of Nature, both the debt of the French and the gratitude of humanity. [Paris, pp. 158–60]

The speech was followed by a "Hymn to Jean-Jacques," composed by Marie-Joseph Chénier, brother of the guillotined poet, sung by the older men, the mothers of families, and the citizens of Geneva.

Thus the official Rousseau and his powerful aura were tucked away, in a ceremony befitting the author of the *Lettre à d'Alembert sur les spectacles*. Cambacérès, man-for-all-seasons, stamped "paid" to the debt France owed to Rousseau, virtue had undone the monarchy, women were lactating on command, and the apotheosis was over. It was time to turn to other business.

In the years that followed, however, before Bonaparte set his foot firmly on the nation's neck, an occasional echo of the old dream was sounded, as individuals still reverted, from time to time, to that compelling vision which had dominated the landscape of France during the period of Jacobin hegemony. François-Valentin Mulot [Mullot], the radical Jacobin who had been denounced as having ordered the massacres at Avignon,[17] turned his mind, in 1797, to the question of a new "institution" for disposing of the dead in a way that would lead the living to virtue. Rousseau, in a little-known passage from his *Institutions chimiques* which Jean Starobinski quotes in *La Transparence et l'obstacle* (p. 303), had speculated that the human body was actually reducible to glass: *"Man is glass and he can return to glass, just like all the other animals."* Rousseau went on to comment "One could conserve the ashes of one's ancestors by substituting, in a matter of hours, clean and shining vases, made of a beautiful transparent glass, for disgusting and hideous corpses. The glass would not be that green color which comes from vegetal glass, but a milky white touched with a light shade of narcissus."

Mulot wrote a pamphlet, turning Rousseau's idea into an "institution" for leading men to virtue.[18] "A man's body makes about twenty-eight ounces of glass," he pointed out, and from this "crystal" heads could be made resembling the deceased. "A gallery of these busts in a family, would that not be a true temple? Would morality not profit? If a monster should deviate from the path of virtue, deny him the honors of vitrification" (p. 8).

A last, lingering revery; the patriot surrounded by milky, narcissus-tinted heads crystallized from the decaying bodies of his ancestors, presiding over his own glass menage, could only remember those frenetic times when virtue had been "the order of the day."

[17]See Décembre-Alonnier, 2: 43–44.
[18]*Vues d'un citoyen sur les Sepultures* (n.p., 1797), an otherwise unmarked brochure at the Harvard Library.

Works Cited

Eighteenth-century works

Andrieux, François-Guillaume. *L'enfance de Jean-Jacques Rousseau, comédie en un acte, melée de musique*. Paris: chez Madaran, 1794.

Aude, Joseph. *Saint-Preux et Julie d'Etanges, Drame en trois actes et en vers; représenté sur le théatre de la Comédie italienne, le 6 février, 1787*. Paris: n.p., 1787.

Barère de Vieuzac, Bertrand. *Mémoires*. 3 vols. Paris: J. Labitte, 1842.

Barruel-Beauvert, Antoine Joseph. *Vie de J.-J. Rousseau*. Londres et Paris: chez tous les Marchands de Nouveautés, 1789.

Bernardin de Saint-Pierre, Jacques-Henri. *Vie et oeuvres de Jean-Jacques Rousseau*. Paris: Cornély, 1907.

Berthier, Père Guillaume-François. *Observations sur le contrat social de J.-J. Rousseau*. Paris: Mérigot, 1789.

Billaud-Varenne, Jacques-Nicolas. *Eléments du républicanisme*. Paris: chez citoyen, l'an I. (BN microfiche 6106), [Barny 1977: 6042].

Bouilly, Jean Nicolas. *J.-J. Rousseau à ses derniers moments; trait historique, en un acte et en prose*. Paris: Brunet, 1791.

Brard, A. J. *Le Réveil de J.-J. Rousseau, ou particularités sur sa mort et son tombeau* (P. A. J. Bxxx. D. V....), Geneva, 1784.

Bricaire de la Dixmerie, Nicolas. *Dialogue entre Montagne [sic], Bayle et J.-J. Rousseau*. Amsterdam: Valleyre, 1781.

Brissot de Warville, J.-P. *De la Vérité ou méditations sur les moyens de parvenir à la vérité dans toutes les connaissances humaines*. Paris: Desauges, 1782.

——. *Mémoires*. Paris: Lescure, 1877.

Buzot, François-N.-L. *Mémoires sur la Révolution française*. Paris: Pichon & Didier, 1828.

Cambacérès, Jean-Jacques-Régis de. "Discours prononcé par le Président de la Convention nationale, lors de la translation des cendres de Jean-Jacques

Rousseau au Panthéon." Paris: Imprimerie nationale, Vendémiaire, l'an III.

Champcenetz, Louis-René-Quentin de Richebourg, marquis de. *Réponse aux lettres sur le caractère et les ouvrages de J.-J. Rousseau. Bagatelle que 20 libraires ont refusé d'imprimer.* Geneva: N.p., 1789.

Charrière, Isabella de. *Eloge de Jean-Jacques Rousseau, qui a concouru pour le prix de l'Académie française.* Paris: Grégoire, 1797.

Chas, François. *Réflexions philosophiques et impartiales sur Rousseau & Mme de Warens.* Paris: Royer, 1786.

Chénier, André. *Oeuvres complètes.* Paris: Pléiade, 1958.

Cloots, Anacharsis. *Appel au genre humain.* Paris: N.p., frimaire, an II (Nov.– Dec., 1793). BN Lb41. 946.

Corancez, Olivier de, Jean Romilly, and Louis d'Ussieux. *Journal de Paris.* 87 vols. Paris: 1 janvier, 1777–31 décembre, 1811.

D'Alembert, Jean Le Rond. *Oeuvres philosophiques, historiques, et littéraires.* Paris: Bastien, 1805.

Delacroix, Jacques. *Eloge de J.-J. Rousseau.* Paris: Le Jay, 1778.

Desmoulins, Camille. *Discours de la Lanterne aux parisiens.* Paris: Le Jay fils, 1789.

——. *Oeuvres.* Paris: Ehrard, 1838.

——. Vilate and Méda. *Le Vieux Cordelier, l'an II.* Rep. Paris: Baudoin, 1825.

Diderot, Denis. *Correspondance.* Ed. G. Roth and Jean Varloot. 16 vols. Paris: Minuit, 1955–70.

——. "Essai sur les règnes de Claude et de Néron." *Oeuvres complètes.* Vol. 3. Paris: Garnier, 1875.

——. "Réfutation suivie de l'ouvrage d'Helvétius intitulé *L'Homme.*" *Oeuvres philosophiques.* Paris: Garnier, 1956.

——. "Sur les femmes," *Oeuvres complètes.* Vol. 2. Ed. Assézat, Tourneux. Paris: Garnier, 1875–77.

Dubrail, ——. *Grande Dispute au Panthéon, entre Marat et J.-J. Rousseau.* Paris: de l'imprimerie des Sans-Culottes, 1794.

Fauchet, Claude. "*Le Contrat social* de J.-J. Rousseau." *La Bouche de Fer.* Ed. Fauchet and Nicolas [de] Bonneville. BN 8° LC 2. 317. (See F. Furet, *Le Cercle social.* Paris: Microéditions Hachette.)

——. "Sur le décret de mort contre le ci-devant roi et son exécution." BR 23: 303.

——. *Journal des Amis.* Paris: N.p. (26 janvier, 1793).

Gin, Pierre. *Des Causes de nos maux, de leur progrès et des moyens d'y remédier.* Paris: Pichard, 1791 [Barny: 6033].

Ginguené [Guingené], Pierre-Louis. *Extraits des lettres sur les Confessions de J.-J. Rousseau* (insérés par M. de la Harpe dans le dernier trimestre du "Mercure de France" de l'année 1792). N.p.: 1792 [pamphlet].

——. *Lettres sur les Confessions de J.-J. Rousseau.* Paris: Barois, 1791 [Barny: 6038].

Gouges, Olympe de. *Les Droits de la femme* (BN: microfiche 14003).

Grimm, Melchior. *Correspondance littéraire.* 17 vols. Paris: Buisson, 1813.

Works Cited

Hébert, Jacques René. *Le Père Duchesne*. *1790–1794*. Reprint Paris: EDHIS, 1969.

Houssaye, Arsène. *Gazette de littérature*. Paris: Veuve Duchesne, June 2, 1787.

Laclos, Choderlos de. *Oeuvres complètes*. Paris: Pléiade, 1944.

Lakanal, Joseph. "Rapport sur J.-J. Rousseau, fait au nom du Comité d'instruction publique…,dans la séance du 29 Fructidor." Paris: Imprimerie nationale, l'an II.

Latour de Franqueville, Mme M. A. M. de. *J.-J. Rousseau vangé par son amie ou morale practico-philosophico-encyclopédique des coryphées de la secte*. N.p.: Au Temple de la vérité, 1779.

Le Blond de Neuvéglise [Abbé Proyart]. *La Vie et les crimes de Robespierre*. Augsbourg: N.p., 1795.

Legros, Charles François. *Analyse des ouvrages de J.-J. Rousseau de Genève, et de M. Court de Gebelin, auteur du monde primitif; par un solitaire*. Geneva: B. Chirol, 1785.

Lenormant, Charles François. *J.-J. Rousseau aristocrate*. Paris: N.p., 1790 [Barny 1977: 6029].

Louis XIV. *Oeuvres*. Paris: Treuttel & Wurtz, 1806.

Malouet, Pierre-Victor. *Mémoires*. 2 vols. Paris: Plon, 1874.

Mercier, Louis-Sébastien. *De J.-J. Rousseau, considéré comme l'un des premiers auteurs de la Révolution*. 2 vols. Paris: Buisson, 1791.

Métra [Mettra]. *Correspondance secrète*. 18 vols. London: John Adamson, 1786–90.

Montesquieu, Charles Secondat, Baron de. *Les Lettres persanes*. Paris: Pléiade, 1956.

——. *De l'esprit des lois*. Paris: Pléiade, 1966.

Morellet, André (Abbé). *Mémoires sur le dix-huitième siècle et sur la révolution*. Paris: Ladvocat, 1821.

Mulot, François-Valentin. *Vues d'un citoyen sur les sépulcres*. N.p., 1797.

Petit, Michel Edme. *Eloge de J -J. Rousseau*. Paris: Droits de l'homme, 1792.

Prudhomme, Louis. *Révolutions de Paris*. 17 vols. Paris: rue des Marais, 1789–93.

Ptivar, —. *La Vérité ou J.-J. Rousseau montrant à Robespierre le livre des destins*. N.p., 1794.

Restif de la Bretonne, Nicolas. *Les Nuits révolutionnaires*. Ed. François Funck-Brentano. Paris: Fayard, 1915.

Ségur, Louis-Philippe de. *Souvenirs et anecdotes sur le règne de Louis XVI*. Paris: Arthème Fayard, 1910.

Soldini, L'Abbé de. "Essai sur la vie de Monseigneur Louis Dauphin, mort à Fontainebleau le 20 de décembre en 1765" (BN Fr. 13784).

Staël, Germaine Necker, mme de. *Lettres sur les écrits et le caractère de J.-J. Rousseau*. N.p., 1788.

Anonymous works, collections of documents and newspapers:

La Chronique de Paris. Ed. A.-L. Millin and J.-F. Noel. August 1, 1790–May 30, 1793.

Eloge de J. J. Rousseau (BN: Lb40.1007).
French Revolution: Documents, 1789–94. Ed. J. M. Thompson. Oxford: Blackwell, 1948.
Jean-Jacques Rousseau raconté par les gazettes de son temps (9 juin, 1762–21 décembre, 1790). Ed. P.-P. Plan. Paris: Mercure de France, 1912.
Jean-Jacques ou le Réveil-matin de la Nation française (BN: Lb39.6823).
Journal de la Montagne. Ed. J. Ch. Laveaux. Paris: 1 juin, 1793–28 brumaire an III (Nov. 18, 1794). 4 vols.
Le Mercure universel. Paris: Cussac [Gazette nationale]. Reprint Paris: 1850–1870. 32 vols.
Principes de J.-J. Rousseau pour l'éducation des enfants, ou instruction sur leur éducation physique et morale depuis leur naissance jusqu'à l'époque de leur entrée dans les écoles nationales. Paris: Aubry, l'an II.
Le Rayonnement de Rousseau jusqu'à la fin de la Révolution. Catalog of exposition of the Bibliothèque nationale, *Jean-Jacques Rousseau.* Paris: BN, 1962.
Recueil des Jeux floraux (1784–1788). Toulouse: N.p., 1788.
Robespierre vu par ses contemporains. Ed. Louis Jacob. Paris: Colin, 1938.

Post-Revolutionary critical and historical works

Abray, Jane. "Feminism in the French Revolution." *American Historical Review,* 80 (1975), 43–62.
Albertson, M. "Enlightenment and Revolution: The Evolution of Condorcet's Ideas on Education." *Condorcet Studies 1.* Ed. Leonora Cohen Rosenfield. Atlantic Highlands, N.J.: Humanities Press, 1984. Pp. 131–44.
Ansart-Dourlen, Michèle. *Dénaturation et violence dans la pensée de J.-J. Rousseau.* Paris: Klincksieck, 1975.
Aulard, Alphonse. *Le Culte de la raison et le culte de l'Etre Suprême (1793–1794).* Paris: Alcan, 1892.
Baczko, M. B. *Rousseau: Solitude et communauté.* Paris: Mouton, 1974.
Barny, Roger. "Jean-Jacques Rousseau dans la Révolution française, 1787–1791: Contribution à l'analyse de l'idéologie révolutionnaire bourgeoise." Diss. University of Paris, 1977.
———. *Le Rousseauisme.* Paris: Microéditions Hachette, 1978. 35 documents on microfiche.
———. "Les Aristocrates et Jean-Jacques Rousseau dans la Révolution." *AHRF,* 50 (1978), 534–68.
———. "Rousseau dans la Révolution." *Dix-huitième siècle,* 6 (1974), 59–98.
Barthes, Roland. *Le Degré zéro de l'écriture.* Paris: Seuil, 1953.
Baudoin, François Jean. *Honneurs publics rendus à la mémoire de Jean-Jacques, étude historique.* Geneva: Carey, 1878.
Benrubi, I. *L'Idéal moral chez Rousseau, Mme de Staël et Amiel. AJJR,* 27 (1938), 7–304.

Works Cited

Besnard-Coursodon, Micheline. "The Problem of a Filiation: Diderot and Danton as Seen by the Nineteenth Century." *DHS*, 10 (1978), 329–44.

Biou, Jean. "La Théorie politique de Rousseau." *AHRF,* 50 (1978), 501–33.

Bloch, Jean. "Women and the Reform of the Nation." *Woman and Society in Eighteenth-Century France.* London: Athlone, 1979.

Blum, Carol. *Diderot: The Virtue of a Philosopher.* New York: Viking, 1974.

——. "Styles of Cognition as Moral Options in *La Nouvelle Héloïse* and *Les Liaisons dangereuses.*" *PMLA*, 88 (1973), 289–98.

Bouloiseau, Marc. *La République jacobine.* Paris: Seuil, 1972.

Brinton, Crane. *A Decade of Revolution, 1789–1799.* New York: Harper, 1934.

Brooks, Richard. "Robespierre's Antifeminism in the *Lettre à d'Alembert* and *Emile.*" *Literature and History in the Age of Ideas.* Ed. Charles G. S. Williams. Columbus: Ohio State University Press: 1975.

Brown, Frederick. *Theater and Revolution.* New York: Viking, 1980.

Bruun, Geoffrey. *Saint-Just, Apostle of the Terror.* Hamden, Conn.: Archon. 1966 [1932].

Buffenoir, Hippolyte. *Les Portraits de Robespierre.* Paris: Leroux, 1910.

——. *Robespierre.* Paris: Dentu, 1882.

Burgelin, Pierre. "L'Education de Sophie." *AJJR*, 35 (1959–62), 113–37.

——. *La Philosophie de l'existence de Jean-Jacques Rousseau.* Paris: PUF, 1952.

Butwin, Joseph. "The French Revolution as *Theatrum Mundi.*" *Research Studies*, 43 (September, 1975), 141–52.

Cahen, Louis. *Condorcet et la Révolution française.* Paris: Alcan, 1904.

——. "Rousseau et la Révolution française." *Revue de Paris*, June 15, 1912, 745–66.

Campardon, Emile. *Le Tribunal révolutionnaire de Paris.* 2 vols. Paris: Plon, 1866.

Carr, J. L. *Robespierre: The Force of Circumstances.* London: Constable, 1972.

Cassirer, Ernst. *The Myth of the State.* New Haven: Yale University Press, 1946.

Cerati, Marie. *Le Club des citoyennes républicaines révolutionnaires.* Paris: Editions Sociales, 1966.

Champion, Edme. *J.-J. Rousseau et la Révolution française.* Paris: Armand Colin, 1909.

Charvet, John. *The Social Problem in the Philosophy of Rousseau.* Cambridge: Cambridge University Press, 1974.

Clément, Pierre-Paul. *J.-J. Rousseau, de l'Eros coupable à l'éros glorieux.* Neuchâtel: Baconnière, 1976.

Cobban, Alfred. *Aspects of the French Revolution.* New York: Braziller, 1968.

——. *The Debate on the French Revolution.* London: Kaye, 1950.

——. *Rousseau and the Modern State.* Hamden, Conn.: Archon, 1964 [1934].

Conlon, Pierre. *Ouvrages français relatifs à Jean-Jacques Rousseau (1751–1799): Bibliographie chronologique.* Geneva: Droz, 1981.

Cotta, Sergio. "La Position du problème de la politique chez Rousseau." *Journée d'Etudes sur le "Contrat Social" [JECS].* Paris: Société des Belles Lettres, 1964.

Courtois, L.-J. *Chronologie critique de la vie et des oeuvres de J.-J. Rousseau*. *AJJR*, 15 (1923), 1–342.

Crocker, Lester G. *Rousseau's Social Contract: An Interpretive Essay*. Cleveland: Case Western Reserve University Press, 1968.

Cuénin, Micheline. *Le Duel sous l'ancien régime*. Paris: Presses de la Renaissance, 1982.

Curtis, Ernest. *Saint-Just, Colleague of Robespierre*. New York: Octagon, 1973 [1935].

D'Alméras, H. *Les Dévotes de Robespierre: Catherine Théot, et les mystères de la Mère de Dieu dévoilés*. Paris: Soc. fr. d'imp. et de lib., 1905.

Darnton, Robert. *The Great Cat Massacre and Other Episodes in French Cultural History*. New York: Basic Books, 1984.

——. "A Spy in Grub Street." *The Literary Underground of the Old Regime*. Cambridge: Harvard University Press, 1982.

Décembre-Alonnier. *Dictionnaire de la Révolution française*. Paris: Administration, 1866–68. 2 vols.

Della Volpe, Galvano. *Rousseau and Marx*. London: Lawrence and Wishart, 1978 [1964].

Delon, Michel. "1878—Un Centenaire ou deux?" *AHRF*, 50 (1978), 641–63.

Derathé, Robert. *Jean-Jacques Rousseau et la science politique de son temps*. Paris: Vrin, 1970.

——. "Réfutations du 'Contrat social.'" *AJJR*, 32 (1950–52), 7–54.

Desné, Roland. "L'Individu malheureux." *Europe*, nos. 391–92 (1961), 22–33.

Devance, Louis. "Le Féminisme pendant la Révolution française." *AHRF*, 49 (1977), 341–76.

Dorigny, Marcel. "Les Girondins et J.-J. Rousseau." *AHRF*, 50 (1978), 569–83.

Dowd, D. L. *Pageant Master of the Republic: J.-L. David and the French Revolution*. Lincoln: University of Nebraska Studies, 1948.

Duhet, Paule-Marie. *Les Femmes et la Révolution*. Paris: Juillard, 1971.

Dupeyron, Georges. "Jean-Jacques et la sexualité." *Europe*, nos. 391–92 (1961), 33–42.

Duruy, Albert. "Les Fêtes nationales pendant la Révolution." *Revue de France*, July 15, 1878.

Ellrich, Robert. *Rousseau and His Reader: The Rhetorical Situation of the Major Works*. Chapel Hill: University of North Carolina Press, 1969.

Fabre, Jean. "Deux Frères ennemis, Diderot et Rousseau." *Diderot Studies*, 3. Geneva: Droz, 1961.

——. "Le J.-J. Rousseau de Lester Crocker." *Revue d'Histoire Littéraire*, 75 (1975), 799–826.

——. "Réalité et utopie dans la pensée politique de Rousseau." *AJJR*, 35 (1959–62), 181–216.

Fairchilds, Cissie. *Domestic Enemies: Servants and Their Masters in Old Regime France*. Baltimore: The Johns Hopkins University Press, 1984.

Falvey, John. "Women and Sexuality in the Thought of La Mettrie." *Women and Society in Eighteenth-Century France*. London: Athlone, 1979.

Fellows, Otis. "Diderot and the Mystery of Women." *Forum* (University of Houston), 16 (Winter and Spring, 1978 [1980]).

Fortunat, Françoise. "L'Amitié et le droit selon Saint-Just." *AHRF,* 54 (1982), 181–95.

Fox-Genovese, Elizabeth. Introduction to *French Women and the Age of Enlightenment.* Ed. S. I. Spencer. Bloomington: Indiana University Press, 1984.

Françon, Marcel. "La Condamnation de l'*Emile*." *AJJR,* 31 (1946–49), 209–45.

Furet, François. *Penser la Révolution française.* Paris: Gallimard, 1978.

Gagnebin, Bernard. "L'Etrange Accueil fait aux 'Confessions' de Rousseau au XVIIIe siècle." *AJJR,* 38 (1969–71), 105–26.

———. "Jean-Jacques Rousseau: Sur le péché d'Adam et le Salut universel." *DHS,* 3 (1971), 41–50.

———. "Le Rôle du législateur dans les conceptions politiques de Rousseau." *JECS.* Paris: Les Belles Lettres, 1964.

Gallois, Léonard. *Histoire des journaux et des journalistes de la Révolution française.* 2 vols. Paris: Schleicher, 1846.

Gay, Peter. *The Party of Humanity.* New York: Knopf, 1964.

Geoffroy, Annie. "Le 'Peuple' selon Saint-Just." *AHRF,* no. 191 (1968), 138–44.

Gershoy, Leo. *Bertrand Barère: A Reluctant Terrorist.* Princeton: Princeton University Press, 1961.

Gilchrist J., and W. J. Murray. *The Press in the French Revolution.* London: Ginn, 1971.

Gobel, Gundula, and Albert Soboul. "Les Almanachs de la Révolution (1788–1795)." *AHRF,* 50 (1978), 608–40.

Godechot, Jacques. "L'Historiographie française de Robespierre." *Actes du Colloque Robespierre.* Paris: Société des études Robespierristes, 1967 [ACR].

Goldberg, Rita. *Sex and Enlightenment: Women in Richardson and Diderot.* Cambridge: Cambridge University Press, 1984.

Goldschmidt, G.-A. *Jean-Jacques Rousseau ou l'esprit de solitude.* Paris: Phoebus, 1978.

Goldschmidt, Victor. *Anthropologie et politique: Les principes du système de Rousseau.* Paris: Vrin, 1974.

Gottschalk, Louis. *Jean-Jacques Marat.* New York: Blom, 1966 [1927].

Gouhier, Henri. *Les Méditations métaphysiques de Jean-Jacques Rousseau.* Paris: Vrin, 1970.

Goulemot, Jean-Marie. "*Les Confessions:* Une Autobiographie d'écrivain." *Littérature,* 33 (Feb., 1979), 58–74.

———. "De la polémique sur la Révolution et des lumières et des dix-huitiémistes." *DHS,* 6 (1974), 235–42.

Graham, Ruth. "Loaves and Liberty: Women in the French Revolution." *Becoming Visible: Women in European History.* Ed. Renate Bridenthal and Claudia Koonz. New York: Houghton Mifflin, 1977.

———. "The Revolutionary Bishop and the *Philosophes.*" *ECS,* 16 (Winter 1982–83), 117–40.

———. "Rousseau's Sexism Revolutionized." *Women in the Eighteenth Century and*

Other Essays. Ed. Paul Fritz and Richard Morton. Toronto: Hakkert, 1976.

——, ed. *Women and History: Women and the Enlightenment.* 9 (Spring, 1984). New York: Institute for Research in History and Haworth Press.

Greer, D. *The Incidence of the Terror during the French Revolution.* Cambridge: Harvard University Press, 1935.

Grimsley, Ronald. *Rousseau: The Religious Quest.* Oxford: Clarendon Press, 1968.

Groethuysen, Bernard. *Jean-Jacques Rousseau.* Paris: Gallimard, 1949.

——. *Philosophie de la Révolution française.* Paris: NRF, 1956.

Gross, Jean-Pierre. *Saint-Just: Sa Politique et ses missions.* Paris: Bibliothèque nationale, 1976.

Guéhenno, Jean. *Jean-Jacques.* Vol. 1: *En marge des "Confessions," 1712–1750;* Vol. 2: *Roman et vérité, 1750–1758;* Vol. 3: *Grandeur et misère d'un espirit, 1758–1778.* Paris: Grasset, 1948–50; Gallimard, 1952.

Gutwirth, M. "Mme de Staël, Rousseau, and the Woman Question." *PMLA,* 86 (1971), 100–109.

Hamel, E. *Histoire de Robespierre.* 3 vols. Paris: Lacroix, 1865.

Hampson, Norman. *Will and Circumstance: Montesquieu, Rousseau, and the French Revolution.* Norman: University of Oklahoma Press, 1983.

Hofstader, Douglas. *Godel, Escher, Bach: An Eternal Golden Braid.* New York: Basic Books, 1979.

Howard, Dick. "Rousseau and the Origin of Revolution." *Philosophy and Social Criticism,* 6 (1979), 349–70.

Huet, Marie-Hélène. *Rehearsing the Revolution: The Staging of Marat's Death, 1793–1797.* Berkeley: University of California Press, 1982.

Hufton, Olwen. "Women in Revolution, 1789–1796." *French Society and the Revolution.* Cambridge: Cambridge University Press, 1976.

Jacobs, Eva. "Diderot and the Education of Girls." *Women and Society in Eighteenth-Century France.* Ed. Eva Jacobs, et al. London: Athlone, 1979.

Jimack, P. D. "The Paradox of Sophie and Julie." *Women and Society in Eighteenth-Century France.* London: Athlone, 1979.

Jones, James F. "The *Dialogues* as Authobiographical Truth." *ECS,* 14 (1985), 317–28.

Kafker, Frank. "Les Encyclopédistes et la Terreur." *Revue d'Histoire Moderne et Contemporaine,* 14 (1967), 284–95.

——, ed. *The French Revolution: Conflicting Interpretations.* New York: Random House, 1968.

Kateb, George. *Utopia.* New York: Atherton, 1971.

Kavanagh, Thomas. "Rousseau's *Le Lévite d'Ephraim.*" *ECS,* 16 (1982–83), 141–61.

Kelly, George. "Conceptual Sources of the Terror." *ECS,* 14 (1980), 18–36.

Keohane, Nannerl O. *Philosophy and the State in France: The Renaissance to the Enlightenment.* Princeton: Princeton University Press, 1980.

Kleinbaum, Abby R. "Women in the Age of Light." *Becoming Visible.* Boston: Houghton Mifflin, 1977.

Works Cited

Lacour, Léopold. *Trois Femmes de la Révolution*. Paris: Plon, 1900.

Laere, François Van. *J.-J. Rousseau, du phantasme à l'écriture, les révélations du "Lévite d'Ephraim."* Paris: Minard, 1967.

La Fontainerie, F. de. *French Liberalism and Education in the Eighteenth Century.* New York: Franklin, 1971.

Laponneraye, Albert. Intro. to *Oeuvres de Maximilien Robespierre*. Paris: chez l'éditeur, 1840.

Launay, Michel. "L'Art de l'écrivain dans le *Contrat social.*" *Jean-Jacques Rousseau et son temps*. Paris: Nizet, 1979.

———. *Jean-Jacques Rousseau, écrivain politique (1712–1762)*. Grenoble: ACER, 1971.

———. *Le Vocabulaire politique de J.-J. Rousseau*. Geneva: Slatkine; Paris: Champion, 1977.

Lecercle, J. L. "Réflexions sur l'art de Rousseau." *Europe*, nos. 391–92 (1961), 89–99.

———. "Rousseau et Marx." *Rousseau after Two Hundred Years*. Cambridge: Cambridge University Press, 1982.

Leduc-Fayette, Denise. *J.-J. Rousseau et le mythe de l'antiquité*. Paris: Vrin, 1974.

———. "Le Matérialisme du Sage et l'art de jouïr." *Revue Philosophique*, 3 (1978), 326–42.

Lefebvre, Georges. "Sur la loi du 22 prairial, an II." *AHRF*, 24 (1952), 253–55.

Lenotre, G. *Le Mysticisme révolutionnaire, Robespierre, et la "Mère de Dieu."* Paris: Perrin, 1926.

Levy, Darline, Harriet Applewhite, and Mary Johnson. *Women in Revolutionary Paris: 1789–1795*. Urbana: University of Illinois Press, 1979.

Ligou, Daniel. "Bertrand Barère et Jean-Jacques Rousseau." *Jean-Jacques Rousseau (1712–1778)*. Gap: Louis-Jean, n.d.

Lucas, Colin. "Nobles, Bourgeois and the French Revolution." *French Society and the Revolution*. Cambridge: Cambridge University Press, 1976.

Maday, André de. "Rousseau et la Révolution," *AJJR*, 31 (1946–49), 169–207.

Marejko, Jan. *Jean-Jacques Rousseau et la dérive totalitaire*. Lausanne: L'Age d'Homme, 1984.

Masters, Roger D. *The Political Philosophy of Rousseau*. Princeton: Princeton University Press, 1968.

Mathiez, A. *Autour de Robespierre*. Paris: Payot, 1926.

———. *Etudes sur Robespierre*. Paris: Editions Sociales, 1958.

———. *Origines des cultes révolutionnaires*. Paris: Cornély, 1904.

———. "Robespierre et la Commune le 9 thermidor." *AHRF*, 1 (1924), 289–314.

———. "Robespierre et la procès de Catherine Théot." *AHRF*, 6 (1929), 392–97.

———. "Robespierre. L'Histoire et la légende." *AHRF*, 49 (1977).

May, Gita. *De Jean-Jacques Rousseau à Mme Roland*. Geneva: Droz, 1964.

McCannell, Juliet Flower. "The Post-Fictional Self: Authorial Consciousness in Three Texts by Rousseau." *MLN*, 89 (1974), 580–99.

McDonald, Christie V. *The Extravagant Shepherd*. Oxford: Voltaire Foundation, 1973.

McDonald, Joan. *Rousseau and the French Revolution: 1762–1791*. London: Athlone, 1965.

McNeil, Gordon H. "The Anti-Revolutionary Rousseau." *American Historical Review*, 58 (1953), 808–23.

——. "Robespierre, Rousseau, and Representation." *Ideas in History*. Durham: University of North Carolina Press, 1965.

Meynier, Albert. *Jean-Jacques Rousseau, révolutionnaire*. Paris: Schleicher, 1912.

Michelet, Jules. *Histoire de la Révolution française*. 2 vols. Paris: Pléiade, 1961.

Moravia, Sergio. "La Société d'Auteil." *DHS*, 6 (1974), 181–91.

Moreau, François. "Les Inédits de Rousseau et la campagne de presse de 1778." *DHS*, 12 (1980), 411–25.

Morellet, André, Abbé. *Mémoires*. Paris: Ladvocat, 1821.

Mornet, Daniel. *Les Origines intellectuelles de la Révolution française: 1715–1787*. Paris: Colin, 1933.

Moses, Claire. "The Legacy of the Eighteenth Century." *French Women and the Age of Enlightenment*. Ed. S. I. Spencer. Bloomington: Indiana University Press, 1984.

Munteano, Basil. "La Solitude de Jean-Jacques Rousseau." *AJJR*, 31 (1946–49), 76–168.

Niklaus, Robert. "Diderot and Women." *Women and Society in Eighteenth-Century France*.

O'Brien, Conor Cruise. "Virtue and Terror." *The New York Review of Books*. October 14, 1985. Pp. 28–31.

Ollivier, Albert. *Saint-Just et la force des choses*. Paris: Gallimard, 1954.

Orlando, Francesco. "La Découverte du souvenir d'enfance." *AJJR*, 37 (1966–68), 149–73.

——. *Infanzia, memoria e storia da Rousseau ai romantici*. Padua: Liviana, 1966.

Palmer, R. R. *The Age of the Democratic Revolution*. Princeton: Princeton University Press, 1959.

——. *Twelve Who Ruled*. Princeton: Princeton University Press, 1941.

Pappas, John. "La Campagne des philosophes contre l'honneur." *SVEC*, 205 (1982), 31–44.

Parfait, Noël. *Notice bibliographique sur A.-F. Sergent*. Paris: n.p., 1848.

Paris, J.-M. *Honneurs publics rendus à la mémoire de J.-J. Rousseau*. Geneva: Carey, 1878.

Payne, Harry. "The Philosophes and Popular Ritual: Turgot, Voltaire, Rousseau." *SECC*, 14 (1985), 307–16.

Perkins, Jean. "Rousseau jugé par Du Pont de Nemours." *AJJR*, 39 (1972–77), 171–95.

Peyre, Henri. "The Influence of Eighteenth-Century Ideas on the French Revolution." *Historical and Critical Essays*. Lincoln: University of Nebraska Press, 1968.

Polin, Raymond. *La Politique de la solitude*. Paris: Sirey, 1971.

Works Cited

Pomeau, René. "Foi et raison de Jean-Jacques." *Europe*, nos. 391–92 (1961), 57–65.

——. Introduction to *La Nouvelle Héloïse*. Paris: Garnier, 1960.

Poulet, Georges. *Studies in Human Time*. New York: Harper, 1956.

Proyart, Abbé. *Louis XVI détroné avant d'être roi, ou tableau des causes de la Révolution française*. Paris: Hôtel de Picardie, 1803.

Proyart, J. M., Abbé. *La Vie de Maximilien Robespierre*. Arras: Théry, 1850.

Racz, Elizabeth. "The Women's Rights Movement of the French Revolution." *Science and Society*, 16 (1951), 151–74.

Raymond, Marcel. "Rousseau et Genève." *Jean-Jacques Rousseau*. Neuchâtel: Baconnière, 1962.

Revault D'Allonnes, M. "Rousseau et le Jacobinisme." *AHRF*, 50 (1978), 584–607.

Rex, Walter. "On the Background of Rousseau's *First Discourse*." *SECC*, 9 (1980), 131–50.

Robespierre, Maximilien. *Mémoires authentiques*. Paris: Moreau-Rosier, 1830 (apocryphal).

Rosbottom, Ronald, and Michel Launay. "Autour de l'article 'Economie politique' de l'Encyclopédie." In *Jean-Jacques Rousseau et son temps*. Paris: Nizet, 1969.

Roussel, Jean. "Le Phénomène d'identification dans la lecture de Rousseau." *AJJR*, 39 (1972–77), 65–77.

Rousset, Jean. *Forme et signification*. Paris: Corti, 1962.

Rudé, Georges. *Robespierre: Portrait of a Revolutionary Democrat*. New York: Viking, 1975.

Schatz, R. J.-J. *Rousseau's Einfluss auf Robespierre*. Borna-Leipzig: Noske, 1906.

Schinz, Albert. *La Pensée de Jean-Jacques Rousseau*. Paris: Alcan, 1929.

Schwartz, Joel. *The Sexual Politics of Jean-Jacques Rousseau*. Chicago: University of Chicago Press, 1984.

Senior, Nancy. "Aspects of Infant Feeding in Eighteenth-Century France." *ECS*, 16 (1983), 367–88.

Shklar, Judith. *Men and Citizens: A Study of Rousseau's Social Theory*. Cambridge: Cambridge University Press, 1969.

Showalter, English. *Madame de Graffigny and Rousseau: Between the Two Discourses*. Oxford: The Voltaire Foundation, 1978.

Simons, Madeleine. *Amitié et passion: Rousseau et Sauttersheim*. Geneva: Droz, 1972.

Soboul, Albert. "Classes populaires et Rousseauisme sous la Révolution." *AHRF*, 34 (1962), 421–38.

——. "J.-J. Rousseau et le jacobinisme." *JECS*. Paris: Les Belles Lettres, 1964.

——. *Maximilien Robespierre*. Paris: Union rationaliste, 1958.

——. *Mouvement populaire et gouvernement révolutionnaire en l'an II (1793–1794)*. Paris: Flammarion, 1973.

——. *Le Procès de Louis XVI*. Paris: Julliard, 1966.

——. "Robespierre et les contradictions du jacobinisme." *AHRF*, 50 (1978), 1–19.

Sozzi, Lionel. "Ínterprétations de Rousseau pendant la Révolution." *SVEC*, 64 (1968), 187–223.

Spencer, Samia I. "Women and Education." In *French Women and the Age of Enlightenment*. Bloomington: Indiana University Press, 1984.

Starobinski, Jean. "J.-J. Rousseau et le péril de la réflexion." *AJJR*, 34 (1956–58), 139–73.

———. *Jean-Jacques Rousseau: La transparence et l'obstacle*. Paris: Gallimard, 1957.

———. "La Mise en accusation de la société." *Jean-Jacques Rousseau*. Neuchâtel: Baconnière, 1978.

———. "La Prosopopée de Fabricius." *Revue des Sciences Humaines*, 161 (1976), 83–96.

———. "'Rousseau's Social Contract' de Lester Crocker." *AJJR*, 37 (1966–68), 262–65.

———. "Tout le mal vient de l'inégalité." *Europe*, no. 391–92 (1961), 135–49.

Taine, Hippolyte. *Les Origines de la France contemporaine: La Révolution, la conquête jacobine*. Paris: Hachette, 1911.

Talmon, J. L. *The Origins of Totalitarian Democracy*. New York: Praeger, 1960.

Theuriot, Fr. "Saint-Just: Esprit et conscience publique." *AHRF,* no. 191 (1968), 120–37.

Thompson, J. M. *Leaders of the French Revolution*. Oxford: Blackwell, 1963.

———. *Robespierre*. 2 vols. New York: Howard Fertig, 1968.

Trahard, Pierre. *La Sensibilité révolutionnaire*. Geneva: Slatkine, 1968.

Trousson, Raymond. *Rousseau et sa fortune littéraire*. St. Médard en Jalles: Ducros, 1971.

Valéry, Paul. *Oeuvres complètes*. Paris: Pléiade, 1942.

Vernes, Paule-Monique. *La Ville, la fête, la démocratie*. Paris: Payot, 1978.

Waldinger, Renée. "Condorcet: The Problematic Nature of Progress." In *Condorcet Studies I*. Ed. Leonora Cohen Rosenfield. Atlantic Highlands, New Jersey: Humanities Press, 1984.

Walter, G. *La Conjuration du neuf thermidor.* Paris: Gallimard, 1974.

———. *Répertoire de l'histoire de la Révolution française*. Paris: BN, 1941. Works relative to Robespierre, pp. 457–74.

———. *Robespierre*. 2 vols. Paris: Gallimard, 1961.

Williams, David. "The Influence of Rousseau on Political Opinion, 1760–95." *English Historical Review,* 48 (1933), 414–30.

———. "The Politics of Feminism in the French Enlightenment." *The Varied Pattern: Studies on the 18th Century*. Ed. Peter Hughes and David Williams. Toronto: Hakkert, 1971.

Zimmermann, E. M. "'Vertu' dans *La Nouvelle Héloïse*." *MLN,* 76 (1961), 251–59.

Index

Index

Solitude: of primitive man, 89, 97; imposed on Rousseau by evil others, 98

Sophie (Emile's wife), 122–123, 136–137

Sovereign: as people, 160; Jacobin definition of, 166

Sozzi, L., 28n

Sparta, Spartans, 41, 115; Diderot on, 115, 119; Frey on, 150; Billaud-Varenne on, 183; laconism, 188; virtue of, 201; women of, 210; Robespierre on, 241

Spectacles, republican, 71

Staël, Mme de (Germaine Necker): and Rousseau's children, 75; admires Rousseau's making virtue a passion, 143

Starobinski, Jean: on Rousseau and Terror, 18, 218; on L. Crocker, 30n; on identification with Rousseau, 35; on the "Prosopopée de Fabricius," 41; on aspects of Rousseau's understanding of virtue, 49, 50, 80, 94, 98; on Rousseau's idea that the body is reducible to glass, 281

Ste-Aldegonde, Comte de, 134

Supreme Being, Festival of, 239–255; Robespierre's isolation at, 252

Taine, Hippolyte, 16; virtue as hypocrisy, 30–31

Tallien, Jean-Lambert, 262

Talmon, J. L., 17, 32

Tears: women's, 48; as erotic substitute, 49; Rousseau enjoyed, 85; and feeling of inner worth 86

Terror: as "order of the day," 202; and women, 212; and xenophobia, 217; as symbolic theater, 218; Robespierre's justification of, 244

Théot, Catherine: trial of, 265–266

Thibault, Anne-Alexandre-Marie, 220

Thompson, J. M., 154, 162

Thuriot, Jacques-Alexis, 217

Tocqueville, Alexis de, 25

Totalitarianism, 32

Trénard, Louis, 28n

Tronchin, Dr. Théodore, 74

Trousson, Raymond, 14, 31, 34, 65n, 135

Truth: accessible through inner feelings, 79–82; and Law of 22 prairial, 257–258

Universal opinion: analogous to general will, 213

Vendée: revolt in, 223

Vernes, Paule-Monique, 245n

Vilate, Joachim, 266

Villette, Charles, 148; survival strategies of, 228

Violence: and Rousseau, 130–132; of Robespierre and Saint-Just, 151, 167; of the Gironde, 169–170; of Marat, 201; and virtue, 202, 236

Virtue, 13–14; as self-hatred, 25; as "soul of the republic," 27; as "order of the day," 27, 227; redefined in materialist terms, 28; and revolutionaries, interpretations of, 28–35; and terror, 30, 31, 259; as opaque sign, 30; as hypocrisy, 31; as state of being, 37; as Julie's voluptuous pleasure, 64; no v. without religion, 70; making v. reign, 72, 114; as political self-absorption, 115; and education, 117; and sexual segregation, 125; holy rage of, 128; synonym for morality, 150; Saint-Just on, 163; Republic is v., 166; insulted by Louis XVI, 179; and violence, 199; and persecution, 199, 247; and impunity, 199; as impetuous passion, 201; and Supreme Being, 240; not a phantom, 241, vice and v. struggle for the world, 242; essence of the Republic, 242; emotional fusion in, 243; "celestial voluptuousness" of, for Robespierre, 254; a natural passion, 273

Volland, Sophie, 88

Voltaire, 16; in Geneva, 56; L'Ingénu, 45; and virtue, 58; satire of La Nouvelle Héloïse, 64, 68, 79, 82; Poème sur le désastre de Lisbonne, 105; condemns church-state alliance, 112; status under Jacobins, 228–229

Waldinger, Renée, 185n

Walter, Gérard: Robespierre bibliography, 153; on Billaud-Varenne, 183; on report of 18 floréal, 238n; on Robespierre's religion, 240; Robespierre and dying, 247; on Law of 22 prairial, 255; on Robespierre's withdrawal from government, 268

War: Jacobin endorsement of, 216

Warens, Mme de, 39, 59

Wetnurses, 47

Williams, David, 121n

Wits (beaux esprits), denounced, 234

‘

Library of Congress Cataloging-in-Publication Data

Blum, Carol, 1934–
   Rousseau and the republic of virtue.

   Bibliography: p.
   Includes index.
   1. France—History—Revolution, 1789–1799—Causes. 2. Rousseau, Jean-
Jacques, 1712–1778—Political and social views. I. Title.
DC138.B55   1986   944.04   86-6396
ISBN 0-8014-1857-7 (alk. paper)

DATE DUE

DEMCO 38-296

Please remember that this is a library book,
and that it belongs only temporarily to each
person who uses it. Be considerate. Do
not write in this, or any, library book.